Contents

Each of these excerpts is taken from *BTEC National Business*, written by Rob Drans-field *et al* and published by Heinemann Educational Publishers in 2004

Preface

This Study Guide for the BTEC National in Business has been published to give you a flavour of the resources that are available to support your course.

A good textbook fulfils many roles. If you have forgotten something your tutor told you in class, you can look it up in the book. If there is something you are not quite sure about or don't quite understand, you can get to grips with it at your own pace and in your own time. If you are unfortunate to miss a class then you can probably read about the topic you missed in the textbook.

Texts also have activities and case studies for you to do so you can see how much you have understood. If you realise you need help, you can then go back to your tutor. Activities also give you the opportunity to practise the skills you will need for assessment.

And most texts will take you beyond their covers! They give you useful websites to explore, they will suggest journals and magazines that will widen your researches and they will have lists of other books to read if you want to explore an issue in greater depth. Make the most of all these leads to broaden your horizons. You will enjoy your course more and you are likely to get better grades.

This Study Guide covers only four of the units you may study for your BTEC National but we hope you will find it useful and will want to make further use of the book that is presented here.

THE SMART WAY TO ACHIEVE YOUR BTEC NATIONAL

We all know people who seem to do well almost effortlessly – at work, at college and even when they are just enjoying themselves. Some of them may be clever or talented but not all of them – so what is their secret? And how does this relate to your BTEC National course?

Every year thousands of students enrol on BTEC National courses. Most are successful and obtain the full qualification. A few do not - either because they don't complete the course or because they don't achieve all the units they need. In some cases students who are successful are still disappointed because they don't achieve the grades they wanted. This can have serious consequences if their offers of a university place are based on the achievement of specific final grades.

The difference between students who don't do as well as they had hoped, and those who do well, rarely has anything to do with brain power. After all, they were all accepted as suitable for the course in the first place. The difference is usually because some work efficiently and some do not. In fact, some students seem to go through college continually making life difficult for themselves – and then wonder why they have problems!

Students who work efficiently are **smart**. The strategies they use mean they are more likely to stay on the course (even if they have problems) and they regularly achieve better grades than other students.

So what do *you* need to do to be smart? First: read this guide. Second: follow it! Third: keep it safely and re-read it at regular intervals to refresh your memory.

The smart way to learn to be smart

1

BTEC National Study Guide: Business. See page 185 for order details of individual texts

1

> ### *In a nutshell*
>
> Working in a smart way means you are more likely to stay on your course, even if you have problems. You will also achieve better grades for doing the same amount of work!

Be smart about your course

There may be quite a gap between your interview at college and the date you start on your BTEC National course. In that time you will probably have forgotten a lot about what you were told. So the first thing to do is to re-fresh your memory and find out *exactly* what your course entails. You can do this by re-reading college information and also by logging onto the Edexcel website at www.edexcel.org.uk.

- There are three types of BTEC National qualifications and each has a different number of units.

  - The BTEC National Award has 6 units
  - The BTEC National Certificate has 12 units
  - The BTEC National Diploma has 18 units

  You should already know which type of BTEC National you are taking and how long your course lasts. It is useful to find out how many units you will study each term and how many units you will complete each year if you are on a two-year course.

- Every BTEC National qualification has a set number of **core units**. These are the compulsory units which every student must complete. There is also a range of **specialist units** from which you may be able to make a choice. These enable you to study particular areas in more depth. You need to check:

  - the title of each core unit and the topics it contains
  - the title of each specialist unit and the area it covers
  - whether you can choose any specialist units you want, or whether your choice is restricted. This may be because of the structure of the qualification or because your college does not offer the full range.

Knowing all about your course means that you are more likely to choose the most appropriate specialist units for your own needs and interests. You will be more mentally prepared and know what to expect. This also enables you to relate your everyday experiences to the topics you will be learning. You can then be alert to information that relates to your studies, whether you are watching television, reading an article, talking to your family or working – even in a part-time job a few hours a week. The more alert you are to these types of opportunities, the more you will benefit.

> ### *In a nutshell*
>
> Log on to www.edexcel.org.uk and check the exact content of your BTEC National course. Download the *Student's Guide* for your course which describes the course structure and the unit titles and check with your tutor which you will study each term. Check the course specification to find out the exact content of each unit and check the specialist units that are offered at your college before you select your specialist units. Always be alert to all sources of useful information that relate to your course.

Be smart about resources

A resource is anything that helps you to achieve your goal and so, generally speaking, the more you have the better! You will be introduced to many college resources during your induction, such as the library, the learning resource centre(s) and the computer network. However, most students never actually sit down and list all the resources they have. This is worthwhile because you will probably have far more than you realise. The easiest way is to divide up your resources into different categories and make a list under each heading.

BTEC National Study Guide: Business. See page 185 for order details of individual texts

2

There are two aspects to resources. Knowing what they are and using them properly! The main types of resources to consider are given below.

- **Course materials**   These include this Student Guide, all the materials on the Edexcel website, all the information given to you during induction, the textbook(s) you use for particular units, the handouts you are given in class and the notes you make in class. They also include resources you are asked to provide yourself, such as lined paper, folders for storing notes, dividers for sub-dividing topics in your folders, pens, pencils, a hole punch, calculator and a good dictionary. These, by the way, are all essential resources – not optional extras you can scrounge from someone else!

  If you are smart then you always have the right resources for each lesson or session because you get organised in advance. You also file handouts and notes *promptly* in the right place in the right folder so that you can find them again quickly. You have clearly labelled dividers and your notes have a clear heading so that you can find information easily. If you are writing up your own notes from research then you will have made a clear note of the source of your information. How to do this is given in the IVA guide *Ten Steps to a Great IVA*.

- **Equipment and facilities**   These include your college library and learning resource centre(s); the college computer network; other college equipment you can use, such as laptop computers and photocopiers; electronic information resources, such as Internet access, electronic journals and CDs; equipment you have at home – such as a computer; specialist equipment and facilities relevant to your particular course.

  Libraries can be baffling if you don't understand the system used to store books: your college computer network is of limited use if you don't know the difference between an Intranet and the Internet or realise that information is stored on CDs as well as in books. Library and resource centre staff are employed to give you help and advice if you need it – so don't hesitate to ask them! You also need to find the recommended way to transfer data between your home computer and college if your options are limited because of IT security. It is also very important that you check the regulations or guidelines on using the Internet and computers in your college so that you make the most of the equipment without falling foul of any of the rules that apply.

- **People**   These include your tutor(s), specialist staff (such as library and resource centre staff), your employer and your colleagues at work, your relatives and friends who have particular skills or who work in the same area you are studying.

Smart students have their own resources

BTEC National Study Guide: Business. See page 185 for order details of individual texts

3

Most people will be keen to help you if you are courteous, well prepared and are not trying to get them to do the work for you! Prepare a list of open questions if you want to interview someone. These are questions that can't be answered with a 'yes' or 'no'. Work down your list but aim to get the person talking freely whilst you make notes. Unless they wander far from the topic you will find out more this way. Then do a final check that you have covered all the areas on your list and get a contact number in case you need to speak to them again. Don't forget to say thank you – and try not to overuse one particular person.

One word of warning! Be careful about asking for help from a friend who has already done the same course and *never* be tempted to borrow their assignments. Tutors can soon tell if the work isn't in your own personal style, or if it varies in style. In addition, assignments are normally changed each year and answers are expected to be up-to-date, so an answer from a previous year is unlikely to be of much use.

- **Your own skills and abilities**   Obviously if you have excellent IT skills then you will produce your written assignments more easily. You will also be better at researching online if you know and understand how to use the Internet and have included useful sites in your Favourites list. Other vital skills include being able to recognise and extract key information from a book, being able to summarise and able to type up your work relatively quickly and accurately. As you will see as you work through this Guide being well-organised and using your time wisely are also invaluable skills and can make all the difference to your final grades.

You can assess yourself as you read this Guide by listing those areas in which you are weak and need to improve your skills. Then talk to your tutor about the best way to do this.

In a nutshell

Resources are vital because they help you to succeed. If you list your resources you may find there are more than you think. Then you must use them wisely. This includes storing handouts safely and thanking people who help you. You also need to develop skills and abilities which will help you to work more easily – such as improving your Internet and typing skills.

Be smart about time

Some weeks you may find you have very little to do – so you can manage your workload easily. Then everything changes. In a short period of time you seem to be overwhelmed with work to do. If you are unlucky, this will coincide with a time when you also have family, personal or work commitments as well. So – how do you juggle everything and still stay in control?

There are several skills you need to be able to do this.

- **Record important dates in advance**   Keep a homework diary or (even better) a wall chart and mark all key dates in colour. You can devise your own system but it is useful to enter assignment review dates with your tutor in one colour and final deadline dates in another. Keep your chart up-to-date by adding any new dates promptly every time you are given another task or assignment. This gives you prior warning when important dates are looming and, if nothing else, stops you from planning a heavy social week for the same time!

- **Prioritise your work**   This means doing the most important and urgent task first. This is normally the task or assignment with the nearest deadline. The exception is when you have to allow for the availability of other people or other resources. For example, if you have two assignments to do and one involves interviewing three people, it is sensible to schedule the interviews first. If you need to send off for information it is also sensible to do this promptly, to allow plenty of time for it to arrive. It also means allowing enough time to print out your assignment well before the deadline – unless you are prepared to join the long queues of students who have the same deadline as you and who are all trying to print out their work at the last minute!

- **Plan your work**   This means analysing each task and estimating how long it will take. For example, you may estimate that an assignment will take you one hour to plan, six hours to research, four hours to type up

BTEC National Study Guide: Business. See page 185 for order details of individual texts

4

Be smart about time

and one hour to check. In this case you need *at least* twelve hours to do the work. If you are sensible you will allow a little more, in case you encounter any problems or difficulties. It is wise to schedule fixed times to work and then plan to give yourself time off when you have completed a task or are 'between' tasks or assignments.

- **Regularly review your progress**   You need to check regularly that you are on schedule. It is easy to spend much longer than you think on some tasks – either because you get bogged down or because you become too absorbed. This will mean you have to do the rest of the work in a rush and this may affect your grade.

- **Be smart – but be kind to yourself too!**   If you are over-conscientious you may be tempted to burn the midnight oil to keep up-to-date. This isn't wise on a regular basis because no-one does their best work when they are over-tired. In this case remember to *target* your efforts where they will count most – rather than try to have everything perfect. Schedule in some breaks and relaxation time too; you are allowed a treat from time to time! If your problem is just the opposite – and you struggle to stay focused if you're not in the mood for work – then you need to practise a little more self-discipline. One trick is to find an aspect of a task that you will find easy or really enjoy. Then start with this to get yourself going. Aim to complete a fixed amount of work before you give yourself a small reward – such as a fifteen-minute break or a bar of chocolate!

You can find more detailed information on planning your work and reviewing your progress in the IVA Guide *Ten Steps to a Great IVA.*

BTEC National Study Guide: Business. See page 185 for order details of individual texts

5

We all need a treat from time to time

In a nutshell

Your workload may be unpredictable and some weeks will be worse than others. You will cope better if you note down all key dates in advance, prioritise properly, plan realistically the time work will take and regularly review your progress. Target your efforts so that you can take sensible breaks and start with tasks you enjoy to motivate yourself.

Be smart about assignments

Assignments are the main method of assessment on all BTEC National courses. Edexcel specifies the exact **assessment criteria** for each unit in a grid. In plain English, this is the list of skills and knowledge you must demonstrate to achieve a pass, merit or distinction. You will find these in your course specification immediately after the content of each unit.

There are two types of assignments.

- There are those that are **internally set**. In this case the assignments are set and marked by your own tutors. Each assignment will include tasks and activities that enable you to produce evidence directly linked to the assessment criteria for a particular unit. Most units have internally set and assessed assignments.

- Alternatively there are **externally set** assignments. In this case an **Integrated Vocational Assignment (IVA)** is set by Edexcel.

In both cases Edexcel checks that centres are assessing assignments correctly and that all centres have the same standards.

Many people panic at the thought of assignments, but being smart means you are well-prepared and won't break any golden rules!

- Always check the assessment criteria grid for the unit in advance, so that you know what to expect.

- The grid is divided into three main columns which state what you must do to achieve a pass, a merit and a distinction grade. The main word, which tells you what to do, is called a **command word**. You must understand the command word *and obey it* to obtain a specific grade. This is dealt with in more detail in the next section.

- Read the assignment brief *thoroughly* and query anything you do not understand with your tutor.

- Check those tasks which must be all your own work and which (if any) you will complete as a member of a group. If you are asked to do any work as a member of a team then you must always identify your own individual contribution to each task.

BTEC National Study Guide: Business. See page 185 for order details of individual texts

6

- *Always* remember that plagiarism (copying someone else's work) is an extremely serious offence and will result in disciplinary action. *Never* be tempted to share your work (or your disks or CDs) with anyone else and don't ask to borrow theirs!

- Check the other rules that apply. These will include

  - whether you can discuss your research or draft answers with your tutor – and when you must do this
  - the college-set deadline date for submission – and the penalties for handing in work late (this might mean your assignment not being assessed)
  - what to do if you are absent when the assignment is due or have a serious personal problem which affects your ability to complete the work on time. There is normally an official procedure for obtaining an extension. This is only when mitigating circumstances apply and can't be used just because you fail to plan properly!

- Make sure you answer every question fully and present your information according to the instructions. You may, for instance, have to provide information in a table or report rather than simply answering questions. You will get a lower grade if you ignore important presentation instructions.

In a nutshell

The assessment criteria grid for each unit states what you must provide evidence against to achieve a pass, merit or distinction grade. It is important that you read and understand this, as well as the assignment brief, and obey all the instructions. Check you know any other rules that apply, such as how to apply for an extension to the deadline if you have a serious personal problem. Then answer the questions fully and present the work as required.

Sadly, over-sleeping doesn't count as a serious personal problem

BTEC National Study Guide: Business. See page 185 for order details of individual texts

Be smart about command words

Command words are used to specify how a question must be answered, eg 'describe', 'explain' or 'analyse'. These words are often related to the level of answer required. You will therefore find these command words in the assessment grid and you will usually see, for example, that 'describe' will get you a pass grade. However, you would need to do more than give a straightforward description to get a merit or distinction grade.

Many students don't get the grades they should for an assignment because they do not realise the difference between these words. Instead of applying their knowledge (for a merit grade) they simply give a brief explanation or a list. Just listing *more* facts will not improve your grade; you must show you can use your knowledge.

The chart below shows you what is usually required when you see a particular command word. You can use this, and the answers below, to identify the difference between the types of answers required for each grade. Remember these are just *examples* of acceptable answers to help you. The exact response required will often depend upon the way a question is worded so check with your tutor if you are unsure what it is you have to do.

To obtain a pass grade you must prove your knowledge and understanding by giving the relevant facts clearly and concisely.

If it says:	This means you should:
Describe	Give a clear description that includes all the relevant features. You might want to think of this as 'painting a picture in words'.
Define	Clearly explain what a particular term means and give an example, if appropriate, to show what you mean.
Design*	Create a plan, proposal or outline to illustrate a straightforward concept or idea.
Explain	Set out in detail the meaning of something, with reasons. This is more dif-
how/why	ficult than 'describing' or 'listing' so it can often help to give an example to show what you mean. Start by introducing the topic and then give the 'how' or 'why'.
Identify	Point out (ie choose the right one) or give a list of the main features.
Illustrate	Include examples or a diagram to show what you mean.
Interpret	Define or explain the meaning of something.
List	Provide the information in a list, rather than in continuous writing.
Outline	Write a clear description but not a detailed one.
Plan	Work out and explain how you would carry out a task or activity.
State	Write a clear and full account.
Summarise	Write down the main points or essential features.

Q   Describe the Apple iPod.

Below is an example answer that would achieve a pass grade.

A   The Apple iPod is a digital player on which music can be stored and played without the need for CDs or tapes. Music is stored on an iPod by transferring MP3 music files that have been downloaded from the Internet or copied from a CD. The Apple iPod with the largest capacity will store up to 10,000 songs and costs about £420. A mini version is much cheaper but stores far fewer – about 1,000 – for about £180. Both have been praised in reviews for their excellent sound quality, ease of use and stylish design.

* You may also find the word 'design' at merit level, as you will see below.

BTEC National Study Guide: Business. See page 185 for order details of individual texts

8

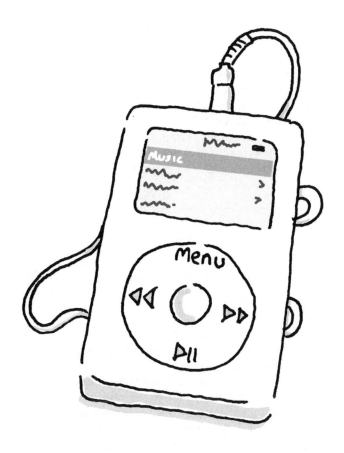

To obtain a merit grade you must prove you can apply your knowledge in a specific way.	
If it says:	This means you should:
Analyse	Identify separate factors, say how they are related and how each one contributes to the topic. This is one step up from the explanation you gave at pass level.
Compare/contrast	Identify the main factors that apply in two or more situations and explain the similarities and differences or advantages and disadvantages.
Demonstrate	Provide several relevant examples or related evidence which clearly support the arguments you are making. If you are doing a practical subject, this might be, e.g. showing your computer or coaching skills.
Design	Create a plan, proposal or outline to illustrate a relatively complex concept or idea.
Assess	Give careful consideration to all the factors or events that apply and identify which are the most important and relevant.
Explain in detail	Provide details and give reasons and/or evidence to clearly support the argument you are making.
how/why Justify	Give reasons or evidence to support your opinion or view to show how you arrived at these conclusions.

Q   Analyse why Apple iPods are so popular.

Below is an example answer that would achieve a merit grade.

A   Apple is one of several brands of MP3 players on the market. Rivals include the iAudio player and the Sony net walkman. Some rivals are cheaper than the iPod, so price is not the main reason for Apple iPod popularity. The iPod took off because its stylish design looked so good and there was some great

BTEC National Study Guide: Business. See page 185 for order details of individual texts

9

advertising that turned it into the 'must have' item as early as Christmas 2003. It was also praised more by reviewers than other digital players. The Apple iPod stores music on a moving hard disk whereas some players store it on computer chips. Hard disk players have better sound quality and greater storage capacity. The Apple is also easy to use. Apple then developed the brand by adding accessories and introducing the mini iPod which comes in five different colours. Apple is also popular because it was the first to develop a portable MP3 player and supports its customers with its iTunes music store online. Downloads from the site aren't compatible with other players and so iPod users are tied to the iTunes site. Many people have criticised this. Apple, however, is the brand that is cool to own – so much so that over 10 million Apple iPods were sold in 2004 out of total sales worldwide of between 20 and 25 million portable music players.

To obtain a distinction grade you must prove you can make a reasoned judgement based on evidence.

If it says:	This means you should:
Appraise	Consider the plus and minus points and give a reasoned judgement
Assess	Must make a judgement on the importance of something. It is similar to 'evaluate' (see below).
Comment critically	Give your view after you have considered all the evidence. In particular decide the importance of all the relevant positive *and* negative aspects.
Criticise	Review a topic or issue objectively and weigh up both plus and minus points before making a decision. It is similar to 'comment critically'.
Draw conclusions	Use the evidence you have provided to reach a reasoned judgement.
Evaluate	Review the information and then bring it together to form a conclusion. Give evidence for each of your views or statements.
Evaluate critically	Decide the degree to which a statement is true or the importance or value of something by reviewing the information. Include precise and detailed information and assess possible alternatives, bearing in mind their strengths and weaknesses if they were applied instead.

Q   Evaluate the effect of Apple iPods on the music industry.

An example answer that would achieve a distinction grade:

A   Apple iPods – together with other digital music players – have helped to give the music industry a new lease of life. In the late 1990s music companies were alarmed that the Internet could ruin their business because of illegal file sharing and they forced the Napster website to close down. This site had allowed music fans to log on and exchange songs free of charge. Music companies also took legal action against private individuals. A famous case was of an American girl of 12 whose mother had to pay $2,000 in fines, which frightened other parents. However, the development of portable digital music players has boosted the popularity of legal download sites such as Apple iTunes, MyCokeMusic and the new Napster subscription service, which sell tracks for about 80p each. These enable music fans to select and store only the tracks they want to hear, rather than have to spend money on a CD album that may contain many tracks they don't want. In Britain in 2004, 5.7 million download tracks were sold compared with virtually none in 2003 and sales are predicted to double in 2005. This growth is being fuelled by global sales of portable music players – the most popular of which is the Apple iPod. The music industry is taking advantage of the trend by pre-releasing tracks online and there is now an official download chart. By 2009, experts predict that the digital market could be worth 25% of total music sales, compared to a mere 1.5% in late 2004. There is no doubt that the Apple iPod, and other portable digital music players, have been a major factor in this huge growth rate.

BTEC National Study Guide: Business. See page 185 for order details of individual texts

10

In a nutshell

The assessment criteria grid for each unit states what you must know to get a pass, merit or distinction grade. It is vital that you understand the command words used and obey them or you will not achieve the best grade possible.

Be smart about your grades

On the Edexcel website you can download a form called *Recording Your Achievement*. This enables you to record the grade for each unit you complete. The form also tells you how many points you achieve for gaining a Pass, Merit or Distinction for each unit and how these are added together to obtain your final grade(s). You obtain *one* final grade if you are taking a BTEC National Award, *two* final grades if you are taking a BTEC National Certificate and *three* final grades if you are taking a BTEC National Diploma.

This is very important information, because it helps you to plan where to target your efforts, particularly later in the course.

- Remember that you will obtain more overall points if you divide up your time so that you put the most effort and work into areas where you are weak, rather than spending the most time on assignments you enjoy or find easy! Although it is tempting to keep working on something you like doing, even when you have already done a good job, the danger is that you then don't do so well in other assignments that you have neglected or where you have cut corners. The secret is to put in the right amount of effort in *every* assignment to get the grade you need. For topics you find easy, this may mean you need to spend less time on the assignment than for work you find difficult – despite the fact that you may be tempted to do exactly the opposite! If you do consistently well in all your assignments you will find that this results in higher overall grades than if you do very well in some but poorly in others.

- Keeping your grade profile up-to-date and discussing it with your tutor at regular intervals is an excellent way of keeping yourself on track throughout the course.

In a nutshell

If you are smart you will plan to manage your grades and your overall profile. Do this by recording your grades, spending more time on important or difficult assessments and discussing your profile, as you go, with your tutor.

Be smart at work or on work experience

On some BTEC National courses there is a vocational element and you will need evidence from work or work experience to prove your skills and abilities. In this case your tutor will give you a logbook to keep. On other courses, workplace evidence is not essential but the knowledge and practical experience you gain is still extremely useful, if not invaluable. This only applies, of course, if you are smart enough to recognise the opportunities that occur. Relevant events are likely to include:

- your induction and any subsequent training courses you are asked to attend – even if these are only very short, work-based sessions

- any performance reviews or appraisals you have with your supervisor or boss

- your dealings with customers of the organisation – particularly if you had to respond to a difficult enquiry or solve a problem.

BTEC National Study Guide: Business. See page 185 for order details of individual texts

Your tutor will tell you how to get a witness statement

- the rules, regulations or guidelines that you must follow. You should think about why these have been put in place as well as the consequences of not abiding by them

- your own duties and specific areas of responsibility

- your relationships with your colleagues and how you resolve any problems or difficulties that occur

- skills you have learned or developed by being at work – from time keeping to achieving targets.

If you have to provide formal evidence then one method is to ask your manager, supervisor or colleagues for a **witness statement**. This is a formal document that confirms something you have done and when you did it. Your tutor will give you a form for this. It is also useful to keep your own work diary and to jot down important things that happen that you could use as evidence in current or future assignments to support your arguments for a merit or distinction grade question.

In a nutshell

Work experience may be an essential part of your BTEC National course. Even if it is not, you will gain many useful skills at work that can help you to achieve your award. Make a note of all key events and activities you are involved in. If you need formal evidence, ask your boss for a witness statement.

BTEC National Study Guide: Business. See page 185 for order details of individual texts

12

Be smart about key skills

Key skills are so-called because they are considered invaluable to everyone at work. Most BTEC National students study for a key skills award and in this case the majority of key skills will often be integrated into your main programme of study. This not only helps you to improve your skills, it also means you have the potential to achieve additional points when you submit your UCAS application. Unfortunately not all students complete their key skills awards and so fail to achieve their maximum points score. This is less likely to happen if you are smart and get key skills to work for you, and don't simply see them as more work to do!

- Always check the tracking sheet you are given with your assignments to see which key skills are covered by that particular piece of work.

- Take advantage of any specific classes for key skills, particularly Application of Number, unless you have passed a GCSE Maths examination that exempts you. Otherwise use the classes to improve your abilities.

- There are dozens of benefits if you can communicate effectively and there are almost endless opportunities for practice. You communicate every day – with your friends, family, tutor, boss and colleagues at work – in a variety of different ways. You spend time writing notes in class and writing up researched information. You prepare written documents for your assignments. You work with your classmates when you are doing role-plays or preparing a presentation. If you communicate effectively you will be able to make better presentations, ask the right questions when you are interviewing and write clearer answers to your assignments. You will then gain better grades for your BTEC National as well as your key skills award!

- Information technology is a crucial tool for completing work related tasks. If you develop your word processing skills and your Internet research skills you will produce better, more professional assignments more quickly and more easily. If you intend to continue studying you will find that good IT skills are invaluable at university. If you hope to start working in business when you leave your course then you can expect your future employer to take a keen interest in your IT abilities.

Make key skills work for you

BTEC National Study Guide: Business. See page 185 for order details of individual texts

- The 'wider' key skills are Improving own learning and performance, Working with others and Problem solving. These are likely to be required in many of your assignments. You will also demonstrate these skills if you go to work or are on work experience. Talk to your tutor about how you can use evidence from the workplace to help you to achieve your key skills award.

In a nutshell

There are many advantages to developing your key skills and achieving your key skills award. You will find this easier if you take advantage of all the opportunities you can to develop your key skills and use naturally occurring situations to provide much of the evidence.

Be smart if you have a problem

Many students have personal problems when they are studying. Knowing what to do in this situation makes all the difference. It also means you have one less thing to worry about when life is going wrong.

- Check your college induction information carefully. This should give you detailed information about the people you can talk to if you have a problem. Normally your personal tutor will be the first person on your list but there will be other people available, too, in case your tutor is absent or if you would prefer to talk to someone else in confidence.

- If you cannot find the information you want, ask a tutor you like and trust for advice – or visit the central student support area instead and ask there.

- All colleges have sets of procedures to cover different events. These include the following.

  - **The appeals procedure**   This tells you what to do if you feel that an assignment has been unfairly marked. The obvious first step in this situation is to ask your tutor to explain the grade you have been given, and how this links with the assessment grid. Do this before you think of taking formal action. If you are unhappy with the tutor's explanation then talk to your personal tutor. If you are still unhappy then you have the right to make a formal appeal.
  - **Student complaint procedures**   This is normally the 'last resort' for a student and is only used when a major worry or concern can't be resolved informally. You therefore have the right to make an official complaint but should only do so when you have exhausted all the other avenues open to you. It is not normally used for trivial matters.
  - **Student disciplinary procedures**   This tells you what to expect if you are disciplined for any reason. Although it is wise to avoid trouble, if you do break a rule then it is sensible to read these procedures carefully. Always remember that an honest confession and an apology will normally count in your favour, so if you do have this type of problem, don't be tempted to make matters worse by being devious.

- All colleges will arrange confidential counselling for you if you have a serious personal problem. The counsellor is a trained expert, not a member of the teaching staff. Without giving away any personal details, your counsellor can ensure that you receive the additional support you need from the teaching team – such as more time for an assignment or time off for personal commitments.

- *Never* be tempted to keep a serious worry or problem to yourself. In this situation your concentration is affected, your time is more precious and allowance must be made for this. Being smart about the way you handle problems will enable you to stay on the course and means the problems will have far less impact on your final grades.

In a nutshell

All colleges have a wide range of support mechanisms and procedures in place that are invoked when problems occur. Take advantage of all the help you can get if you have serious personal difficulties. This can be used to support you on the course until the problem passes and your life is nearer to normal again.

BTEC National Study Guide: Business. See page 185 for order details of individual texts

This unit explains what is meant by a business, and introduces the range of businesses in the public, private and voluntary sectors at local, national and global levels. It then goes on to show how businesses set out aims and objectives which give them a sense of purpose, and strategies which enable them to achieve their objectives. Finally, the unit explores plans for the survival and growth of a business.

Unit 1 is divided into four main sections:

- 1.1 Business activity
- 1.2 Strategic aims and objectives
- 1.3 Functional activities
- 1.4 Survival and growth.

Business activity

What is a business?

A business is any organisation that supplies us with a **product** or **service**. A **product** is something offering benefit that we can touch and see, for example a bottle of cola, or a packet of crisps. However, the term 'product' is also often used for things such as a mortgage or insurance policy. In contrast, a **service** is an activity that is carried out for a person or organisation – such as a taxi or bus journey, or the use of a cash machine at the bank.

Wherever we live, businesses are all around us – the local ice-cream van, corner shop, High Street fashion boutique, shopping mall, restaurant, cinema complex, sandwich bar – these are all familiar, everyday examples of business activity, all trying to provide things people want.

What do businesses do?

- McDonald's sells products such as burgers and cola to consumers, while also providing them with a service – a place where they can sit down and chat with their friends.

- Travel agents are service providers, arranging people's holidays to a range of interesting locations.

What types of products and services does McDonald's provide?

BTEC National Study Guide: Business. See page 185 for order details of individual texts

15

○ Internet cafés provide consumers with a product and a service. Customers can surf the Net, play games and e-mail their friends (services), while consuming products such as a cup of coffee and doughnut.

○ The local bus company provides the service of transporting people to and from their homes and places of work, and perhaps to do some shopping in the town centre.

Practice point

Visit a well-known landmark in your area and look around for examples of businesses. These could be corner shops, other retail outlets, restaurants, pubs, cinemas, factories, parks, leisure centres, Internet cafés, and so on. Draw a sketch map of these businesses and state whether they provide a product or a service.

Of course, today you don't need to go to the High Street or local retail park to find businesses. With the rapid development of e-business in recent years you can now access the services of the most weird and wonderful organisations at the click of a mouse.

We also see business activity all around us in terms of advertising, whether in magazines, on billboards, on TV or on the radio. In each of these cases, the businesses are providing products or services to meet the demands or wants of their **market** or likely **consumers**.

Thinking point

Choose three promotional advertisements on TV, in magazines or on posters.

Using the information that you have collected in the Practice point above, set out a box using the template below and fill it in with examples:

What do businesses have in common?

Businesses all provide us with things we want. Some of them are only local, like corner shops. Some of them are the local outlets of nationwide chains like Next or Pizza Express. Some are local outlets of famous global businesses like McDonald's, Burger King or KFC.

Some are owned and run by small private companies, others by large well-known businesses. Other types of business are run by local and national government departments, by charities and voluntary organisations. These will be studied in more detail later on.

Businesses typically concentrate in areas where the owners have spotted a market opportunity. For example, it makes sense to set up a sandwich bar close to where there are many busy working people, who want to buy a ready-made sandwich. Dentists' surgeries are typically located near to densely populated areas. It would make little sense to open a sandwich bar or set up a dental surgery in a remote village.

Thinking point

Make a list of ten products or services that a lot of people use regularly in your local area. Identify the businesses that have been set up to supply these market needs. Are any such products not supplied in your locality? Perhaps this could provide a new business opportunity!

You will have friends, family and neighbours involved in business activities through their work.

Business activity	What is the product or service involved?	What is the name of the business providing it?	Who are the likely consumers or market for this product?
1 Local business			
2 Promotional advert			

BTEC National Study Guide: Business. See page 185 for order details of individual texts

16

Identify three relatives or friends who are at work. What is the work they do – how does their work help to satisfy somebody else's want or need?

The case study below highlights the activity of a new start-up business in Nottingham. It emphasises the importance of being able to meet the needs of the market better than competitors.

Local, national and global businesses

Some businesses simply serve a local market, such as your local dentist or corner shop. Local businesses require a relatively small amount of money to start up but they must need the meet of their customers if they are to succeed.

Other businesses operate on a national scale – for example there are a number of bus companies covering national routes, and many retailing chains such as Sainsbury's and Tesco concentrate on the UK market.

However, in the modern world big business is increasingly carried out on a global scale. For example, the Nissan motor company, which is Japanese-owned, has its main European factory in Sunderland in the north-east of England. From there it ships out many cars to the European market. Nissan is a global company with manufacturing plants in Europe, Asia and America, and sells cars around the world.

A company that produces and sells goods and services across the globe is called a multinational company. Examples of well-known multinationals

Case study   PROvision

Adam Harris and Adam Brodie set up their own company, PROvision, after spotting a gap in the market in the East Midlands. They had studied business and information technology at Nottingham Trent University and had carried out a research project which identified the importance of care for the environment by business. They also knew that the government was bringing in new laws governing the disposal of electronic equipment and computers.

After carrying out market research they found that there were a lot of businesses with surplus computers they needed to dispose of, while others were seeking to buy value-for-money equipment. The two Adams therefore set up PROvision to strip down, recycle and upgrade unwanted computer equipment. They also sell new computer systems to domestic users and businesses as well as providing computer training. Within two years they have built up a million-pound turnover, and won the regional final of the Shell LiveWire competition for enterprising young people.

1 What is meant by a gap in the market?
2 Why was the idea such a brilliant one?
3 Can you identify a gap in the market which you think could be turned into an exciting business idea?
4 What market research would you need to do to develop your idea into a winning company like PROvision?

BTEC National Study Guide: Business. See page 185 for order details of individual texts

are Shell (oil and gas), GlaxoSmithKline (pharmaceuticals), Cadbury Schweppes (confectionery, food and drinks) and Coca-Cola.

Coca-Cola is a good example of a global business. From its headquarters in the United States it produces marketing and advertising campaigns which are rolled out across the globe. On every continent it works with bottling and canning plants, and with local distributors to get its drinks to consumers. One of its slogans is 'within an arm's reach of desire'. In other words, it intends to make sure that wherever people are they have ready access to Coca-Cola drinks – in their local shop or supermarket, at the leisure centre, at sports events, in vending machines, in restaurants, and so on.

Examples of European businesses that trade globally are Nestlé, the Swiss food company producing a range of products from baby food to coffee and chocolate, and Unilever, the Dutch company that produces a variety of products from Wall's ice cream to almost half of the soap powders available in your supermarket. Examples of British companies with a global presence include Manchester United and Rolls-Royce, the engine manufacturer.

Most of today's giant companies started out on a small scale, often with an individual entrepreneur (risk taker) developing a good idea. For example, Coca-Cola was invented in 1886 by Dr John Styth Pemberton in a backyard in Atlanta, Georgia. Nokia was established as a small local forest enterprise in 1885. Michael Marks (the founder of Marks and Spencer) started out as a door-to-door trader in needles, ribbons and bows in the nineteenth century. More recently, Richard Branson created Virgin from a single record store.

Each of these businesses was set up from a good idea, from the hard work of the original entrepreneur, and from a good understanding of the market that the business was operating in. Knowledge of your market is essential – the entrepreneur needs to be able to calculate whether the business will be a success by

examining wider trends in business activity, such as total sales nationwide. This is particularly important today because businesses don't have just local competitors, they also compete with national and international businesses. At one time the local corner shop competed with neighbouring stores. Today, it competes with national supermarket chains like Tesco and Sainsbury's, and increasingly with international chains like the American Walmart company (which owns Asda), and European rivals like Aldi.

Information about business trends

People thinking of setting up a new business and those who are already in business need to have a clear idea about:

- general conditions in the business world – for example, is the economy booming, or is it depressed?

- trends in the particular market sector that they are interested in, such as the fortunes of the fast food sector.

The government regularly analyses business activity and publishes the results in collections of statistics. These are large reference books that are often available in local and college libraries or learning centres. Increasingly this information is available through government reports that can be downloaded from the Internet.

Practice point

Carry out an Internet search looking at National Statistics Online. Access the part of this site that deals with Social Trends (*www.statistics.gov.uk/*, go to 'Social and Welfare' then click on 'Social Trends'). Look at the introductory material to Social Trends – what does it tell you about the types of trends which are covered in the survey?

Case study Identifying a business trend

According to a report in November 2003 by retail consultants Verdict, today's children are becoming 'Generation XL'. Many large clothing companies are struggling to cope with the variety of children's sizes today. Surveys by consumer groups have repeatedly warned that the number of children with weight problems has doubled in the past 20 years.

More than a third of ten-year-olds are overweight, and experts predict that today's children's lives will be shorter than their parents'.

Figures published in November 2003 showed that children approaching their teens were a stone heavier than those 30 years ago.

As body shapes change, retailers are finding it difficult to produce clothes for tall, thin children as well as short, round ones while protecting their profit margins.

The Verdict report questioned whether some major chains should consider no longer selling children's wear and free up their shop floors for items that yield better and easier sales volumes. At the same time, other retailers are looking at the idea of introducing 'outsize' ranges for overweight children, many of whom already buy clothes designed for older children or adults.

1 Why is information like that produced by Verdict helpful to retailers in making business decisions?
2 Explain two contrasting reactions of businesses to the information provided by Verdict, as reported in the case study.

Examples of useful government publications include:

● Social Trends – draws together social and economic data from a wide range of government departments and other organisations. It paints a broad picture of British society and how it is changing, covering 13 main areas.

● Monthly Digest of Statistics – summary information on monthly economic trends.

● Family Expenditure Survey – a continuous survey which ran from 1957 to March 2001. The data continues to be collected in the Expenditure and Food Survey. Provides information about spending patterns in the United Kingdom.

● Regional Trends – regional profiles, households, labour, living standards, and so on.

● Labour Market Trends – detailed statistics showing employment in different industries, levels of unemployment, wages, and many other useful figures.

● Annual Abstract of Statistics – population, social conditions, production, prices, employment.

● Census of Production – data about production by organisations in all industries.

● Business Monitors – statistics on output in different business sectors. The Retailing Monitor is of particular interest, covering retail sales by region.

Businesses sometimes commission specialist studies of developments in their particular market from market research organisations. Some of the best known of these are Mintel, Dunn and Bradstreet, and Datastream. Nielsen publishes the Nielsen Retail Index, which continuously monitors trading areas such as:

● grocery

● health and beauty

● confectionery

● home improvements

● cash and carry

5

BTEC National Study Guide: Business. See page 185 for order details of individual texts

19

- sportswear
- spirits
- toys
- electrical goods.

Mintel reports can be accessed on the Internet and provide a wide variety of information on specific consumer trends. For example, in 2002 Mintel produced a report on the football business in the UK, showing that football is the nation's favourite sport, with 36% of the population showing an interest in the game. This was more than ten percentage points higher than the next most popular sport (snooker). The research showed that fans are becoming increasingly wealthy so that they can spend more on playing and supporting the game.

Growing numbers of businesses

There was a marked increase in the number of new small businesses setting up in this country in 2003, at a time when the number of people working for large companies increased very little.

In 2003 the numbers of people in full-time employment fell by 77,000, while the numbers of self-employed people increased by 127,000.

This movement to self-employment includes a broad range of occupations, from computer staff to accountants, from carpenters to taxi drivers. But it is most marked in the professions, in the banking, finance and insurance sectors, in consulting, and in construction. Often people who set up their own businesses have been made redundant and find it impossible to secure a full-time position elsewhere, so they set up their own enterprise using their redundancy pay.

Business purposes

Typically firms supply products and services in order to make a profit. They are able to do so in response to demand from consumers. Demand exists when consumers are prepared and able to back up their want and need for a product with money. For example, when a singer becomes popular there is an increase in demand for tickets to his or her concerts, and sales of his or her CDs will increase. More generally, there has been a rise in demand for sports and leisure activities as people become better off and more health conscious.

A good example of another type of business that has been able to profit from giving the consumers what they want is Richmond Foods, an ice-cream maker with marketing rights over Nestlé brands such as Fruit Pastilles lollies. It also makes own-label products for supermarkets, including Asda Really Creamy.

Between 1999 and 2003 the profits of the company continued to rise. The company's share of the 'take-home' market – the ice cream you buy in the supermarket and which accounts for 80% of Richmond's sales – rose to 28% from 25%.

How do we work out the profits of the company? In simple terms this involves taking away all the costs of running the business (including the costs of making the ice cream) from the money received from sales (which is referred to as turnover or sales revenue).

Richmond Foods profit and loss account for 2003

	£ million
Turnover (sales)	127
All costs	117
Operating profit	10

Richmond Foods' revenue was £127 million for the year, while the costs amounted to £117 million, giving a profit from the activity of making ice cream of £10 million in 2003.

In 2004 the company expects that new products (such as Yorkie ice creams) will help it to grow its sales. However, it is worried about the rising costs of ingredients, with cream in particular becoming more expensive.

Practice point

1 If Redbury Ice Creams made a profit of £2.1 million out of total sales (turnover) of £30 million, what is this as a percentage?

Use a calculator. Set out your calculation in the following way:

$$\frac{\text{Profit (£2.1 million)} \times 100}{\text{Turnover (£30 million)}} = ?\%$$

2 Your answer should be 7%. Assume that this figure is typical for an ice-cream manufacturer. How much did you last pay for an ice-cream product? How much of this would have gone to the manufacturer as profit?

3 Who else would you expect to have taken a profit from the process of supplying you with an ice cream?

Making a profit is an important aim of most businesses, because if they fail to make a profit they will not be able to do many of the other things that a good business should do.

For example, a good professional football club may have a number of objectives (things that it wants to achieve):

● to play football that people will pay to watch

● to win trophies and important competitions

● to get involved in community projects, for example helping to raise the self-esteem of young people

● to develop young players in the neighbourhood.

However, the football club that is struggling to survive because its revenues fail to cover its costs may find it difficult to meet all of these desirable objectives.

In 2002, 2003 and 2004 most football clubs failed to make a profit, and as a result they struggled to meet their other objectives.

Not all business activity is carried out on a profit-making basis. For example, there are also not-for-profit businesses such as charities which aim to provide a service and to cover their costs or to make a surplus which can be put back into providing community services.

Types of business

To understand how businesses work and what they set out to achieve you first need to have an understanding of the fundamental differences in law between the main types.

There are three main types of organisation in this country, public sector organisations and two types of private sector organisations.

Public sector organisations are run by the government for the people. Examples are government departments such as the Inland Revenue, which collects taxes, and public corporations owned by the government which provide goods and services, such as the BBC (providing broadcasting services).

Private sector organisations are made up of:

● businesses that seek to make a profit for their owners

● not-for-profit organisations such as charities.

Public sector	Private sector	
Government owned	Privately owned	
	●	for profit
	●	not-for-profit

Business aiming for profit

The main types of business in the profit sector are:

● sole traders

● partnerships

● companies

● franchises.

The differences between these are discussed on page 40.

Not-for-profit businesses

Another world of business activity is what we call the **voluntary sector**. This consists of

7

BTEC National Study Guide: Business. See page 185 for order details of individual texts

21

organisations whose main aim is to provide a service rather than to make a profit. Many of these are charities, and they may use the services of volunteer staff but most of their staff are employed on a professional basis.

In recent times new government legislation has been introduced to tighten up the rules about charities. The prime aim of a charity should be to serve the wider community. Under new legislation, the objects of a charity which are recognised as being lawful are:

- the prevention and relief of poverty
- the advancement of education
- the advancement of religion
- the advancement of health
- social and community advancement
- the advancement of culture, arts and heritage
- the advancement of amateur sport
- the promotion of human rights, conflict resolution and reconciliation
- the advancement of environmental protection and improvement
- other purposes beneficial to the community.

An example of a charity is ChildLine, the free 24-hour helpline for children and young people in the UK. Children and young people can call the helpline on 0800 1111 about any problem, at any time – day or night.

Oxfam is an international charity that works with others to overcome poverty and suffering.

Practice point

Carry out an Internet search to find out about one other not-for-profit organisation, such as War Child or Amnesty International. How does the organisation raise funds? What are its stated aims?

Public sector businesses

A local example of public sector activity is some of the services provided by the local authority where you live.

Thinking point

What is the name of the local government authority where you live? And what are some of the local services it provides?

A national example of a public sector business is the BBC. Check out *www.bbc.co.uk*. The BBC charges an annual licence fee to watch TV programmes; you might have seen some of the adverts on TV warning people against the risk of being caught without a TV licence. These cost £121 a year. The purpose of the BBC is not to make a profit, but to broadcast a wide range of information and entertainment. If it aimed just to make a profit, it wouldn't allow students to freely download study guides from the Internet to accompany its GCSE Bitesize series, which is shown in the afternoons.

Another example of a public sector business is the local hospital; this will be operated by a 'trust' like St George's Hospital Trust in south London, which is part of the National Health Service. This organisation is funded by central government to enable it to provide services. If you were to ask a doctor and nurse how they feel about being business people, they might wonder what you meant ... but they do provide key services. Our definition of a business is a broad one and includes all types of organisations that deliver services.

Thinking point

All sorts of people provide or deliver services on behalf of the government. Inland Revenue workers check tax returns, midwives deliver babies, teachers educate you, and so on. Make a list of six other groups of people who deliver services on behalf of the government for you.

Key stakeholders

So far we have been talking about businesses as if they have a life of their own. In fact there are many different groups of people with a stake or interest in how a business organisation runs. Taking a **stakeholder** view of the organisation involves taking notice of these groups. The following diagram shows some of the stakeholders in a company producing fashion clothes.

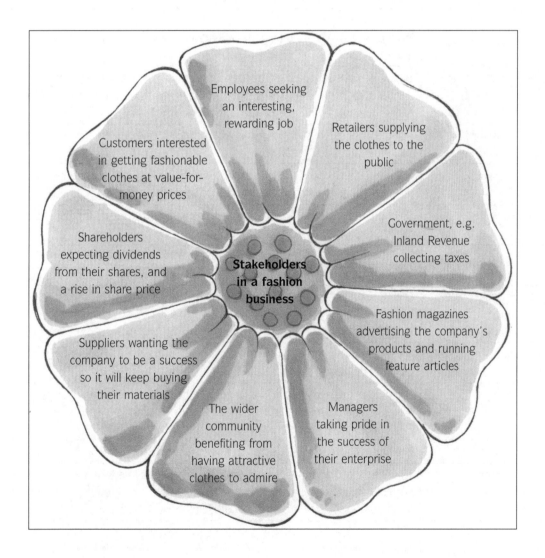

9

BTEC National Study Guide: Business. See page 185 for order details of individual texts

23

Real lives   Dairy Crest

Dairy Crest is a business that supplies milk every day to people's doorsteps. The various groups of people who have a stake in this business are shown in the following table. If the business were to disappear overnight, many of these stakeholders would be affected – as would competitors.

Dairy Crest stakeholders	Reasons for stakeholder interest in the business
Customers	Customers choose to have milk delivered to their door instead of buying it from local shops. If Dairy Crest stopped delivering, those people would have to go to a shop for their milk as they do for other things.
Staff	Delivery and other staff depend on this demand for their employment and income. If Dairy Crest no longer needed them they would have to find other jobs.
Trade unions such as the Transport and General Workers' Union	Trade unions represent the interests of the workers. If Dairy Crest staff were in danger of losing their jobs, the union would fight for those workers to keep the jobs or possibly be offered new jobs in a similar industry.
Local community	Some people see milk deliveries as part of their local community life, like daily postal deliveries to their house.
Pressure groups	Many people are keen to see local community services survive and not be replaced by giant corporations like Tesco, Sainsbury's and Asda.
Suppliers	Dairy companies supply milk to delivery firms. If Dairy Crest closed they would have to find other customers.
Bankers	Banks make money from handling Dairy Crest's account. Without Dairy Crest they would have to find other customers or risk shrinking.
Delivery truck makers/mechanics	Few businesses use electric trucks like milk floats. Without Dairy Crest, truck companies might close their electric truck production and maintenance facilities.
Shareholders	These are owners of the Dairy Crest company who have invested money in the business by buying shares.
Financial institutions	Dairy Crest might have paid into a pension fund like Prudential Assurance so that its staff have pensions when they retire. If Dairy Crest closed, the Prudential would have less savings deposited with them.
Local councils	The local council would lose out on taxes if Dairy Crest closed.
Local Chamber of Commerce	This is an association which speaks up for businesses in a local area and encourages trading conditions that will support business growth. It would have fewer businesses to represent without Dairy Crest.
Property owners/ freeholders	Dairy Crest uses depot space, some of which might be rented or leased from a property owner or freeholder. Closing down might mean that land becomes vacant.
Competitors	Other milk delivery companies might be keen to take over Dairy Crest's share of the doorstep milk delivery market.
Local shops	Local shops would sell more milk if Dairy Crest stopped doorstep deliveries.

BTEC National Study Guide: Business. See page 185 for order details of individual texts

24

Real lives   Michael Moore

Michael Moore, author of the best-selling book *Stupid White Men* and maker of the documentary film *Bowling for Columbine*, used to be a car worker in the city of Flint, Michigan, USA. Almost everyone in Flint either worked for the car company General Motors (makers of Vauxhall cars) or had something to do with the auto industry. In the late 1980s, General Motors closed down 13 car plants in Flint and made 30,000 workers redundant at a time when it was one of the most profitable companies in the world.

Moore spent a year following Roger Smith, the Chief Executive of GM, trying to get him to spend a day in Flint to see the effect of his actions. This is a sad tale of the impact of a business decision on a firm's stakeholders.

Thinking point

Imagine that your college or school closed down tomorrow. Draw a spider diagram of as many stakeholders as you can think of and explain how and why each one would be affected.

Pressure groups

A pressure group is an association of people who get together to put pressure on another group of people to change some aspect of how society works. Amnesty International is an example of a pressure group already mentioned. Compassion in World Farming, Action on Smoking and Health, and the Child Poverty Action Group are all examples of pressure groups.

Compassion in World Farming campaigns to end the factory farming of animals and long-distance transport of livestock, through hard-hitting political lobbying, investigations and high-profile campaigns.

Practice point

Look up either Action on Smoking and Health, or the Child Poverty Action Group. Find out about who they put pressure on and why.

Adding value

One of the most important processes that a business carries out to create profit is termed 'adding value'. This involves turning your inputs into more valuable outputs.

An example of this is a carpenter shaping a number of pieces of wood (inputs), and then fashioning them into a chair (output). Adding value is often far more sophisticated than this, and producers constantly seek to capture value – to make sure that they take for themselves the profits gained from adding value to a product.

One of the most important values added to a product or service is the brand. See the case study on the Coca-Cola brand on the next page.

There are other ways of adding value to a product, such as:

- by giving high quality service to customers
- by offering extras as well as the core product.

The supply chain

A number of stages are involved in bringing a product to the end consumer. We can think of the supply chain as consisting of a number of links, depending on the product.

11

BTEC National Study Guide: Business. See page 185 for order details of individual texts

25

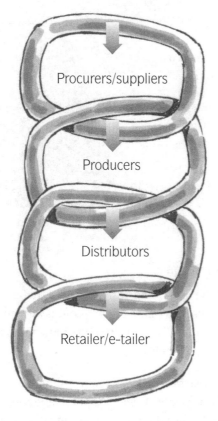

Procurers/suppliers

Producers

Distributors

Retailer/e-tailer

The supply chain

Take, for example, the case of a large confectionery company. The company could possibly be a vertically integrated one – which means that it handles each of the links in the chain itself. However, many businesses nowadays prefer to stick to the stage in the chain that they do best, and to allow other specialist firms to manage the other links.

A confectionery producer makes sweets and chocolate bars in large factories. It buys in supplies of chocolate, sugar, flavourings and other ingredients from a procurer – a specialist firm that buys and sells huge quantities of raw sugar, cocoa and so on.

When the confectionery producer has made, wrapped and boxed the sweets and chocolates, it hires the services of a specialist distribution company to get the products to its own customers – shops and supermarkets who buy in bulk. These customers (supermarkets like Tesco and Asda) are retailers – they break bulk to sell to the end consumer, often in single packets.

Case study   Adding value through the Coca-Cola brand

Coca-Cola is primarily made from sugar, carbonated water, and one or two other ingredients. The same can be said of Pepsi, Mecca, or Virgin Cola. However, what gives Coca-Cola the edge is the well-known brand which is recognised throughout the world, so that Coca-Cola is the second-best-known global phrase after OK.

People are prepared to pay a relatively high price for Coca-Cola because of the brand name and image which is promoted and advertised through global marketing campaigns. The brand is symbolised by the Coca-Cola logo, and the distinctive shape of its bottles.

Thus it is not the water, the sugar, or the secret ingredients that add the most value to the drink, but the brand. The Coca-Cola company has the sole rights to the brand, which it vigorously protects against any form of copying. Next time you buy a Coca-Cola bottle or can, consider how much you are paying for the brand, and how much for the rest of the offering.

1 Can you name other brands where the brand name contributes a substantial amount of the value added to the product?
2 How distinctive is the logo associated with these brands?

BTEC National Study Guide: Business. See page 185 for order details of individual texts

An increasing amount of retailing is now done through the Internet. This is referred to as 'e-tailing' (electronic retailing). For example, Amazon.com is one of the largest booksellers in the world, operating through an e-tailing system.

Practice point

Check the website of Amazon.com to find out whether it stocks this book. What would be the advantage to the consumer of buying this book through Amazon?

Outcome activity 1.1

Pass

Describe the ways in which the business activities of two contrasting organisations meet their stated business purposes. For example, you could contrast a profit-making and a not-for-profit organisation (a well-known PLC and a charity). You could contrast the activities and objectives of businesses in different sectors, such as a retailer and a manufacturing company.

Merit

Explain the way business activities contribute towards achieving stated business purposes. Examine contrasting organisations such as a profit-making company and a charity, or a manufacturing organisation and a services organisation, and explain how their business activities help them to achieve their stated business objectives.

Strategic aims and objectives

The section that follows will:

- explain what is meant by business aims and objectives

- outline a range of contrasting business objectives.

Aims and objectives

All businesses have an aim or purpose. This could be to survive, to grow, to become a market leader, to develop a long-standing family tradition, to provide excellent service, or to create a reputation as the best in their field.

Most commercial businesses want to make a profit; most public sector, voluntary or not-for-profit businesses want to provide a certain standard of service. Sometimes businesses have **service level agreements** where they agree to provide a certain standard of service. A security company might, for example, agree to provide four random security checks on an office building or factory every night between 7 pm and 7 am.

Aims are general, broad statements of purpose. For example, the courier firm Federal Express quotes its aims as 'the world, on time!' These aims can sound impressive and give a rough idea of what a firm does. In practice, though, they have to be turned into objectives if they are to mean anything. An objective is a much firmer statement of purpose and we often say that these have to be SMART. This stands for:

- Specific
- Measurable
- Achievable
- Realistic (or Relevant)
- Time-related.

For a courier firm, specific objectives might be set out in a statement like the following:

> To ensure that 99% of all packages received at our offices by 18.00 are delivered to their final destination before 10.00 the following day within Europe.

You can see that this provides a SMART set of objectives.

- It gives specific objectives related to delivery times.

BTEC National Study Guide: Business. See page 185 for order details of individual texts

27

- Success in meeting objectives is measurable – it will be the difference between 98%, 99% and 100%.

- A 99% success rate may be an achievable objective – whereas 100% may not be.

- The managers of the organisation will know whether a figure of 99% is realistic given previous performance.

- The objectives are related to specific time periods. Typically SMART objectives need to be achieved within a given period of time.

You can see that these SMART objectives give far more precision to an overall business aim.

Practice point

Choose one or two companies that you are interested in and find out more about their aims and objectives. Carry out a web search by using the key words 'aims' and 'objectives' alongside the company name.

Service provision

It is much easier to set SMART objectives for traditional manufacturing industries than it is in modern service organisations.

Societies like our own go through a number of stages or waves of development. Until the second half of the eighteenth century, the UK was an agricultural society (growing things). In the second wave, from 1760 until the Second World War, manufacturing (making things) became very important.

Today we are a service economy in which economic activity is dominated by services such as banking, entertainment and insurance rather than manufacturing products.

SMART objectives can quite easily be set out for manufacturing industry. In book publishing an objective could be to produce 20 new books, to be advertised in a catalogue in March. In car manufacture, an objective could be to produce a new family saloon to capture 20% of the market within three years.

However, it is more difficult to apply SMART objectives to service industries such as those providing health care, education, cleaning or security. In cases like these, business organisations such as hospitals or security firms may have service level agreements (see page 13) where they have to provide a clearly defined level of service for a given period of time.

The hospitals example in the case study on the next page shows that it is possible to establish objectives for service provision. These objectives create targets that managers can work towards, and they are able to measure the success of their actions by comparing performance with targets.

Another example of measuring the success of service provision is in education. Schools and colleges are ranked in league tables each year according to their success in terms of performance indicators such as exam results, truancy rates, and so on. Schools which are persistently poor performers when compared with organisations of a similar type may be inspected and required to implement special measures to improve performance within a specified time period.

The voluntary sector can also use service level agreements as a way of setting and monitoring objectives.

First wave Second wave Third wave

Agricultural society Manufacturing society Service society

Societies go through a number of stages or waves of development

14

BTEC National Study Guide: Business. See page 185 for order details of individual texts

28

Case study   Patient care in the Health Service

Each year key national performance measures are set which are aimed at improving standards of patient care and providing support to NHS staff. For 2002/03 there were nine measures for hospitals:

- emergency admission waits
- total time in the emergency department
- cancelled operations not admitted within 28 days
- financial management
- hospital cleanliness
- improving working lives
- number of inpatients waiting longer than a set length of time
- number of outpatients waiting longer than a set length of time
- number of cancer patients waiting longer than two weeks.

Hospitals must provide information on their success in meeting objectives under each of these headings. Hospitals which are successful in meeting targets are then given more freedom to manage their own affairs in succeeding years.

1 How SMART are the objectives outlined above?
2 Do you agree with the principle of measuring service provision in organisations such as hospitals?

Quality assurance is an important approach to ensuring high quality service provision. This involves teams of employees being given responsibility for making sure that a high level of service is provided. These employees are given training and the responsibility to work together to guarantee high standards. For example, in local authority Social Services departments, teams of employees will regularly meet to discuss ways of providing a better service to clients. Each employee is encouraged to suggest ways of making improvements.

Concentrating on meeting the needs of customers lies at the heart of service provision. In the private sector, businesses will seek to make a profit while doing so. As a result, most of the time services will be produced above cost, that is the price of a service will be more than it costs to provide.

In contrast, some services in the public and voluntary sectors may be provided below cost – they are subsidised services. An obvious example is a charity offering help to children with special needs. Such a service is financed by donations from sympathetic donors. There are many other examples of below-cost provision – for example, in many parts of the country air ambulances transport people to hospital at a commercial loss, because this is an important social service.

In the public and voluntary sectors many activities are charged at above cost prices, but many are subsidised because the aims and objectives of such services have a wider social dimension than simple profit making.

Thinking point

Think of examples of activities run by a public sector organisation such as a hospital or school that are charged at above cost, and those that will be below cost. Explain why these activities fit under the two headings.

Breaking even

Any business that fails to cover its costs will find itself going down a slippery slope. Breaking even is therefore an important business objective, and one that ensures survival at least in the short term.

15

Break-even analysis shows how a business will cover costs or make a profit/loss at different levels of operation.

Let's look at this by examining how a fictional business – Donald's Kebabs – can break even.

Donald's Kebabs sells one main type of kebab, which costs £2 to produce.

The costs that go directly into making each kebab include:

- raw materials – pitta bread, meat and salad
- staff wages – which are based on how many kebabs each employee sells.

The kebabs are sold for £3 each.

On the face of it, it seems that the business is making a profit of £1 on each kebab sold (£3–£2).

That kebab will make a contribution of £1 to my fixed costs.

That will be £3, please!

Variable costs of kebab = £2

However, we haven't accounted for all the costs yet. So far we have only accounted for what we call **variable costs** – how much it costs directly to produce each kebab.

These are called variable costs because they vary directly with the numbers of items produced or sold:

	Variable cost
1 kebab	£2
2 kebabs	£4
3 kebabs	£6

However, we haven't included the overhead or **fixed costs** which are the costs of running the business, regardless of how many kebabs we produce.

These overheads include the rent on the shop, local business taxes, fuel bills, insurance, the manager's salary, and so on. That window smashed last Friday night has to be paid for somehow! Let's say these overheads or fixed costs add up to exactly £20,000 per year. The business has to sell enough kebabs to cover these fixed costs too, or it will make a loss.

As we saw above, every kebab sold brings in (or contributes) £1 towards covering the overheads. This £1 contribution comes from the sale price of £3 minus the variable cost per kebab of £2.

Calculating contribution	
Sale price per kebab	= £3
Variable cost per kebab	= £2
Contribution per kebab	= £1

The business therefore has to sell 20,000 kebabs per year to cover all of its fixed costs (£20,000/£1 = 20,000 kebabs).

If the business is open for 50 weeks in the year (being closed for two weeks' holiday), this means that 400 kebabs will need to be sold each week (20,000/50 weeks). As long as Donald's Kebabs sells 400 kebabs on average each week, it will be safe!

Break-even analysis can be converted into a formula or rule that goes like this:

Break-even sales = fixed costs/contribution

Another way of expressing this is:

Break-even sales = overheads/contribution

In this case, break even = £20,000/(£3–£2 = £1) = 20,000 kebabs.

Let's try these calculations again with a different business example. Imagine you run a hairdressing salon and charge £15 on average to each customer. If the cost per customer in terms of staff wages and materials is £5 and

annual overheads are £50,000, how many customers do you need to serve each year in order to cover your total costs and break even?

Answer: Overheads/contribution = £50,000/£10 = 5000 per year.

If we assume again that your business operates for 50 weeks a year, then you need to serve 5000/50 = 100 customers each week (on average) to break even.

Practice point

Use this formula to work out the weekly break-even sales level for the following three examples, assuming each business operates for 50 weeks per year. You will need to use a calculator. There are three key pieces of information we will be using: fixed costs, variable costs per unit, and sale price per unit.

1   A taxi driver charges an average of £10 per customer for a cost per trip of £5, and has fixed costs of £25,000 per year.

2   A beauty salon charges an average of £12.50 per customer for a cost per visit of £5, and has fixed costs of £100,000 per year.

3   A recording studio charges £25 per customer per hour, with a variable cost of £7.50 per hour and annual fixed costs of £50,000.

This information can be summarised in the following table:

Business	Average charge or sale price	Cost per unit	Fixed costs	Break-even sales level
Taxi driver	£10	£5	£25,000	
Beauty salon	£12.50	£5	£100,000	
Recording studio	£25	£7.50	£50,000	

Work back from the answers below to see how they were worked out.

1   100 passengers per week or 5,000 per year (25,000/(10–5))

2   267 customers per week or 13,333 per year (100,000/(12.50–5))

3   58 one-hour sessions per week or 2,858 per year (50,000/(25–7.5))

BTEC National Study Guide: Business. See page 185 for order details of individual texts

31

Break-even analysis can also be shown on a chart produced either manually or on a computer using a program like Microsoft Excel. We can do it manually by using a sheet of graph paper and plotting sales on the horizontal axis, and costs and revenues on the vertical axis. The numbers to plot can be illustrated by the table below for the kebab shop example used earlier.

We need to plot sales per week up to 800 on the horizontal axis and cost/revenue figures up to £120,000 per year on the vertical axis. This will allow us to draw the following line graphs against weekly sales of 100–800 kebabs:

D: Annual fixed cost

E: Annual total costs = C + D

G: Annual total revenue = A × 3 × 50

You can draw all these lines by mapping the figures in each column against the right sales level.

Let's start with annual fixed costs (line D). We know that these are £20,000, however many kebabs are made and sold. We can therefore plot these as a straight line at £20,000.

Now we can plot annual total cost (line E). Total cost is made up of two parts, total fixed cost (which we have already drawn), and total variable cost. The variable cost is £2 per kebab. We can therefore plot the total cost as a diagonal line starting at £20,000 and rising at £10,000 for every 100 kebabs sold each week. For 100 kebabs, total cost = £20,000 of fixed costs + £10,000 of variable costs (100 kebabs × £2 × 50 weeks).

Now let's take line G (sales revenue). Where sales = 100, plot revenue of £15,000 and mark a small x on the graph paper. Where sales = 200, plot revenue of £30,000. Keep going for the rest of the revenue figures compared to sales and then join all the points up to create a line graph.

We can now illustrate profit or loss at any level of sales. This is simply G (total sale revenue) – E (total costs) at any level of sales.

A	B	C	D	E	F	G	H
Sales output in kebabs per week	Variable costs per week at £2 per kebab	Annual total variable cost (per 50-week year)	Annual fixed costs at £20,000 regardless of sales	Annual total costs (= total variable costs + fixed cost)	Sales revenue per week at a price of £3 per kebab	Annual total revenue (= weekly revenue × 50)	Annual profit or loss (= annual total revenue minus annual total costs)
100	£200	£10,000	£20,000	£30,000	£300	£15,000	−£15,000
200	£400	£20,000	£20,000	£40,000	£600	£30,000	−£10,000
300	£600	£30,000	£20,000	£50,000	£900	£45,000	−£5,000
400	£800	£40,000	£20,000	£60,000	£1,200	£60,000	£0
500	£1,000	£50,000	£20,000	£70,000	£1,500	£75,000	+£5,000
600	£1,200	£60,000	£20,000	£80,000	£1,800	£90,000	+£10,000
700	£1,400	£70,000	£20,000	£90,000	£2,100	£105,000	+£15,000
800	£1,600	£80,000	£20,000	£100,000	£2,400	£120,000	+£20,000

BTEC National Study Guide: Business. See page 185 for order details of individual texts

32

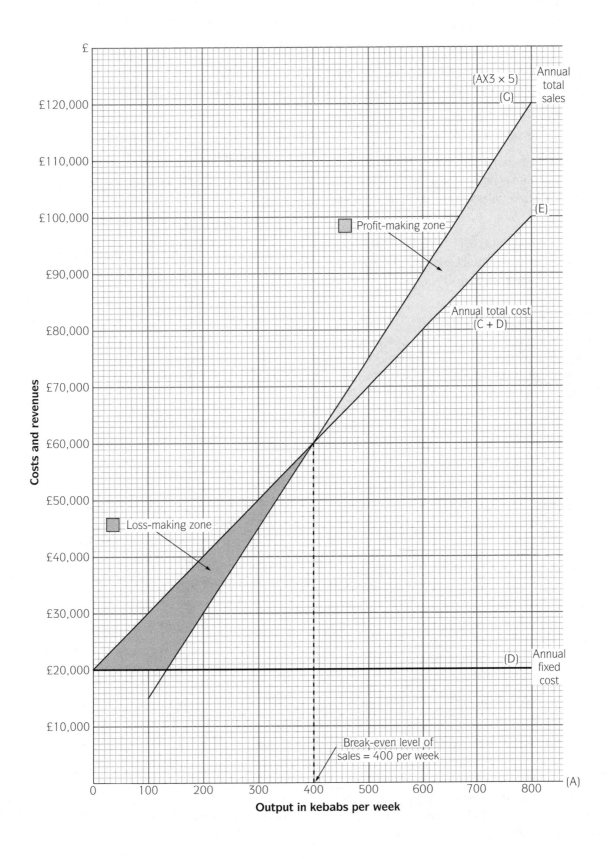

Once you have drawn all the lines you can see:

● the most profitable level of sales is 800 per week

● the break-even sales level which must be met to avoid making a loss is 400 per week

● the way in which total costs and total revenue change as sales rise

● the profit-making zone where the total revenue line is higher than the total costs line (this is where sales are higher than 400 per week)

● the loss-making zone, where the total revenue line is below the total costs line (this is where sales are lower than 400 per week).

Practice point

1 Set out a table for one of the other examples given in the text. Use a piece of paper to graph the costs, revenues, profits and losses at different levels of sales. You could do this as a group with each person doing one set of calculations and drawing one line on a large sheet of sugar paper. Your group could then display the final illustration on the wall.

2 Now try drawing this chart using a software program like Microsoft Excel.

3 Copy the following paragraph and fill in the missing words:

Breaking even is when a business makes sure it covers its _____. Managers take the _____ per unit away from the selling price to get the _____. They then divide their _____ by this figure and find their break-even level of sales, output or service.

Compare what you've written with your friends and see if you agree.

So far we have examined breaking even for relatively small business enterprises. For global companies like Coca-Cola, achieving break-even will involve selling millions of units of their products. This is because fixed costs are so high for global companies. They will include:

● marketing overheads for global advertising campaigns

● distribution costs for global distribution networks

● production overheads for giant production complexes.

Here is an example for a pen manufacturer.

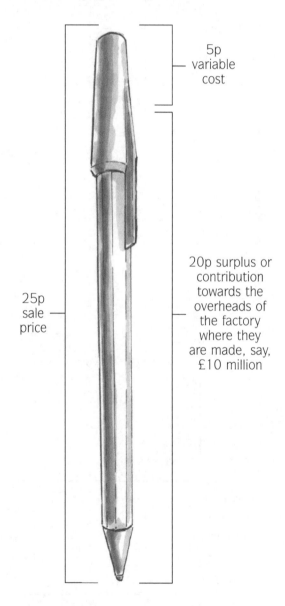

25p sale price

5p variable cost

20p surplus or contribution towards the overheads of the factory where they are made, say, £10 million

Break-even output for pens = £10 million/£0.20 = 50 million.

Profit maximisation

Profit maximisation means the process of trying to raise profit to its highest possible level. This is often achieved by raising sales in situations where each additional unit of a product sold brings in a surplus of revenue over unit cost.

Another way of raising profit levels is to lower costs per unit.

How can we raise sales?

A firm like Bic, making millions of pens, can increase its sales by:

- improving the quality of its product, for example making a longer-lasting pen than competitors
- successful promotion and advertising
- entering new markets, such as new countries
- producing new product ranges, such as more expensive pens.

How can we lower costs?

A firm like Bic can lower its costs per unit sold by:

- buying raw materials from cheaper sources
- paying less for resources such as staff or materials
- producing more efficiently, for example by generating less waste
- increasing output in order to benefit from economies of scale.

Bic is a good example of a business that makes large profits because of economies of scale (as well as other factors such as high-quality production). Economies of scale are the benefits of producing goods in larger quantities, which enable a firm to lower its unit costs of producing and selling goods.

Bic produces hundreds of millions of standard pens. The economies of scale it benefits from include the following:

- Mass production techniques using specialist machinery. It operates large automated factories with efficient modern machinery. A smaller pen producer would work on a smaller scale, often with less efficient machinery. As a result Bic's unit costs are much lower than its rivals.

- Because of its scale Bic is able to raise finance far more cheaply than smaller firms. For example a bank loan for £10 million is cheaper to raise per pound of loan than one for only £1 million.

- Because of its size Bic is able to employ the best international managers, who are attracted by the prestige and pay associated with working for Bic.

- Bic is able to arrange huge discounts when dealing with suppliers of plastic and packaging materials.

In the diagram on page 22 you can see that a firm can break even more quickly, and increase the size of its profits, by raising sales.

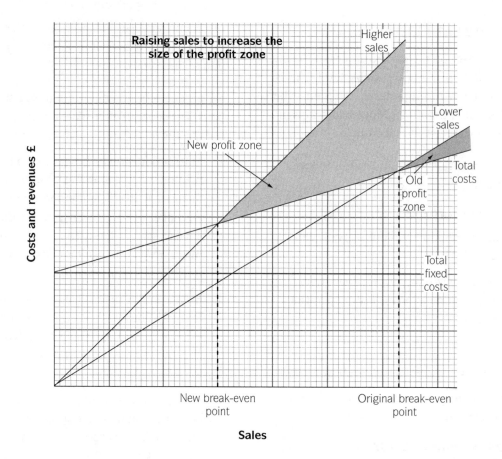

It can also break even more quickly and increase the size of its profits by lowering costs.

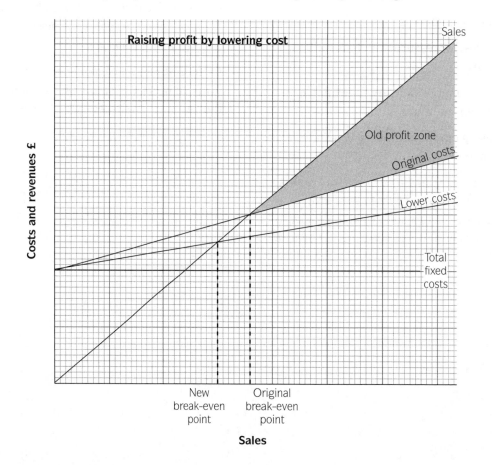

BTEC National Study Guide: Business. See page 185 for order details of individual texts

36

And, of course, it can break even more quickly and increase the size of its profits still further by both raising sales and lowering costs.

Note that when a firm benefits from economies of scale, this will mean producing with higher fixed costs. For example, the overheads at Wimbledon Lawn Tennis Club are much higher than for a local tennis club, and the overheads of a global confectionery company such as Cadbury's are far higher than a small regional sweet manufacturer's. However, where the large company benefits from economies of scale is in having very low variable costs per unit. The large company is also able to spread its fixed costs over millions of units of product. For example, when you buy a can of Coca-Cola, your can will need to pay only a fraction of a penny towards fixed costs because billions of other cans of the drink worldwide are also making a contribution.

If we compare the costs of a small drinks manufacturer with Coca-Cola we will find the points as summarised at the bottom of this page.

The net result is that Coca-Cola's sales are much higher, its costs of production are much lower and profits as a percentage of sales are much higher.

Of course, firms in the real world don't set out purely to maximise profit. It is truer to say that they seek 'satisfactory' levels of profit in the long term. Satisfactory profits are ones that keep stakeholders happy, and particularly shareholders who expect to receive a good return on their shares.

> **Thinking point**
>
> Think of some businesses in your area which have sprung up recently and seem successful. Why do you think they are making a profit?

The dangers of cost cutting

The problem with profit maximisation is that businesses can be tempted to cut corners to reduce their costs. Doing this increases the gap between total costs and total revenue, and therefore increases profit.

Cost cutting can drive firms to pollute the environment rather than spend money on disposing of waste responsibly. A common example is the 'fly-tipping' of waste, such as building materials like earth and rubble, beside public roads.

A more serious problem can be caused by cutting corners on staff health and safety. In Britain today, one person dies at work every working day because of dangerous conditions. Accidents are sometimes due to workers not taking care, but there is no doubt that some employers cut corners on safety, and economise on facilities, protective clothing and training for dangerous duties. The death of 21-year-old student Simon Jones within two hours of starting work at Shoreham docks in April 1998 is a tragic reminder of the need for health and safety at work to be taken seriously. In a recent court case, it was found that London Transport maintenance engineers were expected to work alongside live electrical rails, where they risked fatal electric

	Total fixed costs	Fixed cost per unit	Variable cost per unit
Coca-Cola	Very high, because production is on a very large scale.	Tiny, because fixed costs are spread over billions of units of product sold.	Tiny, because economies of scale lower unit costs of production.
Small soft drinks firm	Relatively high, because there are fewer economies of scale.	Relatively high, because sales are smaller.	Relatively high, because there are fewer economies of scale.

BTEC National Study Guide: Business. See page 185 for order details of individual texts

37

shocks, not to mention being hit by trains. In his findings the judge commented that there was a disregard for health and safety 'from the boardroom [of London Transport] down'. The idea that a job could cost you your life does not seem to worry some employers, for whom profit is more important than people.

Every worker has a legal right to be protected from hazards at work under the Health and Safety at Work Act 1974, and the Employment Act 2002.

Earlier we saw that a business brand is one of the most important ways to add value. Another is good health and safety practice, and concern for employees and consumers. The firm that ignores these concerns risks the value of its brand. For example, in recent times we have seen the value of a number of fast food brands fall considerably as consumers become increasingly concerned about the healthiness of their products.

Practice point

Carry out a risk assessment of your college environment. What sorts of risks do you think that employees and students face there? Do you think better facilities, equipment and training could make it a safer place of work? Quote some details of hazards for discussion in class.

Thinking point

Can you identify practices in the illustration below which involve putting profits before people?

BTEC National Study Guide: Business. See page 185 for order details of individual texts

Poor pay and conditions

Employees can be exploited through working conditions which their managers and company directors would not be willing to share.

They can also be paid wages that are so low that they cannot achieve the basic standard of living enjoyed by most other people.

The national minimum wage applies to most adult workers in the UK and was introduced in 1999. There is one rate for workers between the ages of 18 and 21, and a higher rate for workers 22 and over. The government has also introduced a minimum wage for under-18s, to prevent abuse of youth labour. Employers need to keep records to show that their workers are receiving at least the minimum wage.

A study carried out in 2003 showed that the UK had one of the worst records in the European Union of abuse of the minimum wage, particularly in large cities. Women in particular continue to be exploited and to receive lower pay than men. A survey carried out by the trade union GMB in November 2003 showed that women are still earning almost £100 a week less than men and that full-time women employees received, on average, less than three-quarters of men's earnings.

In 1999 the government also introduced the European Working Time Directive, setting a legal right to a maximum 48-hour week for many workers, although employees can opt out of this agreement if they want to work longer. Increasingly, women are being put under pressure to work longer than 48 hours, particularly in professional jobs. Women are having to work longer hours in order to earn a decent wage. They have had to respond to changes in the job market, and there is increasing pressure for women with young children to get a job. Another survey showed that more than half of working women would like to quit immediately, because they feel pressurised. The following table shows the percentage of employees working more than 48 hours a week:

	Women	Men
Professional	42	27
Managers and administrators	25	20
Other	7	11
Sales	6	3
Clerical/secretarial	5	3
Nursing/care	4	–
Plant and machine operators	4	14
Security	3	3
Craft	3	5
Associate professional and technical	–	8

Source: Labour Force Survey, December 2003

Profits finance growth

Another reason to build up profits is to create finance to pay for growth, development and expansion. Businesses can apply for bank loans but in reality, the main source of finance is often what firms are able to plough back themselves. Banks want to see evidence of **entrepreneurs'** and managers' ability to make a profit on their own before bank money is likely to be invested.

Thinking point

Can you think of businesses in your area that seem to be really successful and to be growing really fast? Where do you think their finance comes from?

An advantage of finding finance without borrowing from the bank is that entrepreneurs then do not need to pay the **interest** due on bank loans. Interest is a key cost, especially for small businesses.

25

BTEC National Study Guide: Business. See page 185 for order details of individual texts

39

Real lives — What do Robbie, Kylie and Madonna have in common?

The finance that firms need for growth can also come through **investment** by outsiders such as friends or family, or finance corporations such as 3i (Investors in Industry). Singers like Will Young and Gareth Gates who win competitions like Pop Idol will get backing or investment from record companies. They will receive recording contracts and the record companies will promote their records on radio and organise TV appearances and concert tours.

It is the same with investors and successful business projects. If you can prove you deserve it, finance companies might come looking to invest in your business. Look at Robbie Williams, Kylie Minogue and Madonna. Artists like these are business propositions – they have a very marketable presence. But remember, finance companies can drop you just as quickly as they take you up!

Another advantage of creating your own finance as an entrepreneur is that you are free to decide how to use your funds. Businesses that owe a lot to the bank have to check every detail of future plans with the bank manager before making decisions. They are less able to follow their business instincts, and have lost some of their freedom.

Thinking point

Can you think of business products which used to be successful but have now died away? A good place to start is with pop artists. How many can you think of who were popular a few months ago but have now vanished?

Share capital

Businesses looking for investment on top of bank loans and their own retained profit may well set up **limited** companies. This is a business structure that allows entrepreneurs to sell **shares** in the business in return for the investment they may need to finance expansion into new markets or to create new products. Most companies are private limited companies, which do not advertise publicly for additional investment but attract investors through private networking.

When a company is set up, the capital invested in it is expressed as a number of shares. These can be bought by investors wishing to put in finance in order to create profit. If a company wants to attract more investment, it can offer more shares for sale. Share owners receive a certificate with details of how many shares they own and their rights within the company, for example to attend the annual general meeting. Owners of shares get a slice of profits at the end of the year in the form of a final dividend, or part-way through the year in the form of an interim dividend.

Each owner of a slice of the company puts in capital in return for shares. Their share of the profit is the dividend that is paid at regular intervals.

Thinking point

If you had £10,000 and wanted to invest in a company that you thought was profitable, which would you choose and why?

Going public

The Stock Exchange is one of the most important institutions in British business, because it provides a means through which investors can buy and sell

BTEC National Study Guide: Business. See page 185 for order details of individual texts

40

shares in hundreds of different public limited companies. Investors know that they can buy shares on the Stock Exchange, and just as importantly they can have their shares sold.

A public company is one that has its shares bought and sold on the Stock Exchange.

Companies can pay to have a full quotation on the Exchange, so their share prices appear on the dealers' visual display screens.

To create a public company, the directors must apply to the Stock Exchange Council, which will carefully check the accounts.

Case study   Share price information

Stock Exchange prices are set out in national newspapers, organised according to the sector the business falls into, such as 'Aerospace and defence', 'Automobiles', or 'Banks'.

The following extract shows how Manchester United's shares appeared, in the sector 'Leisure, entertainments and hotels', on Wednesday, 23 December, 2003. Remember that the newspaper is published on 23 December, so the prices relate to the day before.

52 weeks		Stock	Price	Change	Price/earnings ratio
High	Low				
267	100	Manchester United	267	0.0	18.7

The first two columns (High and Low) tell us the highest price and the lowest price that Manchester United shares have been in the previous 52 weeks, that is from December 2002. Share prices are set out in pence, so the highest price the shares have been is £2.67.

If we look at the Price column for 22 December we can see that it was also £2.67 – so that Manchester United shares were at the highest they had been for 12 months.

The Change column shows any change in price from the previous day. We can see that there was no change, so on both 21 and 22 December the shares traded for £2.67 each.

The price/earnings ratio compares the price of the shares to the earnings on each share in the company. 'Earnings' are the amount of profit that each share makes, and it can be calculated by dividing the profit of the company by the number of ordinary shares in the company.

Earnings per share = profit/number of ordinary shares

The reason Manchester United shares have such a high price/earnings ratio (18.7) is that the share price is high, because investors have confidence in the ability of the club to keep making profits. The share price has risen well above earnings.

So when a business is doing well:

- the share price will be high for a business of its type
- the share price will be nearer the high than the low for the year
- the price/earnings ratio will be high.

1 Look at a recent copy of a national newspaper. What is Manchester United's latest share price?
2 Is it near to its high or its low?
3 What is the p/e ratio?
4 Would the information you have found encourage you to buy shares in Manchester United, given investors' views on its likely future growth?

BTEC National Study Guide: Business. See page 185 for order details of individual texts

Companies wishing to float on the London Stock Exchange have a choice of two markets, the Official List or the Alternative Investment Market (AIM).

The Official List, or main market, is for established companies. There are now over 3000 companies whose shares are traded on the Official List.

The Alternative Investment Market is a market for smaller companies to allow younger and growing businesses to fund their growth. Firms on the AIM have fewer rules to comply with, but they must at all times use the assistance of a firm providing advice, called the nominated advisor.

As well as attracting investment from wealthy individuals, public companies also receive investment funds from professional investors such as insurance companies or pension funds. For example, Manchester United's biggest shareholders in 2003 were two wealthy Irish investors, and a wealthy American. But in addition shares in Manchester United were owned by insurance companies and pension funds.

One way of measuring the performance of a company is by looking at its share price. If a company is doing well or is expected to grow, its share price will rise as new investors become keen to buy those shares.

If, on the other hand, the company has run into difficulties and is expected to do less well in the near future, the share price drops as investors sell the shares and buy others in more profitable

companies. Financial organisations such as pension funds have teams of professional investment analysts who constantly monitor the performance of shares in different markets. They buy shares in companies that are growing strongly and sell shares in companies whose growth has stagnated or even gone into decline. These movements in share prices can have a major impact on companies, because the share price is a very public illustration of how well they are seen to be doing by investors in **the City**.

Share prices rise when the company is expected to do well and fall when it is expected to perform poorly.

Practice point

Study the financial pages of a quality newspaper such as *The Times*, *Independent* or *Guardian* to identify a large public company whose shares are rising or falling significantly. What can you find out about the reasons why?

A major fall in a public company's share price means that its book value falls and it then becomes an attractive target for takeovers. The financial pages of the quality newspapers are full of articles on how well different companies are doing, and takeovers feature regularly.

For example, in the fiercely competitive world of supermarkets, the profits of Safeway fell substantially in 2003 compared with its rivals. As a result the share price fell, as did the price/earnings ratio of the company.

Practice point

The following table compares the share price positions of Morrisons and Safeway in December 2003. How does the information show that Morrisons is in a healthier position, and that Safeway is likely to be taken over?

Food and drug retailers, Wednesday 10 December, 2003

High	Low	Stock	Price	Price/earnings ratio
328	197	Safeway	287	13.3
238	141	Wm Morrison	230	18.8

Growth

We have looked at how profit-seeking organisations often want to maximise profits. We also find that such businesses want to grow as fast and far as possible.

There are two main reasons why it is good for a business to grow:

1 By being large the business is able to benefit from economies of scale, and to spread costs over large outputs. A global brand like Nike is recognised everywhere and its sheer size enables it to engage in huge advertising campaigns and marketing initiatives, as well as to invest vast sums in product research and development.

2 By growing, a business can aim to gain the largest share of its market (**market share**). When a firm gains the lion's share of the market, profits typically follow. The firm that has 51% of the market knows that its nearest rival can gain only 49%.

Case study   Google

Larry Page and Sergey Brin arrived relatively late in the Internet search engine market behind front runners like Yahoo, Altavista and Ask Jeeves. However, as they searched for venture capital to support their enterprise they were convinced that they had stumbled on a Big Idea.

Today, we know that Google has blown the competition out of the water. In 2004, the company is likely to go public to raise even more capital.

Brin and Page set up Google in 1998 in a Silicon Valley garage. Today they are ranked eighth and ninth in the world's richest under-40-year-olds.

Initially the pair were funded by family and friends. Google (the name derives from Googol, the term for a number starting with 1 followed by 100 zeros) handles as many as 75% of all Internet search requests – about 200 million a day. 'Googling' has become second nature to millions of computer users.

Google's major innovation was in searching out web pages according to their popularity and inter-relationship, not just according to key words. The results are therefore more likely to be what the customer needs.

This approach is what has accounted for almost all of Page and Brin's success. One early investor was so impressed that he wrote them a cheque for $100,000 (£60,000) on the spot. The method was then improved further by the speed with which Google managed to present its results.

A major source of revenue for Google is its 100,000 advertisements, which enable the company to make about $150 million in profits on revenues of about $500 million.

1 Why has Google been able to grow so quickly?
2 How would you measure the growth of Google?
3 Why have the owners been so successful?
4 Why do you think that Google has decided to go public?

29

BTEC National Study Guide: Business. See page 185 for order details of individual texts

43

A company like Google with excellent growth prospects is likely to experience a lively interest in its shares. There are many other companies which provide strong growth potential.

Companies with growth potential

Company	Sector	Projects	Likely impact on shares
Google	Information technology	Web browser development	Rush to acquire shares which may be traded on the Internet to gain a global market
BP	Oil and gas	Building huge gas pipeline from Siberia to China (1,300 miles)	Prices will increase on expectation of future growth in profits
GlaxoSmithKline	Pharmaceuticals	Has a large number of new drugs and medicines waiting to be launched onto global markets	Prices will increase in anticipation of future profits

Of course, none of these companies is certain to do well. The high-tech sector is highly competitive, and a rival may launch an alternative to Google. BP's pipeline passes through a number of political hotspots and is open to sabotage; and firms in the pharmaceutical industry have to be very careful about the side effects of 'wonder drugs'.

Internal and external growth

Companies can grow internally by ploughing back profits into the business. This is referred to as 'organic growth', and is an excellent way of growing provided that the business can generate enough profits to finance planned expansion.

However, a problem with this method is that it is relatively slow, and in markets where **competitive advantage** is gained by being bigger, a firm might lose market share to a more aggressive rival.

A quicker way to grow is to take over or merge with other businesses. For example, when Rolls-Royce wanted to expand into the marine (shipping) market, it took over some of the best-known names in this market.

Taking over a company involves buying a controlling interest in its shares. A merger involves two companies voluntarily coming together to form a new enterprise, such as two well-known banks. This form of growth is referred to as 'acquisition'. A company might acquire another business because it does not possess the required skills or resources itself, or because it can buy up a business relatively cheaply if the share price undervalues the potential it sees in the business. Usually when a company decides to take over another one, the share prices of both will increase.

Practice point

Examine reports on a takeover bid in the financial press. Check the share prices of the two companies concerned to see what is happening to their share values.

Ethics

We've taken a look at what business do and how their activities support their aims. We've seen that one of the main aims of commercial businesses is to make as much profit as possible. We've also seen that this can mean cutting production costs and raising income from sales. And as already mentioned (page 23), this can have **ethical** implications.

Many companies state that before they consider the financial objectives of any project they first consider the ethical implications. For example, a gas exploration company might say that it would never consider working on gas reserves in partnership with a government that has a bad human rights record. Working with a corrupt, immoral government is bad ethically, so it is also bad for a company's reputation, and many companies today recognise that to protect their brand they must have the highest ethical standards.

Other organisations take a stand about what is ethical. For example, at the end of 1992 the Co-operative Bank announced a strategy of taking deposits from, and offering financial services to, only organisations that were not involved in controversial activities such as factory farming, blood sports, production of animal fur, manufacture of tobacco or political repression. The bank believes it is necessary to take a stand in order to show the public that it is an ethical company. It does not hide the fact that its ethical stance is also likely to bring in new custom.

More recently the Co-operative Bank has set out policies that are committed to sustaining the environment, in key areas such as the following.

- Financial services – the Co-operative Bank actively encourages its business customers to take a pro-active stand on the environment, and the bank will invest only in companies that do not repeatedly damage the environment.

- Purchasing – the bank welcomes suppliers whose activities are in line with its ethical policies.

- Legislation – the bank supports all government legislation concerning the environment.

More and more companies are giving higher priority to ethical commitments and this is supported by pressure from government, consumers and other interested groups.

In February 2001, the Financial Times Stock Exchange Group put more pressure on big companies to behave ethically by creating the 'FTSE4Good' index. This includes only companies that meet certain ethical standards. For inclusion, companies need to satisfy standards in three areas:

- environmental issues

- social and stakeholder issues

- human rights.

The requirements are tough and companies must also pay to be registered in the index. The registration fee goes to the United Nations children's charity, UNICEF.

Non-ethical behaviour

In 1984, part of a chemical plant operated by the company Union Carbide near the Indian village of Bhopal exploded, giving off large amounts of cyanide gas. Several thousand people in the local community, including workers at the plant, died as a result. Many more were blinded. Union Carbide operated a similar plant in the USA, but this had far better health and safety protection for staff and the local community. Why should health and safety be treated as less important in India than in the USA? Was this an ethical choice on the part of company managers?

Practice point

For more on the Bhopal tragedy, see the archives of newspapers like the *Guardian* at *www.guardianunlimited.co.uk*

Tragic loss of life also occurred at Zeebrugge in 1987, when the cross-Channel ferry *Herald of Free Enterprise*, operated by a company called Townsend Thoresen, sank after setting sail with its bow doors still open. The company had insisted on a rapid turnaround of ferries in the ports in order to increase sales revenue.

And as already mentioned on page 23, Simon Jones, a 21-year-old student, died within two hours of starting work at Shoreham docks in 1998. A lack of health and safety protection, training and supervision cost a young person his life.

BTEC National Study Guide: Business. See page 185 for order details of individual texts

45

About 250 people die at work every year in Britain, many in accidents that could have been prevented with a higher regard for health and safety at work. This illustrates how business decisions can have serious ethical consequences. Spending more on health and safety can reduce profits, but it saves lives. And, of course, when the actions of the companies concerned are exposed in the clear light of day this can have dire consequences for their business prospects. Jarvis, a construction and maintenance company that was held responsible for failing to properly maintain the railway points that caused the Paddington rail crash in 1999, saw its share price plummet in 2003 when the inquiry into the disaster pointed the finger of blame at it.

Outcome activity 1.2

Pass

Explain the role of break-even analysis in supporting the achievement of strategic aims and objectives. Describe the various components of break-even, and show how these would enable an organisation to meet its aims and objectives. One way of doing this would be to do a break-even calculation for a college and show how this enables the organisation to meet its objectives.

Merit

Analyse the importance of break-even analysis in supporting the achievement of strategic aims and objectives. Analyse the way in which the various components of break-even work together – the relationship between costs and revenues, and how this helps the organisation to achieve its aims and objectives. Either use fictional examples, or a real case study for a small organisation such as the college shop.

Distinction

Evaluate the effectiveness of contrasting organisations' business activities in achieving strategic aims and objectives. You will need to consider how well the organisations manage and run their activities, and the types of improvements that could be introduced to make the organisation more effective in achieving its aims and objectives.

Functional activities

Most large businesses can be thought of as having a number of **functions** or specialist areas – a production department, sales department, advertising department, and so on. A hospital might have an accident and emergency department, maternity ward, geriatric ward, and so on.

Interdependent functional activities

The various functions of the organisation can be seen as working together to help the organisation to achieve its overall aims and objectives. For example, in a firm like Gillette, which produces razors and other shaving products, we can see this relationship.

The Gillette example in the diagram opposite shows that while each area has its functional specialism, the functional areas work interdependently to achieve the same organisational aim. Activities are **interdependent** when the various functions work together to achieve shared aims and objectives.

Interdependence in the activities of a small business

Many businesses have a lot of different areas of work to take care of. A corner shop, for example, has to make sure it is well stocked with the right products for its local market. These have to be well laid out and clearly priced in an attractive store with spaces well used.

The store has to be secure when it is closed, so shutters and security grilles might be used. During business hours, it might make use of closed circuit TV (CCTV) to discourage people from shoplifting. The shop has to be staffed by people who know how to deal with the public and can be trusted to handle money. The cash register or till should never be left unattended. Staff working shifts have to be organised – the shop may be open from say 8 am to 8 pm. Staff holidays, rest breaks and sick leave have to be planned for. The stock has to be replaced, and

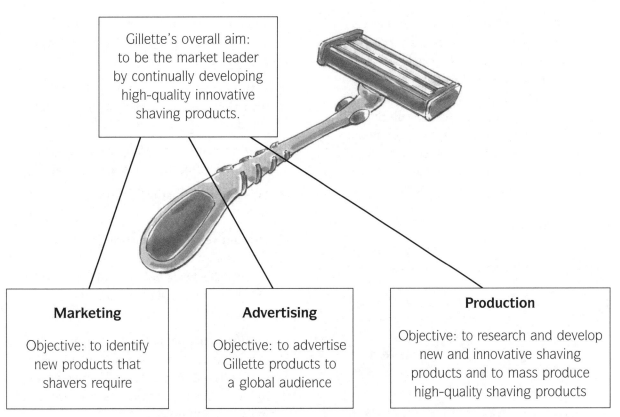

Gillette's overall aim:
to be the market leader
by continually developing
high-quality innovative
shaving products.

Marketing

Objective: to identify
new products that
shavers require

Advertising

Objective: to advertise
Gillette products to
a global audience

Production

Objective: to research and develop
new and innovative shaving
products and to mass produce
high-quality shaving products

Functional areas within Gillette

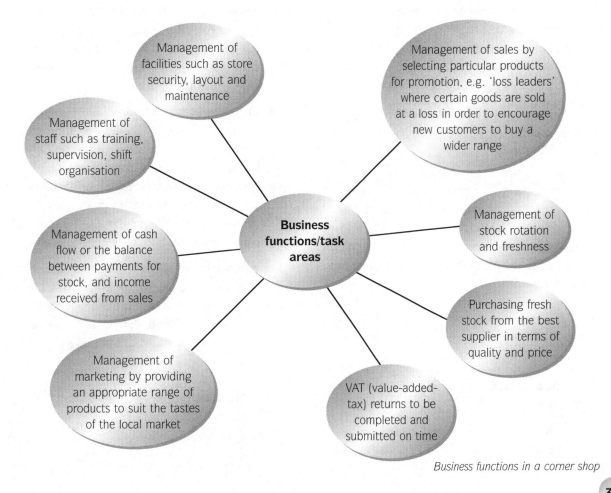

Management of
facilities such as store
security, layout and
maintenance

Management of sales by
selecting particular products
for promotion, e.g. 'loss leaders'
where certain goods are sold
at a loss in order to encourage
new customers to buy a
wider range

Management of
staff such as training,
supervision, shift
organisation

**Business
functions/task
areas**

Management of
stock rotation
and freshness

Management of cash
flow or the balance
between payments for
stock, and income
received from sales

Purchasing fresh
stock from the best
supplier in terms of
quality and price

Management of
marketing by providing
an appropriate range of
products to suit the tastes
of the local market

VAT (value-added-
tax) returns to be
completed and
submitted on time

Business functions in a corner shop

33

BTEC National Study Guide: Business. See page 185 for order details of individual texts

47

perishable food needs to be 'rotated' or moved to the front of shelves so it doesn't get wasted. The business has to be able to keep track of all its sales and has to have enough **working capital** to buy fresh stock from places like cash-and-carry warehouses. The window displays have to have interesting and eye-catching promotions that will encourage new customers to come in and buy. So there's a lot involved in running a successful corner shop.

Practice point

Check out your local corner shop and give it a score out of 10 for each of the areas of functional activity mentioned above. Is it tidy? This is the function of overall management and maintenance of appearance/layout. Is it always properly staffed? This is the function of staffing/employee management. Does some of the stock look old and past its sell-by date? This is the function of stock management/control.

A corner shop can be managed effectively by a family or small team, but they have to be versatile owner-managers or entrepreneurs in order to survive. Some single-person businesses can be simpler than this, such as a taxi driver or ice-cream seller.

Interdependence in the activities of a global business

Motorola is a massive global corporation (ranked 100th largest in the world in 2003). It produces a wide range of electronic equipment like mobile phones, supplies a world-wide market and has annual global revenues of over $30,000 million. It employs people on every continent in factories, offices and sales.

Organisations like Motorola arrange their departments into the most logical functional areas, including:

- **Design:** ideas for new types and styles of products.

- **Marketing:** researching the global market to find out who buys the products, why and what they are looking for in the future. Marketing and design work together to agree new products.

- **Production:** organising the manufacture of the product range to consistently high quality standards.

- **Distribution:** organising the transport and the supply of outlets all over the world.

- **Sales:** organising the local promotion and sale of products.

- **Human resources:** ensuring that the organisation has all the staff it needs to operate effectively, both centrally at head office and locally. Staff training and development is also their responsibility.

- **Finance:** managing the outflow of business expenditure, such as on components, office rent and staff wages. They also manage the inflow of income from sales so that the firm makes a profit overall.

- **Administration:** ensuring the smooth running of the organisation as a whole, making sure that different groups of staff communicate effectively with each other at different times.

- **MIS:** Management Information Services (or Systems). Managing the flow of information through the organisation, using computer-based systems and information and communications technology. Information is a very important ingredient in accurate decision-making so its storage, retrieval and communication have to be managed carefully.

Every department will have targets and goals that flow logically from the overall plan created by the company directors and senior managers. Management is about making sure each task group does what is necessary to make sure targets are met.

Practice point

Research one takeover and give a brief summary of who took over whom, where, when and why.

BTEC National Study Guide: Business. See page 185 for order details of individual texts

48

Case study Targets and goals in confectionery

When the chocolate company Rowntree started selling Kit Kat, Lion Bar and After Eight mints in continental Europe in the mid 1980s, the managers had to be sure this plan to increase sales was going to work well. In fact it worked so well that Rowntree was the target of a takeover battle by the Swiss companies Nestlé and Suchard, who wanted to take advantage of Rowntree's achievements by buying up the whole company. Nestlé won and bought Rowntree for £2.2 billion, over five times its initial book value of £400 million. That's a lot of chocolate!

Drilling down your objectives into functional areas

It is useful to examine the hierarchy of objectives that exist in an organisation at any one time. For example, a global company might be split into divisions: a European, American, and South-East Asian division. Each division might be split into functions such as marketing, production and finance.

We can think of objectives as being drilled down through the organisation so that everyone is pulling in the same direction. Of course, the creation of these objectives would need to be carried out through consultation of headquarters with divisions, divisions with functions, functions with front-line employees, and so on.

Organisational aims/objectives

Divisional objectives

Functional objectives

Objectives for teams and individual employees

Drilling down objectives through the organisation

Organisations operate through directors and owners devising an overall plan. An example of such a plan would be for Ryanair to continue to grow its market share among low-cost airlines. This overall aim is then translated into targets for each department or functional area. Marketing might target three new routes on which to challenge rivals. Sales might target three more effective ways of persuading people to fly with Ryanair. Operations might need to find three ways to improve flight punctuality and reduce waiting times for baggage. Finance might target credit-card fraud as a key way of improving sales income.

Each functional area will therefore have a target or standard for success, so that its contribution to the organisation as a whole can be measured and improved. And of course every employee in each of these functions will be given targets tied in with functional objectives – a sales clerk would be given a sales figure to meet, and so on.

For example, if an organisation has an overall objective of increasing sales by 10% within five years, this 10% figure might be translated into a target for divisions, functions and individuals. Of course it might be more realistic to set some divisions, functions or individuals higher targets than others, depending on what is feasible, in order to achieve the overall objectives.

Interdependence between departments and functional areas is key; they all carry out different tasks but these have to be co-ordinated so that the whole organisation makes progress. There would be no point in designing a mobile phone no one wanted, or stocking up in areas where local

BTEC National Study Guide: Business. See page 185 for order details of individual texts

49

unemployment meant that customers could not afford to buy. So making sure that all these functional areas are working together is one of the key roles of managers.

A non-profit-making, voluntary organisation such as Amnesty International needs to make sure that it campaigns against human rights abuses all over the world in a consistent way. Its activities in Turkey are interdependent with those in Guantanamo Bay in that the organisation as a whole has to operate consistently with its overall aims or mission statement.

Thinking point

Identify a way in which the activities of a department in a business organisation are interdependent with those of another, and explain why.

Contracting out functional areas

Sometimes businesses **contract out** some of their functional activities – in other words they give a contract to a separate company to perform certain functions, such as cleaning. The Dell computer company supplies a worldwide market with personal computers but has contracted out its after-sales operation to call centres in Delhi, India. This has been done to save costs and therefore increase profit, because Indian staff are paid lower wages than English staff would demand. Indian staff may take names like Rose and David and are briefed on developments in *East Enders* and *Coronation Street* in order to be able to relate to English computer customers. This cuts costs for Dell and creates employment in India ... but how do you think UK call-centre workers feel?

Outcome activity 1.3

Pass

Identify and describe connections between the different functional activities carried out in a selected business organisation and its strategic aims and objectives. In a chosen company, describe the functions and show the links between the various functions and how these help the organisation to achieve its objectives.

Merit

Analyse the contribution of different functional activities carried out in a selected business organisation towards the achievement of its aims and objectives. Explain the role of the various functions in a well-known business organisation, and show how these functions work together – production and sales, sales and accounts, and so on. Explain how these functions work together to help the organisation to achieve its objectives.

Survival and growth

So far we have talked about businesses planning for growth. In reality most businesses are in competition with others and are threatened by competition, so they need to make sure they survive. For example, British Airways used to be the dominant UK airline. However, in recent years Ryanair has been far more successful and today its Stock Exchange value is several times that of British Airways, even though it has far fewer planes, less equipment and employs fewer staff.

Ryanair has been successful because it has been able to 'sweat its assets' – the assets being the things it owns like its aeroplanes; it makes them work harder. A Ryanair aircraft will make many more trips each week than a British Airways one, and Ryanair has stripped out unnecessary space such as kitchen areas and some toilets in order to fit in more fare-paying passengers.

Ryanair has therefore been able to take market share from British Airways. British Airways has had to devise a plan to compete with Ryanair and the other low-cost airlines such as EasyJet. It has

BTEC National Study Guide: Business. See page 185 for order details of individual texts

50

decided to focus on the upper end of the market – to be a high-quality airline offering relatively expensive flights with very high levels of service and individual attention to passengers.

If Ryanair is to continue to survive and prosper, it must have a plan to compete with other low-cost airlines. If not, it could fail as a business and become **insolvent**.

Practice point

Research an example of business competition and explain who is competing with whom, for what, and how!

Business organisations can be threatened in many ways. Competitors can take away market share by introducing new products which are more attractive, of better quality and/or cheaper. Tesco television advertisements have featured the actress Prunella Scales playing the role of a fussy mother-in-law phoning other supermarkets to check prices while filling her trolley in Tesco. Record companies compete with each other by

signing boy-bands or girl-bands that meet a market demand for a certain type of music. Car companies compete with each other on grounds of design, speed, safety or price. Bars and clubs compete with each other by having better known DJs, 'hipper' music, endorsement by popular radio stations, and better reputations for smart dress and security.

National and local economic and political conditions can also threaten business survival. When the Millennium Dome closed in 2001, local hotels, bars, restaurants and even taxis in and around Greenwich suffered a drop in takings. Since 11 September 2001, the day of the tragic attack on the World Trade Center in New York, airline travel has dropped dramatically as tourists have begun to fear terrorism in a new way.

Planning for survival

A firm's survival can therefore be threatened by anything that might reduce its income. We have seen that profits are the difference between revenue (or income) and costs (or expenses).

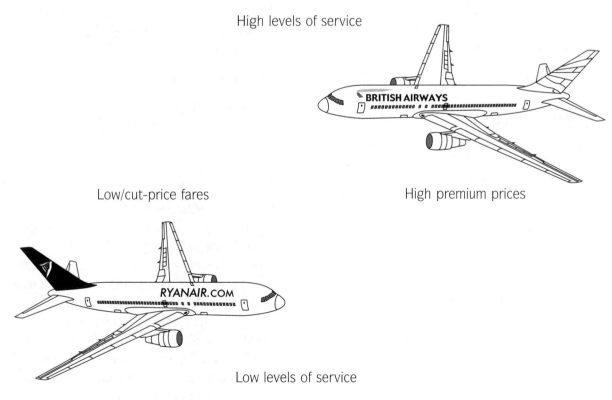

High levels of service

Low/cut-price fares

High premium prices

Low levels of service

The survival route for British Airways

37

BTEC National Study Guide: Business. See page 185 for order details of individual texts

51

If sales revenue falls, because of competition or a move by consumers away from a brand, profit will also fall. Profit can also fall because of a rise in costs. One of the major costs for most organisations is staff wages.

Before the Minimum Wage was introduced, well over a million workers were employed in jobs which paid less than the rate set. Many of these workers would have been young people in part-time or casual jobs with no permanent contract. The minimum wage for 18- to 21-year-olds is £4.10 per hour from 1 October 2004. When it was introduced, certain groups of employers argued that this rise in wage costs would drive firms into bankruptcy. That has not happened. And interestingly, the same argument is not used when senior executives award themselves bonus packages worth millions of pounds!

But anything that raises firms' costs can narrow the gap between income and expenditure to the point of threatening survival.

Another example is the cost of servicing debts in terms of interest payments. Many small businesses express concern at rises in interest rates imposed by the Bank of England. This is because the cost of interest payments on their overheads and bank loans rises as a result. For some, survival is threatened.

Practice point

Research a firm that has become bankrupt or insolvent in recent years and explain why this might have happened.

A firm threatened with bankruptcy or insolvency may try to survive either by cutting costs or by raising revenue. For example, a High Street computer business that offers repairs as well as designing and setting up websites could give up its expensive High Street premises and lay off staff, downsizing to a one-person business operating from home.

SWOT analysis

Many firms keep a constant eye on their market by carrying out regular SWOT checks. A SWOT analysis is a review of strengths, weaknesses, opportunities and threats for an organisation. (It can also be referred to as a WOTS-up analysis!)

Strengths and weaknesses are internal – they are factors relating to the product, or to the firm itself. In contrast, opportunities and threats are external – they relate to factors in the market, or to what the competition is doing.

Let's apply this kind of analysis to a well-known product brand like Police sunglasses. We could identify its SWOT factors to be these:

- **Strengths:** well-known brand, clearly associated with fashion icons like David Beckham and George Clooney

- **Weaknesses:** expensive, beyond the reach of most consumers at £100+ per pair

- **Opportunities:** chance to create a cheaper range of Police brand glasses at an intermediate price, such as £30 per pair

- **Threats:** competition from other designer-branded ranges of glasses such as Armani, DKNY and Adidas.

Thinking point

Carry out a SWOT analysis for another product which is at the heart of a firm's survival – such as a product or service produced by a small local firm.

Increasing output/sales

One way in which firms may try to ensure their survival is by increasing their level of output or sales, thereby spreading their fixed costs. As we have seen, in this way the cost per unit sold drops. An example of this might be a taxi firm employing three drivers for eight-hour shifts round the clock, so that the taxi is always on the road and bringing in revenue to cover the fixed cost of buying it. As Richard Branson has said, 'my planes are not making money if they're not in the air!'

BTEC National Study Guide: Business. See page 185 for order details of individual texts

52

Planning for growth

A more optimistic view is to think about opportunities for growth. Take a local café that offers an all-day breakfast and operates from 8 am to 6 pm. If it is located in a reasonably fashionable part of town where there are nightlife venues nearby, it could expand its business by operating as a more upmarket restaurant or cocktail bar in the evenings. In the first instance, it might try doing this on Friday and Saturday nights, then possibly extend to other nights of the week. This might involve paying additional staff to work evenings, but would bring in additional revenue to contribute towards the fixed costs of rent or lease on the property. Once this business is functioning well, possibly every evening, it could consider the option of buying a similar business in a different locality in order to repeat the experiment and see if it works there.

Many well-known restaurant chains such as Pizza Express have grown in this natural and 'organic' way. A key risk in doing this is the possibility that the successful formula cannot be repeated elsewhere. An idea that works at one end of town might not be successful at the other. Once the business has committed itself to buying a lease on the second outlet it has increased its costs in ways that could threaten its survival unless it can find a way of bringing in extra revenue.

Thinking point

Can you find a local example of a business that has grown significantly? How have they done it?

Taking a risk

Being successful in business involves taking some form of risk. Entrepreneurs put their money at risk, because their business might fail. Volunteers working for aid agencies in war-torn zones often put their own lives at risk.

Real lives   English rugby

You have to take a risk to get rewards. A few years ago the English Rugby Football Union set itself the task of winning the World Cup in 2003. It appointed Clive Woodward as the team coach, an individual known for a risk-taking approach to the game. In the end we know what happened: England were taken to the wire by Australia but managed to win in the last minute of the game with a drop goal by Jonny Wilkinson. In December 2003, English rugby was able to announce a profit of £18.4 million for the year. This profit was up by 21% on the previous year, with turnover increased by almost 50%.

The profit enabled the RFU to wipe out the last £19 million of debt for the development of Twickenham (England's national rugby ground). The building of a new stand is estimated to have increased the ground's capacity from 74,000 to 84,000. At the same time, interest in the game has soared, with Twickenham selling out of replica shirts and other memorabilia faster than they can be manufactured.

Of course, if England had failed, as they so nearly did, all of this would have been different!

39

BTEC National Study Guide: Business. See page 185 for order details of individual texts

53

Choice of legal status

Sole trader is the most common form of business ownership and the easiest to set up. A sole trader is a business owned by one person – though it may employ a large number of people.

To start up as a sole trader all you need to do is inform the tax authorities and open your door. There is no complex paperwork to be filled in beforehand. In addition, you can keep the affairs of your business private, because your are not required to publish reports – simply to fill in your tax return for the Inland Revenue each year.

Typical examples of sole traders are plumbers and small building firms, graphic designers, providers of personal services such as mobile hairdressers, small shops, and a number of information technology services such as web-page design.

Partnerships are business associations between two or more owners of an enterprise. Partnerships usually have between two and 20 members, though there are some that have more. Partnerships are found in many different areas of business where more capital, skill or expertise is required than can be provided by a single owner.

Companies are groups of people who share responsibility for a business venture. The owners (shareholders) jointly put a stock of capital (money) into the business. They are then entitled to a share of the profits in the form of a dividend.

Private (limited) companies issue shares which can be bought and sold only with the permission of the board of directors, who are appointed to represent shareholders. In contrast, a public company (PLC) has shares that are traded on the Stock Exchange, and can be bought and sold freely.

Franchises are a 'business marriage' between an existing, proven business (the franchisor) and a newcomer. The newcomer (known as the franchisee) buys permission to copy the business idea and use the name of the established company in a certain location. The franchisee commits his or her capital and effort. The franchisor commits the trading name and management experience, and often supplies materials and equipment.

Legal structures of business

The legal structure of a business is an important decision. If you start up on your own, the obvious choice is to be a sole trader or sole proprietor. The owner invests his or her own savings, collects the profits, foots the bill for losses and has to meet all debts. For debts, the owner has unlimited liability; this means that the owner has to meet all debts, regardless of how high these rise.

The owner may team up with others in a partnership. Each partner puts in capital and draw profits in proportion to what has been invested. They also have unlimited liability, so they have to meet their debts however high they become.

Setting up a limited company can be done for as little as £200 and allows business people to attract investment by selling shares. They also benefit by having **limited liability** on debts, so they only have to pay up to a limit if they become insolvent. They must register with Companies House, and submit business accounts each year.

Practice point

Contact Companies House and explore the exact cost of setting up your own company. Look in *Exchange and Mart* newspaper to check the prices of 'off-the-peg' companies.

Risk of takeover

One of the risks you take by setting up a PLC is that of being taken over. As mentioned on page 35, the Rowntree chocolate company, which had operated successfully for over 100 years, was taken over by the Swiss giant Nestlé in the 1980s after a takeover battle with Suchard – 30% of its shares were bought up in a so-called 'dawn raid'

BTEC National Study Guide: Business. See page 185 for order details of individual texts

54

lasting 15 minutes. Rowntree directors came to the office to find they now worked for Nestlé.

This is one of the risks of forming a public limited company. Directors of PLCs have to make sure they deliver profit figures which please their shareholders, many of whom are likely to be large financial institutions like insurance companies and pension funds. If they don't do this, shareholders can start to sell and a trickle of share sales can become a flood where the book value of the company, built up over a lifetime, can crash within a day. Some companies are so concerned by this risk that they arrange to buy 51% of their shares on the stock market so they can be protected against the risk of takeover. The American jeans company Levi-Strauss spent $1.5 billion doing this in the 1990s.

Other structures

Some business people set up a company under a franchise agreement where they make, sell or distribute a well-known product in return for a share of the profits (see page 40). Many fast-food companies like KFC, Burger King and McDonald's run at least part of their operation in this way. Other well-known examples include Pizza Express, KallKwik and Prontaprint. You might have to invest several hundred thousand pounds for a 20-year partnership with Pizza Express, for example, but you benefit from the greater market presence enjoyed by a well-known product compared to your chances operating on your own as an unknown.

Another interesting company option is to set up a co-operative. This is where a group of people share the operation of a company, investing capital and taking a share of the profits. An example might be the New Internationalist Co-operative. It produces a monthly magazine mainly concerned with the development of poorer countries. There are about 25 members who take it in turns to edit an issue, commissioning writers from different parts of the world to talk about their experiences or a particular subject. Whereas companies have a

division between owners and staff, co-operatives have a more equal structure, although they frequently appoint managers from within.

Another popular type of business in the public sector is a trust. A local hospital or chain of doctors' surgeries might be set up as a National Health Service trust. This is a non-profit-making body that can receive funds from government for certain clearly defined purposes. All the doctors' surgeries and clinics in a particular area might be financed, for example, by a primary care trust.

Charities, as we have seen, are organisations set up to provide for the welfare of a particular client group. Oxfam, for example, was the first organisation to deliver food to the capital of Cambodia, Phnom Penh, after the country was ravaged by the dictator Pol Pot in the 1970s. One in eight of the population had been killed by the Khmer Rouge and many were starving.

Charities are often companies limited by guarantee, so they cannot become indebted beyond a certain level. Charities usually aim to provide as full a service as possible but may also make a surplus, which can then be ploughed back into better services for the future.

Businesses are likely to choose the structure that offers them the best opportunities for raising capital and protecting themselves against debt. For many small and medium-sized businesses, the popular option is a private limited company.

Business people can get high-quality professional advice on choosing the right structure from commercial solicitors and accountants, but their advice does not come cheap! Small businesses have access to experienced advisers via the Business Link Partnership which has been set up across the country. This is a mentoring scheme where more experienced entrepreneurs can offer guidance based on their valuable local experience. The London Borough of Islington Business Link office caters for the enormously wide range of businesses in an area which includes fashionable upmarket restaurants along

BTEC National Study Guide: Business. See page 185 for order details of individual texts

55

The legal status of businesses

Type of business	Legal status	Advantages and disadvantages of structure
Sole trader	Unlimited liability. Business and owner are the same body in law.	No reports are required so business affairs can be kept private. Business will be small, with limited capital. Owner may have to sell personal possessions to meet debts of business.
Ordinary partnership	Unlimited liability. Set up by Deed of Partnership. Business and partners are the same in law.	Business consists of two or more partners. Business is relatively small with limited capital. Owners may have to sell personal possessions to pay debts of partnership. Business has to be dissolved when a partner dies or leaves.
Limited liability partnership	Partners have limited liability. Set up by Partnership Act (2002).	Recently introduced to cover large partnerships like accountancy businesses. Partners have limited liability.
Private company	Owned by private shareholders. The company is a separate body from its owners. Shares can only be bought and sold with permission of the Board of Directors. Limited liability.	Shareholders have limited liability. Able to raise more capital than sole traders or ordinary partnerships. Must comply with Companies Act setting out required legal documentation, tax details, and reporting requirements. Pays corporation tax.
Public company	Owned through shares traded on the Stock Exchange. Limited liability status. Must register as a company with the Registrar of Companies and with the Stock Exchange. The company is a body in law in its own right.	Can raise most capital as shares can be bought and sold on the Stock Exchange. Shareholders can lose only the value of their shareholding. Able to buy other companies. Must fill in detailed paperwork for the Registrar of Companies. Pays corporation tax.
Charity	Must be a body set up for charitable purposes. Supervised by the Charity Regulation Authority. Charities with income of more than £1 million must produce a standard information return including details of fund raising and content of work.	Charities with incomes of over £10,000 per year must register. Must pass a 'public benefit test' – showing work is intended to benefit the general public. Registered charities have credibility in fundraising. Exemption from income tax, corporation tax and capital gains tax.

BTEC National Study Guide: Business. See page 185 for order details of individual texts

56

with smaller, more humble firms struggling to survive in highly deprived neighbourhoods.

Most towns also have a Chamber of Commerce which supports local business and offers guidance and advice. Often it supports firms through informal contacts and opportunities to 'network', pool ideas, share experiences and learn from each other's successes and failures. The Small Firms Enterprise Development Initiative is also a source of helpful guidance. See *www.sfedi.co.uk*

Practice point

Check out your local Chamber of Commerce and Business Link Partnership. See what services they offer new businesses.

Business plans

New businesses produce plans to be presented to bankers, investors and other potential stakeholders. Established businesses are also required to do so when borrowing. Most businesses have to undertake business planning to some extent.

A simple business plan should be clearly set out under the following headings.

- **Contents page.** This is useful in any kind of report that is more than two or three pages long.

- **The owner.** This section should give some information about the owner (or owners) including educational background and previous experience. It should also contain the names and addresses of two referees.

- **The business.** This should first show the name and address of the business and then go on to give a detailed description of the product or service being offered, how and where it will be produced, who is likely to buy it, and in what quantities.

- **The market.** This section will describe the market research that has been carried out, what it has revealed, and details of prospective customers – how many there are, and how much they would be prepared to pay. It should also give details of the competition.

- **Advertising and promotion.** This should give information about how the business will be publicised to potential customers. It should give details of likely costs.

- **Premises and equipment.** This section should show that the business has considered a range of locations and then chosen the best site. It should also give details of planning regulations (if appropriate). Costs of the premises and equipment needed should also be included.

- **Business organisation.** This should state whether the enterprise will take the form of sole trader, partnership, company, or franchise.

- **Costings.** The business should give some indication of the cost of producing the product or service, and the prices it proposes to charge. It is then possible to make profit calculations.

- **Finance.** This should give details of how the finance for the business is going to be raised. How much will come from savings? How much will need to be borrowed?

- **Cash flow.** This should list all expected incomings and outgoings over the first year. Cash flow calculations are important, but at this stage can only be approximate.

- **Expansion.** Finally, the business should give an indication of future plans. Does it want to keep on producing a steady output, or is dramatic expansion possible? Does it intend to add to its product range? What kind of new competition is likely to emerge, and how will the business deal with it?

BTEC National Study Guide: Business. See page 185 for order details of individual texts

57

Outcome activity 1.4

Pass

With the use of a commercially supplied template, prepare a business plan to support future survival and growth. Use a simple business plan outline supplied by a High Street bank, or Shell LiveWire, to produce a business plan designed to achieve the survival and growth of a business idea of your choice. You can create your own figures.

Merit

Explain the importance of a business plan to support future survival and growth. Use a commercially supplied template for a business plan to create a business plan of your own for a fictional organisation, and explain how creating the plan will help the organisation to survive and grow.

Distinction

Assess the contribution of functional activities to the success of a business plan in achieving organisational aims and objectives. Using a business plan of your own for a fictional organisation, assess how the different functional activities of the organisation (such as sales and human resources) will contribute to the success of the plan.

Key terms

Breaking even
making sure costs are covered

The City
the part of London in which financial service corporations (e.g. the Stock Exchange, banks and investment companies) are concentrated and have operated for over 300 years

Competitive advantage
all of the ways in which an organisation is able to gain an edge over its rivals by doing something better than them – by having a more recognisable brand, better quality products, more outlets, etc.

Consumers
end users of a product or service

Contracting out
giving a contract to another firm to carry out various activities for a business, e.g. contract cleaning or contract marketing

Entrepreneur
a person who takes risks in setting up his or her own business

Ethics
the ideas people have on what is right or wrong. For many business organisations, the right thing to do is to make as much profit as possible from sales. This is what some shareholders want. This may be fine as long as there are only winners, and no losers. The problem is that some people can be harmed, directly or indirectly, by other people's profit-seeking

Fixed cost
a business cost that does not vary with the level of output or sales

Functions
the components or departments of a business involving some form of specialism, e.g. marketing, accounts or sales

Insolvent
unable to meet current debts; the term for going bankrupt applied to companies

Interdependence
the idea that a chain is only as strong as its weakest link; every member of staff or department has to act as part of a larger organisational team

BTEC National Study Guide: Business. See page 185 for order details of individual texts

Key terms

Interest
the cost of borrowing money – if I borrow £100 from the bank at 10% annual interest, I will have to pay back £110 this time next year

Investment
money paid into a business by outsiders to make it grow, create more profit and pay a share to the investors

Limited liability
being able to set a limit on your total exposure to debt when you set up – doing this means you do not have to pay the full extent of business debts you might run up, and it offers valuable protection

Market
the whole situation in which products and services are traded by buyers and sellers

Market share
the proportion of a market controlled by one particular business. The diamond company De Beers, for example, controls 80% of the worldwide market for raw or uncut diamonds. Stand outside its offices in Charterhouse Street, London EC1 and you are standing on top of a diamond mountain stored in the vaults deep underground

Private sector
owned by shareholders and usually aiming to make a profit

Product
a thing of substance made naturally or manufactured for sale, e.g. eggs, cheese, television sets, cars

Public sector
owned by central or local government or a similar type of public authority – usually aiming to provide a service

Service
intangible item such as legal, medical or financial advice, a haircut, or the local greengrocer delivering your purchases to your home

Service level agreement
a commitment by a business to provide a certain level of service to a client for a certain period of time

Shares
slices of a company

SMART objectives
business aims translated into a set of measurable objectives – the idea is to be able to tell clearly whether they have been achieved

Stakeholders
all the people affected by a business in one way or another

Variable cost
a cost that increases with the level of output or sales

Voluntary sector
the part of the economy made up of voluntary organisations, where the managers and workers are unpaid volunteers

Working capital
money needed for day-to-day running of the business, such as paying wages, buying new stock, and so on

BTEC National Study Guide: Business. See page 185 for order details of individual texts

59

End-of-unit test

1 Classify the following according to whether they are in (a) the public sector, (b) the voluntary sector, or (c) the private sector.

- Manchester United PLC
- the BBC
- Oxfam
- Amnesty International
- Mars (confectionery)
- Coca-Cola
- ChildLine
- Bank of England
- local councils
- McDonald's
- the armed forces
- Orange.

2 List two useful government statistical publications that you would find from searching National Statistics Online. Explain what would be in one of these publications.

3 What is meant by the term 'demand'? If I want a new car, does that constitute demand?

4 If a business has a turnover of £10 million and all of its costs come to £3 million, what is its profit?

5 Who owns public sector businesses?

6 Why might the owners of a private limited company not want to go public?

7 Where would you buy shares in a public limited company?

8 Why might someone whose job has become redundant choose to enter into a franchise agreement rather than another form of business?

9 List four 'objects' of charities that are regarded as lawful.

10 List three groups of important stakeholders in a PLC, and explain what their stake is in the company.

11 Give an example of a pressure group and state what its object is.

12 How can a brand add value to a product?

13 List three stages in a typical supply chain.

14 What is meant by 'e-tailing'?

15 What does the term 'service level agreement' mean?

16 If a business has fixed costs of £100,000, sells its products at £10 each and has variable costs of £5, what is:

- contribution per unit?
- the break-even level of sales?

17 Give three examples of economies of scale for a large hotel chain.

18 What is the European Working Time Directive, and who does it affect?

19 What does the price/earnings ratio of share prices measure? What is this a good indicator of?

20 What is meant by organic growth in a company? Why is this a good way to grow?

BTEC National Study Guide: Business. See page 185 for order details of individual texts

60

Resources

Texts

Bradburn, R: *Understanding Business Ethics*, Continuum, 2001

Cawson, Alan: *The Top 200 Websites on E-commerce*, Kogan Page, 2000

Dransfield, R: *Business Law Made Easy*, Nelson Thornes, 2003

Mellahi and Ward: *The Ethical Business*, Palgrave, 2003

Riddersdale and Nordstrom: *Funky Business*, Prentice Hall, 2000

Magazines

The Economist

Business Review Magazine, available by subscription from Philip Allan Publishers, see *www.philipallan.co.uk*

General Studies Review: provides regular articles on business, with business and economics case studies.

Websites

www.tt100.biz The Times 100 case studies provides a wealth of case study material outlining up-to-date business practice

www.ukonline.gov.uk Government information and services on-line

www.cisco.com Cisco Systems – networking for the Internet

www.easyjet.com EasyJet low-cost airline

www.ibm.com/e-business IBM on-demand business

www.hp.com/ Hewlett-Packard computers

www.guinness.com Official Guinness website

www.waterstones.co.uk Waterstones working with Amazon.co.uk

www.tesco.com Tesco on-line

www.directline.co.uk Direct Line insurance

www.eaglestar.co.uk Eagle Star insurance

www.amazon.com Amazon main site

www.dell.com Dell computers

www.lastminute.com Last-minute travel and entertainment

www.ebay.com Ebay on-line shopping

BTEC National Study Guide: Business. See page 185 for order details of individual texts

61

As human beings we are communicating all of the time, sometimes consciously, sometimes without realising we are doing it. Every message we convey gives an impression of us, and the same message can communicate different meanings to different people. What messages do the following extracts convey to you?

> 'I was sick of lames telling me what to do and giving me their opinions. There was no way a square across a desk was going to tell me about my life and my lifestyle and be able to capitalise off it more than me. That would make me a square.'
>
> *Damon Dash, head of the $300-million Roc-A-Fella record label.*

Does he come over as:

- exciting and go-getting?
- a person to admire and aspire to be like?
- anti-establishment and rude?
- illiterate?

> 'Gordon Brown's record over the last six and a half years has been one of tax and spend and fail. It is the height of hypocrisy for him to make the same claims yet again about tax, public services reform and the economy.'
>
> *Michael Howard, speaking as Shadow Chancellor*

Does he come over as:

- honest and critical?
- giving an objective opinion?
- just another politician complaining about the opposing party?
- desperate?

BTEC National Study Guide: Business. See page 185 for order details of individual texts

> PLZ 4GV ME but i cant W8 2 C U L8R It will B GR8 2 CU@ SKOOL B4 EVRY1 arrives
>
> ILU
>
> C
>
> *If (like me) you need a translation of this, it is:*
>
> 'Please forgive me but I can't wait to see you later. It will be great to see you at school before everyone arrives.
>
> I love you.
>
> C.'

Does this writer come over as:

● hip and trendy?

● tender and affectionate?

● insincere?

● illiterate?

● someone you would long to see?

● someone you would avoid?

Communicating is a real minefield. We try to communicate one message, but sometimes a different one comes over to our audience. Our message is affected by our audience's opinions, experiences, prejudices and state of mind; but the first impression we create is vitally important.

In business we often get only one chance to convince our audience. The impression we want to give is that we are a professional person whom the message receiver should be keen to do business with. But it is so easy to give a very different impression if our business communication skills are poor. That is what this unit of the course is all about – creating positive impressions by presenting information in a professional manner.

In this unit we will be looking at how to gather appropriate information, how to use it well and how to use the different business communication methods in a professional way. We shall also be looking at companies to see how they communicate with us, their prospective customers, in order to create an appropriate corporate image for themselves.

This unit is divided into four main areas:

● 4.1 Gathering relevant and accurate information

● 4.2 How information can be processed

● 4.3 Presentation of gathered information

● 4.4 Creative corporate communication.

BTEC National Study Guide: Business. See page 185 for order details of individual texts

Gathering relevant and accurate information

In order to present a true and accurate picture to the receiver, it is vitally important that the information gathered is accurate and that it is professionally presented. First let us look at the types of information that you may need to gather.

Types of information

Qualitative information

Qualitative information cannot be interpreted in numbers. It informs business organisations about the opinions and preferences of individuals, and helps them to understand their customers. This type of research involves finding out people's opinions, feelings, likes and dislikes and the motivations behind their actions. It is used to find the psychology underlying buying decisions.

Typical methods for the qualitative researcher are:

- surveys and questionnaires – using a set of questions with a range of people

- observation – watching what happens, such as how many people enter a store, what items people buy, etc.

- interviews – a one-to-one question-and-answer session

- focus groups – gathering a group of people together to share views and discuss opinions.

There are problems associated with qualitative research. People often find it very difficult to explain their behaviour or their motivations. Also, many people are reluctant to tell a researcher what makes them do what they do. Sometimes interviewees will try to guess the answers that the interviewer is looking for, and will give the answers they think the researcher wants to hear, whether they agree or not. As a result qualitative researching requires careful planning if the researcher is to find out what truly motivates customers.

Quantitative information

Quantitative information can be examined statistically. Typical quantitative information includes:

- how often people buy a product

- how much they are prepared to pay for the product

- how many people buy the product in a typical week

- any seasonal changes in sales patterns.

Note that all these questions produce answers in numbers, which can be analysed to find historic patterns, and extended into the future to make predictions. This analysis can be used to predict sales, but is also used for:

- analysing and predicting the financial status of the company, such as predicted profits, or the future situation of cash in the bank

- examining staff turnover (how quickly staff leave the firm) and the personnel requirements of the company

- predicting operational needs such as new machinery, additional raw materials and premises requirements.

Practice point

1 You are researching consumer buying patterns and preferences for potato crisps. Write a series of six questions to ask – three should obtain qualitative information and three quantitative information. Ask your teacher or lecturer to check them.

2 Test your questions by asking 10 of your class colleagues to answer them.

3 Examine your questions critically in the light of the responses you have received. How good were they? Did they reveal information that could be used, or would they need amending if they were to be used for a full survey?

Many research methods supply both qualitative and quantitative information, as the two are so

BTEC National Study Guide: Business. See page 185 for order details of individual texts

closely interlinked. For example, they might ask about a person's reasons for buying a certain brand and lead on to how many items are bought.

Features of information

Internal and external information

When we begin to search for information there are basically two places we can look: inside the company (internal information) or outside the company (external information).

Internal information could come from a variety of sources within the firm. Here are some of the main ones.

- The accounts department will have a range of historic figures relating to company performance, such as profit figures and the costs of each department.

- The sales department will carry details of previous sales records for different products or services sold by the firm. Interviewing the sales staff will give you an idea about the prospects for sales in the future, but be careful – sales staff are notoriously optimistic about the possibilities for future sales, so try to verify their estimates by comparing them with the

historic data. Many sales staff love to use the 'hockey stick' prediction method (see the illustration below).

- In a manufacturing company, the production department will be able to give details of production costs along with past and possible future production levels.

- The human resources department can tell the researcher about staff turnover rates, numbers of employees and the skills they have, training needs and the types and numbers of staff that will be required in the future.

- The marketing department can give information about the success of previous marketing campaigns and promotional activities.

- The customer services department can tell you what customers are saying about the company's quality of service or products, and their reactions to new ideas.

External information can be gathered outside the company, either by interviewing customers or examining published data. These are known as primary and secondary research.

The 'hockey stick' prediction method

123

BTEC National Study Guide: Business. See page 185 for order details of individual texts

65

Primary sources

Any information that is original is referred to as **primary data**. It is conducted by or on behalf of the firm, is specific to the firm's needs and will involve methods such as questionnaires, observation, group discussions and interviewing.

Secondary sources

Secondary data has two types of sources: desk research and external data. Any information obtained from sources internal to the firm, such as accounting records, stock records or sales sheets, is described as desk research.

External data is published data that was not gathered specifically for the company but can be used by it. This may involve searching through publications issued by the government, trade associations, media, directories and others. Information can also be obtained from websites or from published sources such as Mintel, a market research company that produces detailed market reports on most industries.

Currency and life expectancy of information

While some facts remain relatively unchanged for many years, we live in an ever-changing world, and what is current and correct today may become outdated very quickly.

Many industries develop extremely fast – you only need to consider how the computing and communications industries have changed beyond recognition in the past 20 years to realise that the currency of our research information (how up to date it is) is vital for ensuring that our conclusions are true and valid. Take care to ensure that the information you acquire is as current as possible. Check publication dates on books, newspapers and journals, and check 'last updated' dates on websites.

Means of communication

Today there are many ways of communicating in business situations, but not every way is suitable in every situation. Here are some of the methods you could choose from:

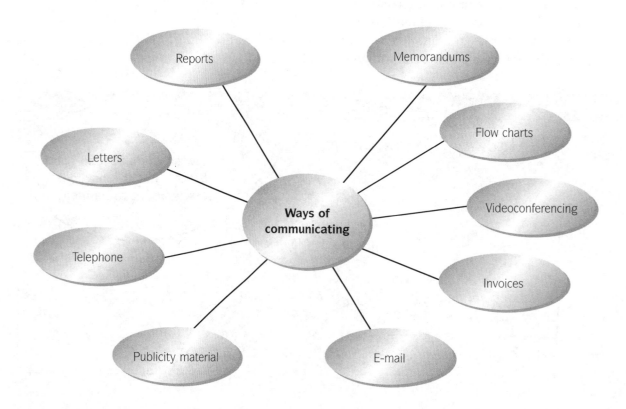

BTEC National Study Guide: Business. See page 185 for order details of individual texts

Telephone calls

The telephone is very useful for fast communication enabling quick feedback and discussion. Modern telephone facilities can allow conference facilities so that a number of people can be involved in the same conversation.

Videoconferencing

Videoconferencing means conducting meetings or conversations through TV screens. It allows people to speak face-to-face with colleagues who are many miles away, even across the world. Such systems used to be only available to companies with a lot of money to invest in fast videoconferencing suites and fast telephone lines, but these days the investment required is minimal. With a simple webcam, a fast Internet connection and videoconferencing software (one version of which is available free from Microsoft), any company can set up videoconferencing facilities.

Business letters

Although letters are relatively old-fashioned, companies still produce vast quantities of them. This is because they are simple and quick to produce, and they also provide a written record of correspondence that can be useful in the event of a dispute. See the example of a business letter style on the next page.

This style may look a little 'boring' and 'stuffy', but it is the style of letter that businesses expect to receive, so it is the style you should adopt for all letters you write during your BTEC National course.

Remember your letter gives messages about you and about your company, so you must take steps to make a good impression. The following guidelines will help you.

- Good business letters should have a structure as follows:
  - introduction: saying what the letter is about and why you are writing
  - details: the main body of the letter should contain the information you wish to convey to your reader
  - the next step: telling your readers what they should do next in response to your letter.

- Remember that when you write a business letter you are not writing to your best friend or your mum! You will not necessarily write the way you speak, as we are all lazy with our conversational English. Instead, you have to be formal and correct. Make sure you use good punctuation and correct spelling. Write in proper sentences – but they don't have to be long. Don't use 20 words when 10 will do. Use proper English and avoid slang words. Your tone should be professional and objective, not chatty, casual or over-friendly. It is better to write:

  'We deeply regret the impolite treatment that you received in our store today. I can assure you that prompt steps are being taken to ensure that this does not happen again.'

  than to say:

  'Sorry about the mix-up. Don't worry, I'm sorting it.'

- Draft your letter first – don't expect to be able to write a good letter first time without any revisions. You should read and re-read your letters to ensure that they make sense. Better still, get someone else to read it for a more objective opinion.

- Always be helpful – you've heard the saying that 'the customer is always right'. Your job is to help at all times, even when you think that the customer is mistaken or rude.

- Avoid irrelevance – stick to the point. Business people are busy and do not want to waste time. A long-winded letter is most likely to end up in the bin.

BTEC National Study Guide: Business. See page 185 for order details of individual texts

67

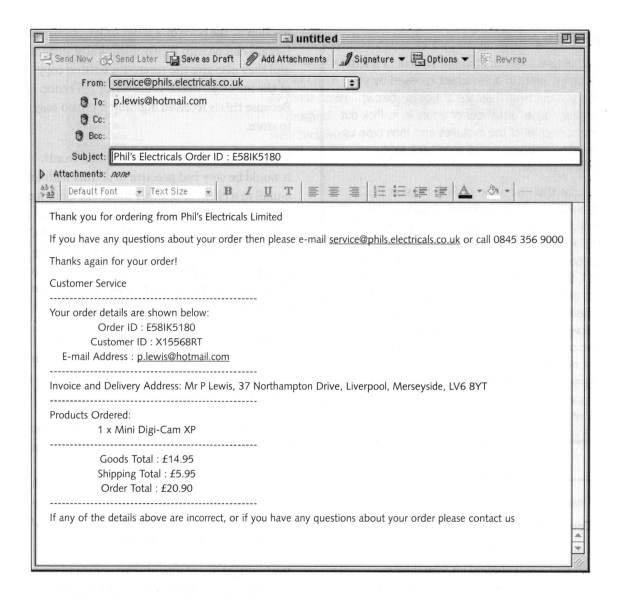

Practice point

Obtain the e-mail address of your tutor and send him or her an e-mail. Outline what you see as the main benefits of using e-mail over other forms of business communication. Also, give details of the e-mail provider company that you use. Explain why you chose that particular company and evaluate the service you receive.

Memorandums

A memorandum is an internal form of communication and is intended for relatively quick messages between members of staff. Unlike a letter, there is no complimentary close and memos are not normally signed unless they are being used to authorise payments. Memos always have a subject (title) and it is common to use simple bullet points in the main text. Here is an example of a typical memorandum:

BTEC National Study Guide: Business. See page 185 for order details of individual texts

70

MEMORANDUM

To: P Blakey

From: G Hawthorne

Date: 21 June 2004

Subject: Consignment of computer spares

Further to our recent conversation, I can now confirm that the consignment that you were expecting has arrived. The consignment consists of:

- four packages marked 'Spares'
- one package marked 'Keyboards'
- seven packages marked 'CPU – Handle With Care'.

The consignment is available for collection during office hours from the depot. If you would like it delivered to your office, please call me on ext 5418 and I will put it on the next delivery truck.

Practice point

Write a memo to your tutor requesting a fresh date for a tutorial. Explain why you were unable to make the appointment given to you this week, and outline the topics you would like to cover in the meeting.

Reports

A report is a very commonly used style of written communication in business. It is a formal response to a task that has been set or investigations that an employee has undertaken.

For example, your manager might ask you to investigate the efficiency levels in the production department and to make some recommendations for improvements. This is a complex investigation and might require you to gather a lot of information before you can make any suggestions. You might need to:

- observe what happens on the factory floor
- interview staff members
- discuss matters with supervisors
- gather the thoughts of senior managers
- investigate new technologies that have become available
- visit different companies to observe different management techniques or working practices.

Once you have acquired the information, you might present the results to your manager in the form of a business report, as follows. Note that a report usually carries these sections:

1.0 Terms of reference

2.0 Procedure

3.0 Findings

4.0 Conclusions

5.0 Recommendations

Bibliography

Appendices

BTEC National Study Guide: Business. See page 185 for order details of individual texts

71

CONFIDENTIAL

For: A Bailey, Production Director   *The person who will receive the report*   Ref: PG

From: P Guy, Production Manager   Date: 18 June 2004

REPORT ON THE EFFICIENCY OF THE PRODUCTION LINE AT PHIL'S ELECTRICALS

1.0   TERMS OF REFERENCE   *The introduction. You should say what you are doing and why*

On 4 May you asked me to investigate production line efficiency on the shop floor. I was asked to comment on the current systems used, the mood among the production team and any recent development that might help to improve performance.

2.0   PROCEDURE   *The steps you took to gather the information*

In order to obtain the relevant information and opinions, I followed the following procedures:

2.1   Observations were made on various occasions on the factory floor.
2.2   Interviews were conducted with staff members on the production line.
2.3   Extensive discussions were conducted with production line supervisors.
2.4   Those senior managers with experience of the production function were interviewed.
2.5   New technologies were evaluated off-site.
2.6   Visits were conducted to RTK PLC and Middletons Ltd (Stockport).

3.0   FINDINGS   *This is the longest report section. It includes all of the information and opinions that you have gathered*

3.1   The mood of the staff on the production line is generally good. The managerial style used by the supervisors seems to suit the nature of the staff employed. However ...

3.2   Procedures implemented in the department work adequately but many of them have not been reviewed for some considerable time ...

3.3   . . . .
3.4   . . . .

4.0   CONCLUSIONS   *This should refer back to your Terms of Reference. What is the answer to the task that you have been set?*

It is clear that the general management of the production function at the company is effective. However, ...

5.0   RECOMMENDATIONS   *What you think should happen as a result of your findings*

As a result of my investigations, I recommend that the Board of Directors give active consideration to the following:

5.1   The introduction of JIT procedures would undoubtedly improve the efficiency of production ...

5.2   A variety of new technologies have become available in recent years, and the following seem to be the best of those available ...

BIBLIOGRAPHY   *List your sources of information. You should use the Harvard Referencing System*

Moyles, PC and Grew, P, 2001 *Production Techniques*. 2nd ed. London: Heinemann.
Turner, E, 2003. *Management of Production*, 7 (4), 17–25.
Guide to Production. Nottingham Trent University. Available from: http://www.ntu.ac.uk/library/

APPENDICES   *Any attached documents referred to in the text should be included at the back of your report*

BTEC National Study Guide: Business. See page 185 for order details of individual texts

72

When compiling reports you should pay careful attention to the layout and the numbering system for the points. Professional business reports can be many pages long, so the numbering of sections and sub-sections is important because people will need to be able to refer to parts of the report easily during managerial discussions.

Practice point

You are a member of the management team at your school or college. Your manager has asked you to write a report about a fight that took place in the canteen today. You will need to invent the details and the investigation procedures that you went through to compile the report.

Invoices

An invoice is a document produced by a firm selling goods or services on credit, and it is normally produced by the sales department when the goods are dispatched to the buyer. It is intended to confirm the details of the goods or services purchased and the details of the payment required – both the total amount and the date when payment is required. Invoices are normally kept for a period of at least six years as they may be needed as evidence of a contract between the firm and the customer if any legal action should be taken over goods or services sold. Here is an example of an invoice:

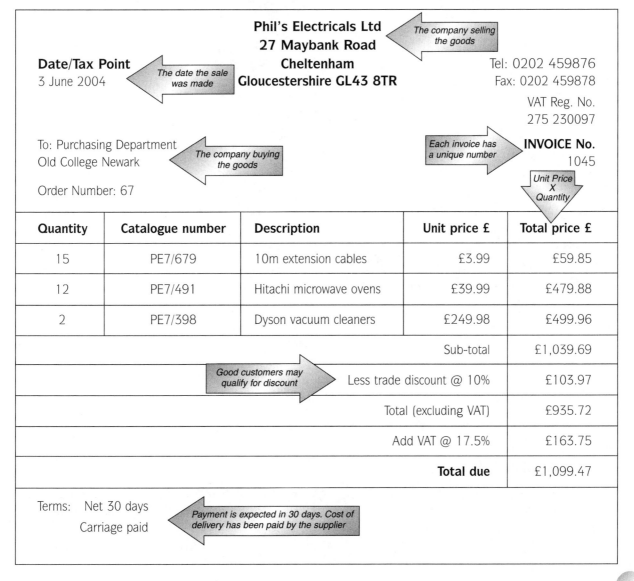

Phil's Electricals Ltd
27 Maybank Road
Cheltenham
Gloucestershire GL43 8TR

The company selling the goods

Date/Tax Point
3 June 2004 — *The date the sale was made*

Tel: 0202 459876
Fax: 0202 459878

VAT Reg. No.
275 230097

To: Purchasing Department
Old College Newark — *The company buying the goods*

Order Number: 67

Each invoice has a unique number

INVOICE No.
1045

Unit Price X Quantity

Quantity	Catalogue number	Description	Unit price £	Total price £
15	PE7/679	10m extension cables	£3.99	£59.85
12	PE7/491	Hitachi microwave ovens	£39.99	£479.88
2	PE7/398	Dyson vacuum cleaners	£249.98	£499.96
			Sub-total	£1,039.69
			Less trade discount @ 10%	£103.97
			Total (excluding VAT)	£935.72
			Add VAT @ 17.5%	£163.75
			Total due	£1,099.47

Good customers may qualify for discount

Terms: Net 30 days
         Carriage paid

Payment is expected in 30 days. Cost of delivery has been paid by the supplier

131

BTEC National Study Guide: Business. See page 185 for order details of individual texts

73

Flow charts

Flow charts are a very useful way of showing a process that takes a number of logical steps and requires decisions to be taken along the way. In a flow chart an oval represents the start or end of the chart, oblong boxes contain instructions and diamonds contain decisions. Here is an example of a flow chart to decide whether a reminder letter needs sending to a customer:

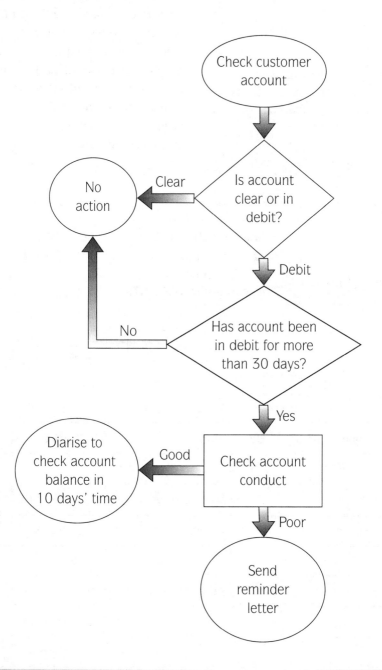

Publicity material

Many forms of **publicity materials** are used by companies, and although they vary greatly they all carry certain qualities:

- they are attractive to the eye

- they are informative

- they enhance the corporate image of the firm (see page 160).

The level of detail varies. Posters and stickers carry only minimal information (but enough to attract attention). Brochures and websites can carry much more for the customer to read.

Posters carry minimum information, but attract attention

Brochures and leaflets carry more information for the customer to read

133

BTEC National Study Guide: Business. See page 185 for order details of individual texts

75

Purpose of information

Information is vitally important to businesses. A company without information is like someone wandering around in the dark; he doesn't know where he is going and if he gets to where he wants to be it is more by luck than good planning. Companies use information for a variety of purposes.

Updating knowledge

Information is gathered so that firms know how their markets are developing, how labour markets are changing, what the economy is doing, what new laws are being passed that might affect the way they do business, and so on. All of this information helps firms to make accurate decisions based on full knowledge – without this, incorrect decisions will be made.

Informing future developments and offering competitive insight

A company that does not change, develop and grow will quickly find itself being left behind by the competition. Developments need to be based on informed decisions, and this is possible only through information gathering. A firm will not launch a new product, for example, unless it has ample evidence that the product is likely to sell. Do you think that Sony Ericsson would have launched the first picture phones if they had not had clear information to suggest that they were likely to sell well?

Sales promotions

If we wish to promote our products and services effectively, we need to know how our customers 'tick'. Good research information will give us an insight into their behaviour patterns and their buying motivations. Information can therefore help companies to sell well.

Inviting support for activities

You may need to communicate with people in your company, or even from other firms, to help in certain tasks. For example, you may need to enlist the support of staff members in a new sales drive, or you may be looking for them to suggest ideas for moving the firm forward. If the activity you are considering involves a lot of expenditure, you may contact organisations outside your company to request sponsorship support. This often happens in the sports industry, where many events would never take place without the financial support of sponsors. Sponsorship can only be gained following extensive communication.

Information gathering

To gather information for business purposes it is essential that a wide range of sources are used. This will be equally true for your assignment work, so there are some important lessons to be learned here for assignment preparation. Make sure that you use a wide variety of sources; too many students assume that the Internet is the first and last word when it comes to gathering information, but if you are to create a complete and accurate picture you should use as many methods as possible. Here is an outline of the range of sources available to you.

Primary sources

Getting first-hand information by conducting questionnaires, observations, focus groups and interviewing will give you an up-to-date picture of how potential customers feel. Carefully targeted primary research should yield new ideas and opinions that you cannot get in any other way. It is time-consuming and sometimes difficult, but the effort is normally well worth it.

Visiting companies to interview members of staff can give you first-hand opinions of recent developments and what is happening in a market. Don't underestimate the value of personal contacts when doing such research. If you have parents, brothers, sisters, friends or relations who work in a relevant occupation, take the opportunity to interview them, preferably at their workplaces. Personal contacts are more likely to be responsive to your approaches and will normally help you to speak to the relevant people and make time to deal with your questions.

BTEC National Study Guide: Business. See page 185 for order details of individual texts

76

The Internet

The Internet is a mine of information, covering every topic you could think of. It is relatively easy to find information on any topic using one of the many **search engines** available. However, Internet searching is not always as easy as we think it might be. Students often say 'I can't find anything on the Internet on that subject'. That statement normally means that the student has tried a couple of queries on a search engine and not found anything relevant straight away. Good searching requires logic and patience – after all, Google claims to be searching over 3.3 billion sites, so to find exactly what you want is never guaranteed to be easy.

How can you improve your Internet researching skills? Here are a few tips:

- Use a variety of search engines. Some of the best search engines are *www.google.co.uk*, *www.altavista.co.uk*, and *www.lycos.co.uk*. There are many others, but try various search engines before you give up.

- Be specific with the words you use in your search. If you are researching sales trends in the potato crisp industry, for example, don't just put in the word 'crisps' – 'sales trends potato crisps' is much more likely to give you something useful.

- Use the '+' symbol to indicate specific words that must appear in your results. 'Sales trends potato crisps' will give plenty of pages that contain only one of these words. Add a plus before each word, '+sales +trends +potato +crisps', and this will give only sites that contain all four of the words.

- Use the '−' symbol to indicate topics that should be omitted from search results. If you wanted to eliminate references to Walker's crisps from the above search, you might search under '+sales +trends +potato +crisps − Walkers'.

Practice point

Use the above techniques to find suitable information to help you plan a trip to London to see a specific sight or show. Your planning should take in travel arrangements and some ideas of where to eat.

Government statistical sources

The government produces a vast amount of statistics that can be very relevant to business investigations. Many are published in the form of booklets and are stocked by most libraries. The website of the Central Statistical Office is very comprehensive and should cater for most needs: *www.statistics.gov.uk*.

News sources

For up-to-date information on how business is changing and events that will affect businesses, there is no better source than newspapers and TV news. Most TV news programmes report on business-related topics. BBC News 24 has business news reports and BBC2 has a daily programme called *Working Lunch*, which can be very useful.

Newspapers are still the best source for business news – all the quality papers such as the *Telegraph*, *Independent*, *Times*, *Guardian* and *Observer* have separate business sections that cover the latest events. Today it is not even necessary to buy the paper, as most newspapers have websites that you can access free. The *Daily Telegraph* site at *www.telegraph.co.uk* has great coverage in the business news section, and a search function that allows you to research previous articles from the past few years. The site for *The Times* is also useful: *www.timesonline.co.uk*.

Trade journals

For the latest thinking from people on the inside of different industries, trade journals are the resource to use. These are published for people who work in the industry, and make excellent research materials.

135

BTEC National Study Guide: Business. See page 185 for order details of individual texts

77

○ *Marketing*, published by Haymarket Publications, gives up-to-date information on the latest ad campaigns, branding methods and which advertisements are making the most impact with consumers.

Marketing

○ *Marketing Week* magazine also covers the marketing industry, featuring in-depth articles outlining the latest techniques of marketers in the UK and abroad.

MARKETING WEEK

○ *Supply Management* is published for the Chartered Institute of Purchasing and Supply, and is aimed at company buyers and contract negotiators. It contains the latest information about buying in retail, service and manufacturing environments.

SupplyManagement

○ *Management Today* looks at employment law and the issues related to the management of people.

Company reports and accounts

Each year, every public limited company publishes a *report and accounts*. These documents are primarily intended to show the company's financial position, and contain details of company balance sheets and cash flow statements. However, they also contain details of new product launches, reviews of the market including the firm's position within that

market, descriptions of the company's products and marketing campaigns. The website *www.carol.co.uk* is a good source for such reports – you can search by company name and obtain copies of the latest reports on your computer screen, free.

Textbooks

With the development of the Internet, some students seem to feel that textbooks are less important, but this is not so. Textbooks are normally written by people with some expertise in the area, which is not always true of Internet authors. Anyone can set up a website and write on it, since the content of the Internet is completely unregulated.

University and college libraries

These carry a wide range of books, journals, statistics, theses and other hard-to-find publications. Large university libraries will probably not allow you to take materials out, but as long as you ask permission you are unlikely to be prevented from reading and making notes.

Validation

Having gathered information, it is important that we determine how valid the information is. In other words, is it accurate and relevant?

Source evaluation and checking

One of the most important questions you should ask yourself in deciding on the validity of your research information is 'Who wrote this information, and what were their motivations in writing it?' A lot of the information you find may be valid, but some may be misleading.

Some sources are clearly more reputable than others. Quality newspapers are generally well researched and articles written in them are likely to be believed, but the same cannot be said of all the tabloids, some of which aim to shock and entertain rather than present an objective and well-informed article.

This problem is much worse on the Internet. There is no regulation of content, so you have to question what you read on websites. Clearly information from reputable, well-known providers, such as *www.bbc.co.uk* or *www.telegraph.co.uk*, are to be trusted, but many others contain inaccurate information, and some are deliberately set up to deceive the reader.

Other sites are not necessarily set up to influence opinion, but are simply 'spoof' sites, set up as a joke. But some of them are hard to detect immediately and it would be easy to believe that some of them give accurate information.

When you are researching on the Internet, the rule is to take care, because not everything you read is true. Remember that much of what you read is opinion, and opinions are not facts. Always read sites critically.

Practice point

Visit the following two websites:
www.wto.org
www.gatt.org

You will find they look pretty similar at first glance, but read the content in more detail and you will find that they have very different messages to give.

One was set up by the World Trade Organisation to outline its policies in encouraging trade between all the nations of the world. The other was set up by anti-globalisation protesters who believe that the policies of the WTO are harming poorer developing nations for the benefit of richer nations, especially the US. The protesters have exactly mimicked the style of the WTO site so that to the casual user it is difficult to tell them apart. It would be easy to stumble on the wrong one and include content from it in a research project, and this would give a very different view of the activities of the WTO from the one you were expecting.

Look at the two sites carefully to distinguish the different points of view.

Practice point

Visit the following sites and complete the tasks in the table.

Site	How convincing is it? Justify your judgement	What clues can you spot that the site is not reliable?
http://home.inreach.com/ kumbach/velcro.html		
www.genochoice.com/		
http://www.malepregnancy.com/		
http://147.129.226.1/ library/research/AIDSFACTS.htm		

137

BTEC National Study Guide: Business. See page 185 for order details of individual texts

79

Facts are definite events, truths that can be verified either through a person's experiences, through research or by observation. Opinions are people's beliefs, and they are not proved – in some cases, cannot be proved.

For example, I may think that my work team is not performing well because they are not paid well enough, so I may try to resolve the situation by gaining a pay rise for them. If, however, the real problem is that I treat them badly, the extra pay will not achieve the desired effect; my opinion has led me to make an incorrect decision.

Basing decisions on facts is therefore much better than basing them on opinions. Unfortunately, the Internet is not regulated and anyone can write anything they want on a web page. If they write in a convincing way, they could fool you into believing something is a fact when it is incorrect, or merely an opinion. This would undermine the value of your research and the decisions that you take as a result of your findings.

Error management

Error management means identifying the causes of errors and taking appropriate actions to ensure that they do not recur. In this context it means changing research procedures to reduce the possibility of errors and to minimise the consequences of those that do occur. For the researcher this means learning from mistakes.

One common mistake that students make when researching on the Internet is not checking the nationality of the information. If you are researching market trends or conditions, it is very easy to find material on the Internet and not realise that it relates to the US market rather than the UK market. Usually when students make the mistake once, they learn and do not make it again. This is an example of error management at work.

Currency

The currency of information means how up to date it is. It is vital to ensure that the information you collect is still relevant. Many books in libraries were printed some years ago, and many

Internet sites were written some time ago and have not been updated. So a thorough researcher should check book publication dates and also the 'last-updated' dates on websites to check for currency.

Consistency of information handling

All the techniques described in this section will help you, but it is vital that you use them consistently. All information needs to be valid, or wrong decisions could be made. Sometimes the information you supply could form the basis of a multi-million pound decision, in which case it is vital that you are presenting an accurate picture or the company could lose substantial sums.

You should therefore get into good habits, remembering to check your information as thoroughly as possible on a regular basis.

Standards and constraints

When you are preparing to present your research information, there are a number of considerations that you need to take into account. Some of what you present may be affected by the law, and there are also voluntary codes of practice that should be observed, along with commonly accepted social, moral and ethical constraints as to what you can write or talk about. You therefore need to consider the following areas when compiling your research and putting the results together.

Legislation

The main pieces of legislation you need to consider are the laws on **copyright**, **patents** and **defamation**.

- **Copyright:** Any original work of literature, art, music, sound recording, film or broadcast is subject to copyright, which means that the original creator of the work has control over people using and making copies of the work. As a researcher you must therefore be sure that material you use is given full credit. You must give full details of sources used and quoted in any assignment or presentation you do.

BTEC National Study Guide: Business. See page 185 for order details of individual texts

80

You are not allowed to copy or use substantial sections of someone else's work unless you have express permission. Note that copyright law extends to material that appears on the Internet – just because it is freely accessible does not mean that you are free to use it without permission. The main legislation covering this area in the UK is the Copyright, Designs and Patents Act 1988.

- **Defamation:** This means saying something damaging about someone else. Libel happens if you write something damaging about someone, and slander is when you speak something defamatory. In business, when writing up your research findings or preparing your presentations, take care not to include any defamatory statements, or you could be dismissed and find yourself in court facing a substantial damages claim.

Voluntary codes of practice

If you wish to investigate a business, you should always *ask permission*. Even if it is simply a case of observing what goes on in a retail store, it is good practice and respectful to ask permission first. A business person has a right not to be observed or questioned, and as a researcher you should respect that right.

Confidentiality is also vital. Depending on the nature of your research you may be asked to keep certain facts or observations confidential, particularly where they relate to specific individuals. In this case you should respect a person's right to confidentiality and ensure that there are no identifying features in your research paper or presentation.

As outlined above, it is important that you give due credit to the original writers of work you have used in compiling your research. The details of references you have used should be listed using the Harvard Referencing System.

In the Harvard system, the references are listed in alphabetical order of authors' names.

Reference to a book

Author's surname, initials, year of publication. *Title*. Edition (if not the first). Place of publication: publisher.

Example:
Needham, D, Dransfield, R, Guy P and Dooley, D, 2000. *Marketing for Higher Awards*, London: Heinemann.

Reference to a journal article

Author's surname, initials, year of publication. Title of article. *Title of journal*, volume number (and part number), page numbers of contribution.

Example:
Page, WP, 1999. Economies of Scale. *Economics Today*, 9 (3), 19-23.

Reference to a newspaper article

Author's surname, initials (or newspaper title), year of publication. Title of article. *Title of newspaper*, day and month, page number(s) and column number.

Example:
The Times, 2003. Growth or Bust. *The Times*, 8 June, p.15a.

Reference to a government publication

Name of issuing body, year of publication. *Title of publication*. Place of publication: Publisher, report number (where relevant).

Example:
Office for National Statistics, 2002. *Labour Market Trends*. London: ONS, ONS/3303/227.

Reference to web pages

Author/editor. (Year). *Title* [on-line]. (Edition). Place of publication, Publisher (if ascertainable). Available from: URL [Accessed date].

Example:
Brown, J (2001). *Business Report* [on-line]. Nottingham, New College Nottingham. Available from: *http://www.ncn.ac.uk/reports/ businessreport.htm* [Accessed 21 June 2004].

BTEC National Study Guide: Business. See page 185 for order details of individual texts

81

Social, moral and ethical constraints

You should always avoid offence in researching, so you need to behave in a moral and ethical fashion when collecting evidence.

Newspaper reporters are often accused of immoral and unethical methods of collecting information about or photographs of famous people. Do not fall into the same trap. Collect from accessible sources, report the facts you collect in an objective way, avoid stereotyping (jumping to conclusions about) people or jobs, and always try to avoid offending.

Access

The information you present should be easily accessible to your audience. Remember that the most important thing about communication is that it should convey a message – the message is more important than the medium by which it is conveyed. The golden rule is to keep it simple and clear.

- Information must be readable. Don't use long words when short ones will get the message across, and avoid ambiguous sentences (ones that could mean more than one thing).

  Make sure that you use good grammar, spelling and punctuation. If you think you are weak in one of those areas, ask your teachers for support.

- Information must be clear and understandable. Make sure that your use of technical language is suitable for your audience.

- Information must be suitable for the audience. Use the right style for your audience – refer back to page 125.

Make sure you treat people in an ethical manner when you are collecting information

BTEC National Study Guide: Business. See page 185 for order details of individual texts

● Ensure that the presentation method is appropriate to the reader, the situation and the type of information being conveyed. You have a wide range of written business formats to choose from, as well as oral presentations, electronic methods (e-mail, videoconferencing) and visual means such as posters, charts and diagrams. Think carefully and choose the most appropriate style or method.

Suitability

It is important to ensure that all the information you present is appropriate for your purposes and that you avoid any extra material that is not relevant to the task in hand. For more details on how to ensure you are achieving this, see 'Synthesising information', page 143.

Thinking point

Listed below are a number of situations in which you will need to communicate. Decide on the method you would use and justify your choice – explain why that is the best one.

	Method chosen	Justification
To warn a staff member formally about poor work		
To reply to a letter of complaint received today		
To discuss a new sales strategy with your fellow directors in Glasgow, Cardiff and Basle (Switzerland)		
To explain to the workforce about the new wage structure		
To confirm a client's availability for your meeting next Friday		
To gain the help of the staff in achieving the new branch sales targets		
To query your latest salary slip which is £500 short		

141

BTEC National Study Guide: Business. See page 185 for order details of individual texts

83

Outcome activity 4.1

You are a market research assistant working for Rapid Research, Market Square, Nottingham, NG1 7RT. Your company has been asked by a local manufacturer, Topfizz Drinks Ltd, to perform some research on its behalf. It is planning to launch a new range of soft drinks but needs more market information in order to decide what to do. You have been asked to gather research information in preparation for a presentation to be given to the staff and directors of Topfizz Drinks.

Pass

Your first task is to collect information from a range of sources about the current state of the soft drinks industry in the UK. Your research must include examples of both primary and secondary information, and it should also show examples of both qualitative and quantitative results.

Merit

Topfizz Drinks is a very important customer for Rapid Research. Your manager, Ray Search, is therefore very concerned that the information you provide to Topfizz is as detailed and accurate as possible. He asks you to send him an extended memorandum explaining the ways in which more accurate business information may be produced from raw data.

Distinction

Your manager, Ray Search, informs you that as a result of your findings, Topfizz Drinks will be deciding whether to make an investment in a new bottling and production plant.

1 Evaluate the significance of the accuracy of business information and explain how different audiences might require different levels of accuracy and detail delivered to them. Give examples to illustrate your comments.
2 Outline how accurate and detailed you think the information needs to be for Topfizz Drinks. Explain your reasons.
3 Explain how accurate and detailed the information you present might need to be if you were to give a presentation on the same topic to:
   - the workers in the Topfizz factory
   - a group of 16-year-olds at the neighbouring college who are investigating local businesses.

How information can be processed

This section of the unit looks at how you can put all the information you have collected into useful formats, and how to present your findings as clearly as possible.

Processing methods

Copy and paste from source

You will have collected information from various sources and one thing you may have to do is to compile the information into one document. This may be a report or PowerPoint slides ready for a presentation. It is easy to copy and paste a variety of information from various electronic sources into one document. You can copy and paste from:

- text documents
- spreadsheets
- databases
- the Internet
- most other programs.

Using the 'Paste Special' and 'Paste Link' function, it is also possible to paste in an item that changes whenever the source file is altered. This can be very helpful when manipulating graphs and figures from spreadsheets.

Practice point

Open up Microsoft Excel and create a simple graph. Experiment using the 'Paste Special' and 'Paste Link' function to copy it into other documents.

You should always take care when you are copying and pasting items that you are not infringing copyright.

Mathematical and graphical manipulation

Primary data that you have gathered from questionnaires or observations, and statistics that you have acquired from the Internet, can also be manipulated mathematically and graphically to make it easy for your audience to pick up the main messages from your research. These techniques are examined in 'Synthesising information', below.

Data handling applications

It is possible to use computer programs to help with processing your data. The two main ones you are likely to use are spreadsheets (such as Microsoft Excel) and databases (such as Microsoft Access). It is not within the scope of this book to teach you how to use these programs, but here is a short summary of the potential of each.

- **Spreadsheets** will manipulate figures for you. If you input figures to a spreadsheet you can program it to do various mathematical operations, including working out averages and interest calculations. Spreadsheets can also be used to produce professionally presented charts.

- **Databases** are used in industry to store collections of data records for accounts, stock management, personnel records, and other record keeping. Databases can be cross-referenced to each other so that information may be collected and manipulated from various data sources.

Synthesising information

Synthesising means combining all the details and information you have discovered into one complete document, in a form that is easy for your reader to understand. This may involve summarising lengthy pieces of text, doing some mathematical or statistical analysis with figures you have collected, or drawing graphs of results.

Synopsis of text

One of the skills a researcher needs is summarising the information collected. This is also called making a synopsis of the information. Many sources that you use will give you a large quantity of information, and one of your jobs is to condense that information into brief, relevant

points for your audience. For example, if you were to consult a Mintel report on a particular industry, you would find multiple pages of densely typed information. Your audience will not need all this, so your job is to extract the relevant points and present them.

Statistical analysis

You can also help your audience to extract useful information from your numerical information and your primary research by doing some simple statistical analysis. The following techniques could be used.

- **Simple rises and falls** If you are comparing results from one year or month to the next, the most obvious analysis is to calculate the size of the rise or fall.

- **Percentages** You can compare results by working out percentages. For example, if a company has these three products selling in one year, you can work out how much each product contributes as a percentage of total sales.

Product	Sales (£s)
Bicycles	125,000
Trainers	275,000
Shirts	200,000

BTEC National Study Guide: Business. See page 185 for order details of individual texts

To work out the percentages, first work out the total sales:

$$125,000 + 275,000 + 200,000 = 600,000$$

To work out what percentage bicycles are of the total, divide the figure for bicycles by the total and multiply by 100:

$$\frac{125,000}{600,000} \times 100 = 20.83\%$$

A calculator will work this out if you key in 125,000 ÷ 600,000 then press %.

Bicycles make up 20.83% of total sales.

Work out the percentages for each of the other products. If you do your sums correctly you should get the following answers:

Trainers = 45.83%

Shirts   = 33.33%

Practice point

Phil's Electricals has branches in five cities in the UK. Sales in 2003 for each of the branches were as follows:

Branch	Sales (£s)
London	1,234,000
Nottingham	567,000
Liverpool	498,000
Norwich	317,000
Exeter	614,000

Calculate the percentages of total sales made by each of the branches.

● **Percentage changes** Sometimes we obtain details of how a particular figure has changed over a period of time. In this situation you might work out the percentage change, in other words how much something has changed in percentage terms. This can be quite important, as a percentage change can give a very different, and possibly more accurate, picture than looking at the raw total. For example, assume that profits at Phil's Electricals have risen as follows:

	Profits (£s)
2002	214,550
2003	216,695

If you were to simply discuss the change in the raw data, you could say that profits have increased by £2,145. This sounds like a good increase, but if we work out the percentage change, we find that it has increased by only 1%, which sounds much less impressive.

We calculate percentage changes by using the following method:

Percentage change

$$= \frac{\text{Difference between figures}}{\text{Original figure}} \times 100$$

With our above figures, therefore, we would do the following:

$$\frac{216,695 - 214,550}{214,550} \times 100$$

$$= \frac{2,145}{214,550} \times 100$$

$$= 1\%$$

BTEC National Study Guide: Business. See page 185 for order details of individual texts

86

Practice point

Here are the total sales of soft drinks in the UK from 1992 to 2002:

Year	Million litres
1992	8,550
1993	8,765
1994	9,285
1995	10,255
1996	10,125
1997	10,590
1998	10,730
1999	11,575
2000	11,900
2001	12,390
2002	13,070

Source: Sucralose Report 2003

Now work out the percentage changes as follows:

Year	Percentage change in soft drink sales
1992 – 1993	
1993 – 1994	
1994 – 1995	
1995 – 1996	
1996 – 1997	
1997 – 1998	
1998 – 1999	
1999 – 2000	
2000 – 2001	
2001 – 2002	
1992 – 2002	

Tally charts Following primary research in the form of questionnaires or observations, you will probably need to make tally charts of your results in order to produce totals for each variable you are observing. Tally charts look like this:

Purchase	Tally	Frequency
Biscuits	⊩Ⅲ III	8
Crisps	I	1
Newspapers	II	2
Fizzy drinks	IIII	4
Other drinks		0
Sandwiches	⊩Ⅲ IIII	9
		Total = 24

The results could be displayed using a table as above, or a graph (see the next page).

Classification and tabulation Research often results in large quantities of data, and one of the researcher's most important jobs is to make sense of this data for the reader. Results can be presented by using classification and tabulation.

This involves arranging the data into classifications. If we have a wide variety of numerical responses, it would be more meaningful to present our results in groups rather than individual results. For example, if we are presenting the ages of people who gave particular responses, we might have a range from age 10 up to, say, age 70. If we give a separate score for each age we will still have a mass of results, all with relative totals. If we group the ages, we will get a good picture of how age affects responses, and it will be much easier to read the information and understand its main messages. Overleaf is an example of classified and tabulated data.

145

BTEC National Study Guide: Business. See page 185 for order details of individual texts

87

Age	Amount purchased (frequency)
10 – 19	23
20 – 29	25
30 – 39	49
40 – 49	46
50 – 59	19
60 – 69	2

There are some important points to note when you create data tables. First, there should not be too many classifications – say a maximum of ten. Second, make sure that the classifications do not overlap. For example, if the first two rows were to read

like this, where would you put the result for a person aged 20?

Age	Amount purchased (frequency)
10 – 20	
20 – 30	

Make your classifications unambiguous to avoid this problem.

Make sure your categories are comprehensive. In other words, there should a classification suitable for every response. If one response will not fit in any category, you need to redesign them. In the table above, if we had an age of 5 or 75 we could not place it.

Wherever possible, make your classifications of the same size.

Classified data can be graphed using a type of bar chart known as a histogram:

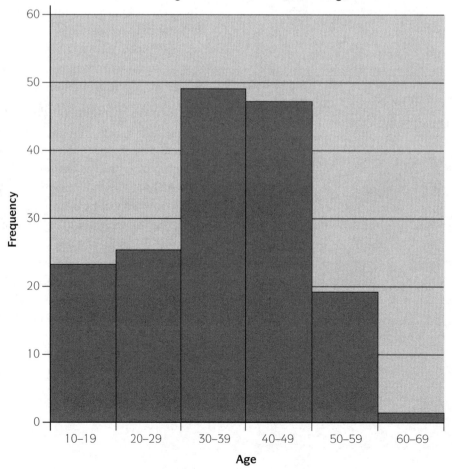

Histogram to show distribution of ages

BTEC National Study Guide: Business. See page 185 for order details of individual texts

Practice point

The following data shows sales of digital cameras in different stores across the UK. Using the set of results, draw up appropriate classifications for the data and use a tally list to tabulate the results.

470	287	45	109	314	100	217	311	180	85
341	121	251	235	71	472	130	50	183	241
199	369	34	141	240	274	90	153	238	290
315	187	201	283	251	403	375	503	325	381

Now produce a histogram of your results.

Note the following points with histograms:

- the columns should be drawn without leaving space between them, because there is a regular scale along the horizontal axis

- the values of the variables are always shown on the horizontal axis

- the frequencies are always shown on the vertical axis.

● **Averages** It is often useful to talk about an average, such as the average number of customers served in a day, the average prices for a product; the average time it takes to make a product, and so on.

The mean is the most commonly used average. To find the mean of a set of numbers, we simply add them up and divide by the number of items in the set.

Find the mean of the following numbers:

2, 4, 6, 8, 9, 12, 14, 17.

$$\text{The mean} = \frac{\text{sum of the scores}}{\text{number of scores}}$$

$$= \frac{2 + 4 + 6 + 8 + 9 + 12 + 14 + 17}{8}$$

$$= \frac{72}{8}$$

$$= 9$$

Practice point

Calculate the mean of the following data:

25 10   4 22 31 39   4 13 19 21

37   4 15 33 40   1 45 11 22   4

● **Simple extrapolation** Extrapolation means identifying a trend that has happened in the past and then extending it into the future, assuming that it will continue. For example, here are the approximate average prices quoted on the stock market for the shares of Games Workshop PLC in 2003:

Dec-02	412
Jan-03	430
Feb-03	425
Mar-03	445
Apr-03	510
May-03	540
Jun-03	575
Jul-03	630
Aug-03	710
Sep-03	730

If you were to create a graph of these figures it would look like the one on the following page.

BTEC National Study Guide: Business. See page 185 for order details of individual texts

89

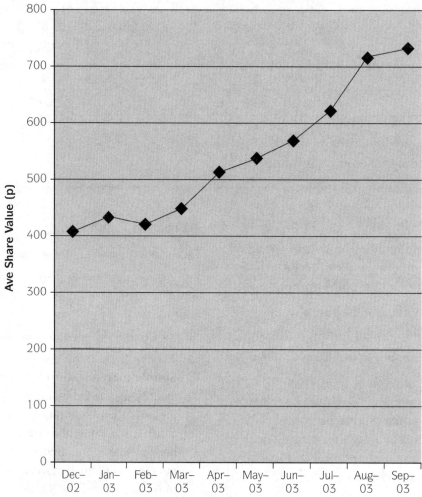

Share Price: Games Workshop PLC

We can identify the trend quite easily from
this graph. If we now extrapolate the trend
into the future, we might draw a line of best
fit on our points and extend it into the future.

BTEC National Study Guide: Business. See page 185 for order details of individual texts

90

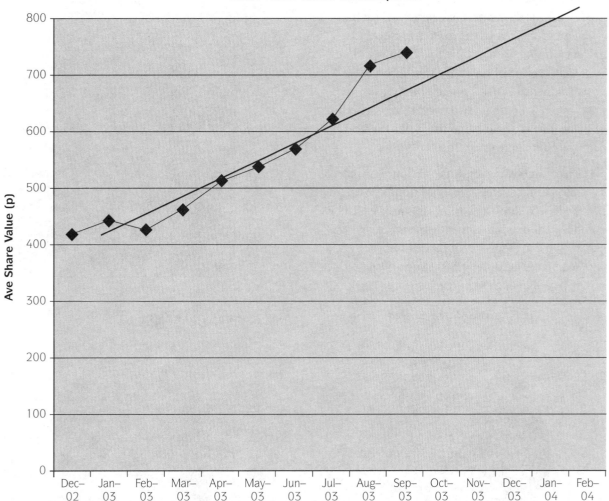

Share Price: Games Workshop PLC

Our simple extrapolation suggests that by January 2004 the price would be well over 800p per share, and that might well encourage you to buy such shares. Although this extrapolation is perfectly reasonable, it illustrates quite clearly the problems with such predictions. Quite simply, predicting the future is very difficult, even with extensive, accurate historic information. Anything could happen in the future, and share prices are particularly hard to predict as they are subject to so many variables. If Games Workshop continued to expand sales well, the share price might continue in this trend, but it could just as easily dip down.

Practice point

What did happen to the Games Workshop share price after this period? How accurate was our prediction?

Graphical representation of results

Using graphs is an excellent way of presenting numerical information to your reader or the person watching your presentation. It is much easier to read information from a graph than from a list or table of figures. It is also very easy to produce professional-looking charts from a spreadsheet such as Microsoft Excel. However, you need to be aware of which chart type to use in which situation. The following page gives some guidance on this.

149

BTEC National Study Guide: Business. See page 185 for order details of individual texts

91

- **Line graphs** may be used to display trends in specific variables. For example, if we had a set of figures for the exchange rate and we wanted to show how this had fluctuated over a period of time, this would best be demonstrated using a line graph. If we wished to compare two trends to see whether one follows the other, putting two lines on one chart may reveal this.

- **Pie charts** show how a total figure is split into various categories. For example, if we wished to show how total sales are shared by different market segments, the whole pie would represent the total sales and each segment would show how much of the total was sold in each segment.

Multiple Bar Chart

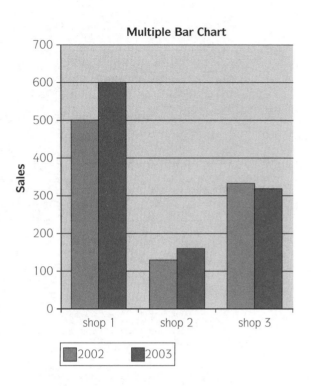

Database Market Shares

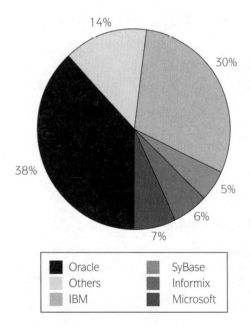

Stacked Bar Chart

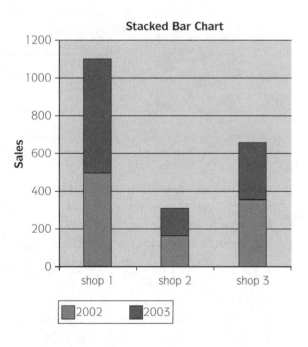

- **Bar charts** are used to compare data totals. A multiple bar chart shows different series of data side by side. For example, if you wanted to compare numbers of customers for different years or across different stores, this would be a good way to show the information. A stacked bar chart shows the different series stacked on top of each other. The advantage of this is that you can read the total number of customers across all the series from the top of the stack.

- **Scatter charts** or scatter diagrams show you whether there is any relationship between two features, such as a product's price and its sales. If the points lie roughly on a straight line, the two are closely related and we say they have a 'strong correlation'.

150

BTEC National Study Guide: Business. See page 185 for order details of individual texts

92

For example, if you wanted to see whether there was a correlation between the amount spent on advertising and the number of sales you achieved, you would plot the data for a number of months or years to see whether a relationship did exist. On the chart below, for example, there appears to be a good correlation and we could say that there appears to be a strong link between advertising and the number of sales – the more we advertise, the more we sell.

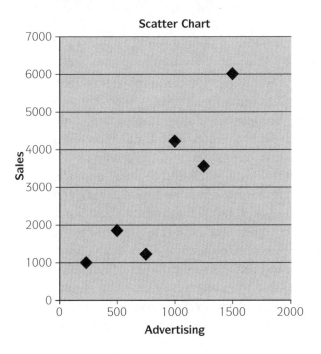

Scatter Chart

Output requirements

When preparing the results of research for an audience, we have seen there are a number of techniques you can use. It is also important to make your final product attractive to the eye and easy to use.

Page layout

Some elements of the page layout should stay the same throughout a document. The main font style and size should not alter throughout the text, and headings should be of consistent styles. Microsoft Word can help with this as it has a number of built-in heading and body-text styles. Using these will give your documents consistency.

However, some variety in the pages can make life easier for the reader. Images can give relief from endless text and, if they are well chosen, they can also aid understanding. Images look good if they have text flowing around them, as in the example on the next page.

You can produce mixed text and graphics pages in a desktop publishing program such as Microsoft Publisher, Aldus Pagemaker or QuarkXPress.

Text formatting

At the top of the screen in Microsoft Word are a number of options for altering the formatting of your text. Clicking on the menu options 'Format' and 'Font' will give you a number of options for altering your text style, colour and size, as well as some specialised styles.

Use of tables

Microsoft Word and other word processors contain powerful table functions. Tables are an excellent way of lining up information in columns and rows, making sure that it is all grouped neatly.

Resolution of images

Images come in various resolutions and generally the higher the resolution you use, the more detailed and high definition your picture will be. Photographs normally require much finer detail than simple drawings. On a computer, picture detail is measured in dpi, or dots per inch.

There is a decision to be made here – a high-resolution image may look great, but if you put a few high-resolution images into a Word document, the file size soon becomes too large. This means having to save it to CD rather than floppy disc, and it also takes longer to load into a computer. The bigger the file size, the more memory the computer needs to handle it, and older machines with slower processors will quickly find the going tough.

You therefore need to ask yourself: how high need my definition be? Take care when shooting with digital cameras or scanning pictures. If you

151

BTEC National Study Guide: Business. See page 185 for order details of individual texts

93

Here is Some Text

text text

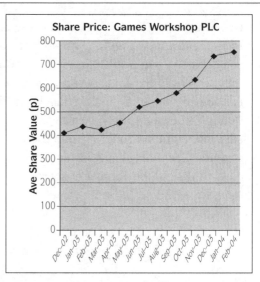

Share Price: Games Workshop PLC

text text text text text text
text text

text text text text text text text text text text text text text text text text text text text text text text text text
text text text text text text text text text text text text text text text text text text text text text text text text
text text text text text text text text text text text text text text text text text text text text text text text text

Text flowing around images can make your page layout more attractive

choose a very high-resolution setting, not only will it take a long time to scan the image or take the picture, but the file size may be unmanageable.

Combining information from a range of applications

Refer back to 'Copy and paste from source', page 142, to remind yourself about this.

Use of specialist software and hardware

A number of computer programs and pieces of specialist equipment may help you to make a better presentation. Here are some ideas.

● **Flip charts** are relatively simple to use and many professional presenters still use them extensively. Remember that not every venue will have high-tech equipment, so being able to use flip charts creatively may become important. A neatly written, colourful flip chart can look visually appealing.

Make the words bold and tall (using a wide-tipped marker pen) – about 5cm is a good size. Avoid using light colours like yellow or orange as your audience may not be able to read them. Use good quality pens and paper so that they don't 'bleed' onto other sheets.

94

Leave plenty of space on the sheets. A crowded sheet is confusing and difficult for your audience to read. If you are going to write on the paper during your presentation, you would do well to rehearse it first to identify any potential problems (such as words you have trouble spelling, or simply running out of room on the sheet).

Using flip charts can give you some advantages over other presentation methods. They allow for spontaneity, and you can get your audience involved by asking them to write on the sheets.

After a session putting ideas onto flip chart paper, you can keep the final results for later analysis. And you don't need to worry about power cuts or whether your electricity extension lead will be long enough!

- **Overhead projectors** are available at many venues and they can add impact to your presentation if used well. Unfortunately, it is easy to use them badly. Practise using the projector before the presentation – find out where the on/off switch is, how to focus it and where to place it so as to make a big enough image.

Leave your slides on the screen long enough for your audience to read them thoroughly and interpret any figures or graphs. Talk about your slides so your audience can take in the information.

Don't keep turning to the screen and turning your back on your audience. If you want to see which point comes next, look down at the transparency on the glass.

Turn the projector off when you have finished using it – they are noisy and hot.

- **PowerPoint** is a program produced by Microsoft to aid presentations. It is very simple to use and you will quickly be able to produce professional-looking slides. If you have never used PowerPoint before, visit *www.microsoft.com/education*. There are useful tutorials that will take you through the program.

PowerPoint and similar programs allow you to put colourful, artistic backgrounds on your slides, and to incorporate sounds, photographic images, animations and web links. A presenter kit will allow you to project your slides onto a screen so that they are very large, suitable for large venues and audiences. It is a powerful tool, but once again, you must practise using the equipment until you are proficient.

Adherence to legislation

Adhering to legislation means working within the law. There are various laws that you will need to consider when preparing and presenting the results of research. These are described below.

Copyright legislation

This was previously discussed in the section 'Standards and constraints', on page 138. You are not allowed to copy or use substantial sections of someone else's work unless you have express permission.

Designs and patents

This area is also covered by the Copyright, Designs and Patents Act 1988. A **patent** gives the inventor of a new product or process the right to stop others from making, using or selling that invention without permission. Any ideas that the researcher discovers must not be passed off as the researcher's own ideas.

W3C

The World Wide Web Consortium (W3C) is an international group of business and academic representatives based at Massachusetts Institute of Technology (MIT). Members of this group work to create and develop common standards for the World Wide Web, but these do not have the force of law.

Disability discrimination

The Disability Discrimination Act 1995 was introduced to combat the discrimination faced by many disabled people. It provides rights in a number of areas, but one of the key ones is in

153

BTEC National Study Guide: Business. See page 185 for order details of individual texts

95

employment. The Act requires that a disabled person not be treated any less favourably than others and requires that companies make reasonable adjustments to working practices or premises to accommodate disabled people (unless there is reasonable justification for not doing this). Adjustments could involve wheelchair ramps or flexible hours to allow for treatment.

Researchers should make sure that disabled people have equal access to the premises in which presentations are to be delivered, for example, and ensure that information is presented in such a way that a disabled person can receive the message as easily as anyone else.

Equal opportunities

The Sex Discrimination Act 1975 and the Race Relations Act 1976 were brought in to encourage people to treat others as individuals and to respect differences. The European Union Equal Treatment Directive now makes it unlawful to discriminate not only on the grounds of sex, race and disability but also on grounds of sexual orientation and religion or other belief. By December 2006, age discrimination will also be unlawful. Researchers must therefore make sure that they respect people's differences in the way they ask questions, decide who to interview and present results.

Outcome activity 4.2

Continue the assignment concerning Rapid Research and Topfizz Drinks Ltd that began in Outcome Activity 4.1, page 142.

Pass

Manipulate the data that you have collected into appropriate formats ready for your presentation. Your work must show clearly that you have synthesised the data well. It should therefore include the use of:

- text (summarised from original data)
- well-laid-out pages
- statistics, including percentages or percentage changes, and at least one average
- tables
- charts
- data combined from various sources.

Presentation of gathered information

É muito importante conhecer suas audiências.

Did you follow that? Unless you speak Portuguese, the chances are that it meant nothing to you. (Even if you do speak Portuguese, my rough translation may still leave you wondering!) In English it should say, 'It is very important to know your audience.' That is what this section is all about.

Writing in an inappropriate language is a pretty obvious error, but other errors are less easy to spot and they can impede communication just as effectively. You must think about the needs of your audience and adapt your presentation in order to help them.

Presentation methods

The first step will be to consider the presentation method to use – different methods may suit different audiences.

Documents

You could use any of the documents outlined earlier in this unit: letters, reports, memoranda, invoices, e-mails, flow charts or publicity materials. But if the audience has difficulty using written documents you may have to consider adaptations. Partially sighted people may need documents to be enlarged or produced in braille, a special type of text that can be read by touch. People with some types of colour blindness may need you to use different colours in your documents. People who do not speak English as a first language may need alternative versions in their languages.

On-screen multimedia presentation

Presentations on PowerPoint or a similar program can use techniques that traditional methods cannot – such as moving graphics, links to the Internet, video and music. Most of these are also visual media, so you could make it easier for someone in your audience who is partially sighted by producing copies of slides to look through during the talk, and providing transcripts of video footage.

Web-based presentation

You could put your presentations on the Internet or a company intranet. The advantage of this is that it can be accessed many times by interested users, and you can also make your research information available to a much wider audience.

A web presentation could simply be in audio, where the receiver clicks on a button on your web page and your recorded voice plays in an audio player program.

Alternatively you could upload your PowerPoint slides to the website so that a reader can go through them one at a time at his or her own pace.

It is also possible to run full video of your presentation on a website. Record the presentation using a digital camera, save it as an MPEG or AVI file, and place it on your site.

Finally you might have a full videoconference presentation. This is a live performance where delegates at a distance are able to watch you and feed back to you. Relatively little equipment is required for such a task – you need PCs with webcams at both ends of the conference, a fast Internet connection and some software such as Microsoft Net Meeting. At a designated time, all the delegates log on to the site and a live interactive presentation can take place.

Multilingual support

It is entirely possible that some members of your audience are non-English speakers, and for many people English is a second language. You might consider:

- asking members of the audience if they would like you to make special arrangements for them

- having paper copies of PowerPoint slides prepared in their languages for them to read during your presentation

- preparing translations of handouts to be used or reports that you have written

- organising an interpreter or English language support worker.

At the very least you should speak at a moderate pace and ensure that you pronounce your words carefully, and offer to send a transcript of your talk.

Style of presentation and images used

These areas are discussed in the following section.

Audience requirements

A professional presenter will ensure that he or she is able to adapt the content of the presentation to suit different audiences, or individuals in an audience. It is very important to obtain some idea of the make-up of an audience before you deliver a presentation, as you may need to make some significant changes to ensure that your audience gets your message. You would be well advised to make inquiries about the people likely to be in an audience beforehand so that you don't get caught out because you had not catered, for example, for someone who is partially sighted.

Here are some of the reasons for changes that may be necessary, and some ideas about how you might cater for the individual needs of your audience.

Age/intellectual development

Young people can usually concentrate for relatively short periods, while older people and those who are well educated are more likely to be able to listen to you for an extended period. Building variety into your presentation is helpful for any audience, but it is vital for the young or less well educated. Young people also respond well to visual stimuli, such as pictures, video and models. The key therefore is to change style during the presentation, perhaps start with a visual stimulus to attract attention, then talk formally for a few minutes, follow that with an activity, more talk, a video, etc.

155

BTEC National Study Guide: Business. See page 185 for order details of individual texts

97

Use of examples – age, gender and ethnicity

A good way to help your audience understand is to give examples to illustrate your explanations, but you may need to adapt these to take account of your audience. Use examples that draw on the lives of your listeners, and reflect their experiences and interests. Examples drawn from different ethnic backgrounds and ones that draw from the experiences of both genders in positive ways are preferable.

Special needs of audience – accessibility

Individuals may have special needs that you need to be aware of. You may need to adapt the environment so that students with special needs sit in appropriate positions in the room. Lip readers, for example, would not want you to be standing in front of a window as they would see you silhouetted against the light, which makes lip reading very difficult.

You may want to consider the need to adapt your materials to make them more legible for your audience. Handouts and PowerPoint presentations, for example, could be done using large font sizes to help the partially sighted. Some visually impaired people also find certain colour combinations, such as green and yellow, to be problematic, so these should also be avoided. For someone with learning difficulties you may also want to adapt the pace of your presentation.

Language and readability

You need to adapt the language you use to suit your audience. Young, less well educated or inexperienced people may want you to use simple language, whereas an older or more professional audience would be comfortable with technical terms and phrases.

Attention span

Professional people and older, educated people are often able to concentrate for much longer periods, so you can give lengthy presentations to such people. This would not be the case with a group of schoolchildren, so adapt accordingly.

Young children would not be expected to concentrate on one topic for a long period

Interest

You need to know how interested your audience is in the topic you are to present. If they are already keen to hear what you have to say, then you don't need to work too hard, but many audiences will need to be won over.

Variety in your presentation can help with this, as can a little humour, but be careful with humour. A good joke at the start of your presentation is a great way of engaging your audience and getting them on your side, but a badly received joke, or worse still one that is offensive, can leave you with a lot of ground to make up. If you are in any doubt at all, don't try humour.

Presenting yourself

If you were to present to a group of manual workers wearing a suit, you would be in danger of creating a barrier between yourself and the audience. You might be seen to be siding with management (who typically wear suits). However, if you were to dress down when presenting to a board of directors, your audience may not hear what you have to say because they considered

BTEC National Study Guide: Business. See page 185 for order details of individual texts

you to be unprofessional. Dressing in a way that is appropriate to your audience will encourage them to listen to you and respect what you have to say.

Business and industry experience and knowledge

Inexperienced people will need the basics explaining first. If you miss this out they will not get anything from your presentation. Equally, if you labour your way through the basics of a topic when you are speaking to experienced business people you will come over as patronising and they are unlikely to listen. By the time you get to the main point, they will already have switched off.

The overall message here is simple: **know your audience!**

Thinking point

You are preparing a presentation to deliver to a professional audience about the new packaging design for a best-selling chocolate bar. You have been told that the presentation will be delivered to the board of directors initially, but you have also been asked to present the same information to the staff later in the day. The staff are aged from 16 to 60, and include one woman who is partially sighted.

Outline in general terms the types of adaptation you would include to ensure that the second presentation goes as well as the first.

Facility management

Equipment required

The types of equipment needed are shown in the diagrams below:

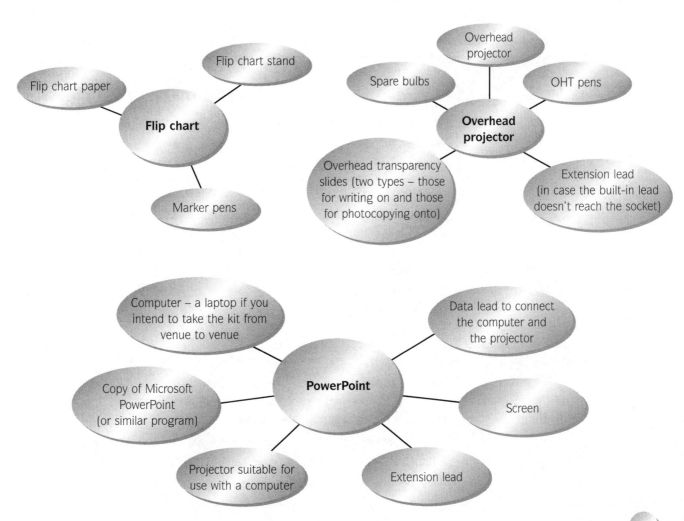

157

BTEC National Study Guide: Business. See page 185 for order details of individual texts

99

Maintenance of equipment

You need to ensure that your presentation equipment is kept in the best possible condition. Tips for maintenance are given in the table at the bottom of the page.

Implications of updating information

One of the main advantages of the PowerPoint system becomes apparent when it is necessary to update the information in a presentation that you have delivered before.

Flip charts would need to be rewritten and new paper, pads and pens would need to be used.

New overhead transparencies would need to be purchased and the slides would need to be re-written.

On a PowerPoint system, however, you can simply change a detail and save it on the hard drive and everything is ready. There is no extra cost and this is much quicker than the other methods. If you use the 'Paste Link' function, the details can be

Case study   PowerPoint

Your manager has asked you to look into the costs of buying equipment for the new company conference room. You feel that it would be a good idea to install a PowerPoint presenter kit system.

Investigate the relative costs of using flip charts, overhead projectors and PowerPoint or similar technology. If you search on the Internet, or visit some office supply stores, you will be able to find out the costs of each piece of equipment.

With the results of your research, prepare a short report that details the relative costs and justifies the purchase of the PowerPoint presenter kit.

Equipment	How to maintain
Flip chart	Check the stand occasionally, but there is little to go wrong. Replenish the paper periodically. Replace marker pens when necessary, although they do last for some time.
Overhead projector	Clean the glass plate of the overhead projector periodically. Make sure you have a spare bulb handy at all times as they do not give any warning before they fail. Bulbs are very easy to replace if you have a spare. Simply unscrew the lid (there is normally one screw on either side of the projector) and lift it off. The old bulb simply pulls out of its housing (take care, it will be very hot) and the new bulb pushes in to replace it. Have a qualified electrician check the equipment for safety every six months. Replace OHT pens periodically.
PowerPoint presenter kit	Clean the projector lens with a lens cloth frequently. If you are using a portable kit, take great care with the data lead that connects the laptop with the projector. It has a number of pins in each socket, and if one of these becomes bent it may be useless. With portable kits, also take great care not to move the projector while the lamp is hot. It is easy to break a lamp while hot and they are costly to replace. Have a qualified electrician check the equipment for safety every six months.

BTEC National Study Guide: Business. See page 185 for order details of individual texts

updated automatically when you make a change in another program. These systems are therefore the most efficient when it comes to improving, updating or amending your presentation materials.

Outcome activity 4.3

Continue the assignment concerning Rapid Research and Topfizz Drinks Ltd from Outcome Activity 4.1 and Outcome Activity 4.2.

Pass

1 Write a letter to the Chief Executive of Topfizz Drinks, Miss D R Pepper, inviting her and her board of directors to your presentation. The address is Topfizz Drinks Ltd, Carbonate House, Lenton, Nottingham, NG5 6TT.

2 Produce a memorandum to be sent to the staff in your office inviting them to the same presentation.

3 Produce a poster to advertise your presentation. This is to be displayed in the office and canteen.

4 Write an e-mail to be sent to the head of estates management at Rapid Research, Mr J Sheridan, asking him to confirm your booking of the conference room for your presentation. You must also inform him of the equipment you will require.

5 Deliver your presentation.

Merit

Miss Pepper is very pleased with your presentation and she has asked you to repeat it for a group of workers from the Topfizz factory. She informs you that the audience will be predominantly young workers, and that one member of the audience is profoundly deaf.

Ray Search (your manager) is keen that this second presentation goes equally well and he has asked you what steps you will take to adapt the presentation to meet the needs of the new audience.

Write a memorandum to Ray outlining to him the adaptations that you will make. You must demonstrate in the memorandum that you are meeting the needs of everyone in the audience. Analyse and justify the presentation methods which will meet the needs of the audience members.

Outcome activity 4.3 *continued*

Distinction

1 Evaluate how accurate and detailed the information you presented was. Consider the reasons why you were asked to deliver the presentation. Was it as accurate and detailed as it needed to be? What areas might have been improved?

2 The presentation that you deliver should make use of creative presentation techniques to enhance the delivery of your messages. The presentation should therefore be made using a PowerPoint presenter kit. Use a selection of the following techniques:

- additional visual aids
- good use of transitions in your PowerPoint slides
- video (recorded or original)
- photographic images (original digital images, stills from film or TV or images from the Internet)
- music or sounds
- animated images (original or found on the Internet)
- other creative methods.

BTEC National Study Guide: Business. See page 185 for order details of individual texts

101

Creative corporate communication

Companies communicate with us every day of our lives, so often in fact that we don't always notice when it is happening. A lot of this communication aims to sell us products and services, but much happens in order to create a **corporate image** for the firm. A company's corporate image is the impression of the firm in people's minds; the image that is created when the firm's name is mentioned. The aim is to achieve a positive image, but it is just as easy to create a negative one.

Corporate image

Corporate image is important as it encourages sales, attracts new and better staff, and encourages people to become and remain shareholders of the company. Companies use a combination of the following tactics to create their corporate images.

Logos

A **logo** is an emblem used as the badge of a company, and it is always to be found on promotional material. Logos can be designed to say something about the company or can just be a unique design that stays in the memory of the potential customer.

They are powerful tools, and many firms have logos that are instantly recognisable to people around the world. A brand logo can give people the confidence to buy new products launched by a company. Logos are used to:

- attract attention
- inform people about the company
- differentiate it from other companies
- allow customers to identify the company.

Practice point

Which of the following logos can you name?

BTEC National Study Guide: Business. See page 185 for order details of individual texts

102

In order to keep your corporate image up to date it is important to keep your logo up to date. For example, what do you think people would think of the Pepsi-Cola company if it was still using the following logo?

This is the logo that it used back in 1905. It would be difficult to continue to portray the company as dynamic, up to date and in touch with young people if it still used the same logo. Consequently the Pepsi logo has evolved over the years:

1973

2003

1998

Thinking point

Consider the four Pepsi logos above.

1 What factors do you feel influenced Pepsi in each of the logo changes illustrated?

2 Which features of the logo have not changed over the years? Why do you think the company decided not to change these?

3 There appear to have been more frequent changes in recent years than in the early years. What factors may have influenced this?

Livery

Livery is a distinctive colour scheme used by a firm on all its vehicles, packaging and promotions. For example, McDonald's uses a red background and yellow text. The distinctive McDonald's livery is used on all of its stores worldwide, and it is also used on all vehicles and packaging.

A unique or unusual livery makes your product instantly recognisable worldwide, encouraging sales.

Uniforms

A distinctive uniform or dress style can also enhance the company image, especially if this is in keeping with the livery and professionalism of the company.

Letterhead and font style

Many companies develop a distinctive, often unique, font style that will be instantly recognisable to customers. For example, Quaker developed a unique font for Sugar Puffs, a style that emphasises the unique qualities of the product and helps to make the product stand out from competitors.

BTEC National Study Guide: Business. See page 185 for order details of individual texts

103

Vocabulary

Vocabulary used in promotional material can enhance a desired image. The City of Birmingham recently decided to promote a new brand image; it was decided to use certain words in all advertising to promote the best aspects of the city. The words chosen were:

- welcoming
- surprising
- creative
- diverse
- dynamic.

These words are now used in all promotional materials. A billboard advertisement for the city reads:

From creativity comes growth

The custard factory is a hotbed of creativity, situated in eastside ... Birmingham's developing new creative learning centre

Note the number of times the word 'creativity' or 'creative' is used in the text.

Practice point

You are in charge of promoting your school or college. Draw up a list of six key words that you could use to promote the establishment.

Draw a poster incorporating those words to advertise your next open evening.

Supporting promotional statements or straplines

A **strapline** is a memorable phrase used by the company to draw attention to the product or to inform the customer. It has a powerful part to play in promoting corporate image, as a well-chosen strapline can make the product or service memorable for the customer. Young people are particularly good at remembering straplines and

the product names associated with them; those products become ingrained in the memories of these potential customers.

Thinking point

Which firms or products use the following straplines? Match the strapline in the left column with the correct name from the right column.

It's not for girls!	John Lewis
Never knowingly undersold	Stella Artois
Reassuringly expensive	Yorkie
Exceedingly good	AA
The Real Thing	Churchill Insurance
Just Ask	Mr Kipling
Give the dog a phone	Cadbury's
Chocolate and a half	Coca-Cola

Some companies choose to put their names in the strapline, thereby making the company even more memorable:

- The future's bright, the future's Orange
- Carlsberg – Probably the best lager in the world
- A to B, we RAC to it
- Why can't everything orange be Fanta?
- It's a Mini adventure!
- Beanz Meanz Heinz.

Endorsements and affiliations

Signing up a famous person to **endorse** your product can enhance public image and improve sales. Care should be taken in choosing an appropriate celebrity, however. The association with the celebrity should enhance the status of the product in the customer's eyes, so the person chosen should be someone admired by the target audience, ideally someone who acts as a role model to those people and who holds the same values.

Multimedia associations

There is much benefit to be gained from bringing your product to the attention of people through either film or music. Both approaches can be subtle and very effective in enhancing product image.

● **Product placement** is where a company pays to have its product appear in films, books, computer games and/or on television. A carefully chosen placement can enhance the public image of a product or company by associating it with a particular type of person or environment to which viewers aspire. For example, in the film *Castaway*, starring Tom Hanks, the firm Federal Express was featured very prominently, and many positive comments were made during the film concerning the quality of the FedEx service.

In 2002 the film attracting the most placements was *Minority Report*, starring Tom Cruise. Included in the film were Oakley, Lexus, Nokia, Reebok, Burger King, Guinness, The Gap and American Express. At one point in the film, Tom Cruise's character is offered a Guinness by name.

During a recent episode of *Will and Grace* in the US, Debra Messing wore a Polo shirt available on Polo.com. Five days later, traffic on the Polo site had doubled and close to 3000 T-shirts had been sold.

Product placement has proved to be a popular method for companies to promote their products, one of the main reasons being cost. Although it is not cheap to get a product placed, compared with the cost of filming and showing advertisements on prime-time TV,

the price is significantly less. All the filming costs involved in a placement are borne by the company making the film.

● **Famous pop songs** have been used in advertisements for many years. The association has a double benefit. A popular song gets plenty of air-play on both TV and radio, so if your product is closely associated with a particular song, every time it is played people think of your product. This is free advertising on prime-time TV and radio! It also works for the musicians, because coverage on the advertisement enhances and even launches musical careers.

Distinctive packaging

Packaging can make your product stand out from competitors on the shelves. It can be used to attract initial attention, or enable a customer to pick out your product as a trusted brand when surrounded by a multitude of similar products in a supermarket. Either way, it can be used successfully to promote increased sales.

When Virgin first launched its Cola, it was faced with the problem of differentiating the product from two massive brands, Coca-Cola and Pepsi-

163

BTEC National Study Guide: Business. See page 185 for order details of individual texts

105

Cola. It also faced the problem that both companies also had products that came in readily recognisable packaging, particularly the traditional Coke Classic bottle.

Virgin's answer was a combination of celebrity endorsement and unique packaging, the 'Pammy' bottle. Virgin Cola was originally endorsed by Pamela Anderson, and the designers developed a 'curvy' bottle that was supposed to mimic Pamela's curvy shape! The promotion worked, and Virgin Cola quickly established itself in a very competitive market.

Pamela Anderson and the 'Pammy' bottle

Practice point

Visit your local supermarket and identify a number of distinctive packaging styles. Note what it is about them that makes them unique and analyse how the packaging has contributed to the distinctiveness of the corporate image of the company.

Sponsorship

This can be used to bring the organisation's name to many new people. It can enhance an established image, or create a new one. For sponsorship to be effective, the event or person sponsored should be in line with the company's desired image. This could involve sponsoring an artistic or sporting event that needs financial backing, or it could mean donating items of equipment or kit to local groups or sports teams.

Examples of sponsorship include:

- Vodafone sponsoring the Epsom Derby
- Flora sponsoring the London Marathon
- Orange sponsoring the British Film Academy Awards
- O_2 sponsoring the Edinburgh Mela
- the Royal Bank of Scotland sponsoring the Royal Highland Show and the Edinburgh Street Party.

Of course, sponsorship will only have a positive effect on company image if it is drawn to the attention of the public, so general advertising literature will normally carry details of the sponsorship agreed.

Manchester United has both a kit sponsor (Nike) and a main team sponsor (Vodafone). McDonald's sponsors sports coaching for young children, while Specsavers sponsors local cricket.

Thinking point

1 Look at each of the above sponsorship examples. What do you think are the motivations behind each example?

2 Care must be taken when choosing sponsorship deals. In 2003 Vodafone, which also sponsors the England cricket team, asked the team not to tour Zimbabwe in winter 2004. Why do you think it asked for this?

On-line activity

Many firms need to trade on-line today to boost sales. Some firms cannot sell directly on-line because of the nature of their businesses, but they may still choose to have an Internet presence to enhance their image. Walker's crisps and Pepsi are examples. These firms have major websites but do not sell through them; they simply use them to enhance their images.

BTEC National Study Guide: Business. See page 185 for order details of individual texts

106

A firm can also enhance its image and encourage use of its website by promoting the web address through traditional channels. This might involve including the firm's web address on packaging, posters, TV ads, carrier bags, free gifts and other traditional promotion tools.

Public relations

Public relations activities are intended to bring the company to the attention of the public for the right reasons, and can be used to enhance the desired image. PR consists of many activities, including:

- press conferences
- Christmas cards
- open days
- supporting local schools and colleges
- publicity stunts
- supporting charities
- photocalls.

Public relations is discussed in detail in Unit 3.

Press releases

Firms will often write articles about themselves and their achievements and submit these to local and national press and TV. If they are considered to be interesting by the editor and are included, this brings free advertising for the company.

Attractiveness of presentation

Clearly an attractively presented piece of promotional material will boost the image of the company. See Unit 3 for more on creative product promotion.

Outcome activity 4.4

Continue the assignment concerning Rapid Research and Topfizz Drinks Ltd from Outcome Activities 4.1, 4.2 and 4.3.

Pass

Miss Pepper has contacted you to say that she feels Topfizz Drinks may need to consider using some more creative communication techniques if it is to be successful in creating a positive corporate image for itself in the market. She has asked you to investigate the methods used by one of the major companies in the market and to send her a detailed report on the techniques it uses. She will use this when deciding what strategies to use for her company.

Investigate either the Pepsi-Cola company or the Coca-Cola company. Research the creative communication techniques used by the firm and the ways it goes about creating a positive corporate image for the company. Produce a report addressed to Ray Search (your manager) that he can present to Miss Pepper. This should fully describe the techniques that your chosen company is using.

Merit

In the 'Conclusions' section of your report, explain why the techniques you described were effective. Analyse the successful strategy of creative corporate communication in your chosen company.

Distinction

In the 'Recommendations' section of your report, suggest additional creative communication techniques that could be used by your chosen company to enhance its corporate image further. Fully justify all your suggestions.

165

BTEC National Study Guide: Business. See page 185 for order details of individual texts

107

Key terms

Company reports and accounts
documents produced annually by each public company giving details of its financial position and a summary of the past year's trading

Copyright
law that states the original creator of work has control over people using and making copies of it

Corporate image
the impression of the firm that is created in the mind of a member of the public

Database
a computer program for storing data records

Defamation
saying or writing something about someone that damages his or her reputation or causes financial losses

Endorsement
paying a celebrity to use your product or service publicly

Error management
identifying the causes of errors and taking appropriate actions to ensure that they do not recur

External information
information found from outside the company

Extrapolation
identifying a trend and extending it into the future to predict what may happen

Flow chart
diagram showing a process that involves a number of steps and a series of decisions

Internal information
information found from within the company

Logo
an emblem used as the badge of a company on promotional material

Patent
registering a patent on an invention prevents others from making and selling it without permission for a period of years

Primary data
original information that you have found for yourself

Publicity material
publications produced by the firm that are intended to attract attention and promote sales

Qualitative information
the opinions and preferences of individuals

Quantitative information
research that produces results in the form of numbers, e.g. how many people buy a product

Search engines
facilities on the Internet that allow you to search for websites dealing with topics of interest

Secondary data
information found from previously published or written sources, either within or outside the firm

Spreadsheet
a computer program that allows the user to manipulate figures and perform complex mathematical tasks

Strapline
a memorable phrase used by a company to draw attention to the product, or to inform the customer

BTEC National Study Guide: Business. See page 185 for order details of individual texts

108

End-of-unit test

1 Explain the difference between qualitative and quantitative analysis. Give examples to support your explanations.

2 Explain the difference between internal and external research information. Give examples to support your explanations.

3 Some researchers believe that you should do secondary research before primary research. Explain the benefits of this approach.

4 What advantages do focus groups have over other primary information methods?

5 How can we check the currency of the information we are gathering? Think of at least four different information sources, and explain how you would check the currency of each.

6 'Telephone technology is so good these days that we don't need to produce written business correspondence any more.' Do you agree with this statement? Give reasons for your answer.

7 'Patents and copyright rules are an incentive to innovators.' Explain why you think these laws are necessary.

8 Sales in each of the branches of your company in the past month were as follows:

Branch	Sales (thousands of pounds)
Cardiff	£25,216
Glasgow	£37,498
London	£49,377
Birmingham	£27,565

Work out the percentage of the total sales made by each of the branches. Give your answers to one decimal place.

9 (a) In 1999 your company had 512 employees; today it has 384. What is the percentage change in staff over those years?

(b) You are expecting to recruit a further 32 staff this year. What will the percentage change be this year?

10 Calculate the mean of the following set of figures.

192	287	36	433	357
398	88	297	250	412
222	154	299	97	101
175	241	376	36	314

11 How much faith can we place in extrapolated figures? Give reasons for your answer.

12 What would be the best type of chart to illustrate the data in Question 8? Explain your answer.

13 Create the graph that you described in Question 12 using a spreadsheet program.

14 Outline three situations when you might choose not to use a PowerPoint projector kit. Explain your reasons.

15 In what ways is PowerPoint a superior medium for delivering presentations? What limitations does it have?

16 Outline the considerations that are important when preparing a presentation to be delivered to a group of schoolchildren aged 11.

17 Design a new logo for your school or college. Explain how it will improve the image of the school or college.

18 Write a new strapline for your school or college. Explain how it will help to improve the image of the school or college.

19 What are the main advantages of product placement over a traditional celebrity endorsement?

20 Identify a number of sponsorship deals that have been agreed with firms in your locality. Explain why these deals help the corporate image of the firms concerned.

BTEC National Study Guide: Business. See page 185 for order details of individual texts

109

Resources

Texts

Carysforth, C: *Communication for Work*, Heinemann, 1998

Matthews and Davies: *The Born Presenter*, Thomson Learning, 2002

Milner, D: *Success in Advertising and Promotion*, John Murray Publishers, 1995

O'Guinn, Allen and Semenick: *Advertising*, South Western College Publishing, 1998

Parry, H: *Successful Business Presentations*, Croner, 1994

Websites

www.google.co.uk Google search engine

www.statistics.gov.uk National Statistics on-line

www.telegraph.co.uk Telegraph on-line newspaper

www.carol.co.uk Company annual reports on-line

www.cia.gov/cia/publications/factbook Country profiles and world facts

www.microsoft.com/education Microsoft training and tutorials

www.bized.ac.uk Biz/ed, business and economics-related subjects

www.mori.com Mori research services

www.mintel.com Mintel, supplier of consumer and product information

www.keynote.co.uk Keynote, market intelligence

www.datamonitor.com Datamonitor, business intelligence

www.adslogans.co.uk/general/students.html Information for students on advertising slogans

168

BTEC National Study Guide: Business. See page 185 for order details of individual texts

110

This unit shows how marketing has an impact on the ability of an organisation to achieve its aims and objectives. It also illustrates that marketing is much more than simply advertising.

After establishing the underlying aims of marketing, the activities associated with marketing in a typical organisation are discussed, alongside the factors that ensure it is conducted in a proper manner.

The sections on marketing research and marketing information show how to collect essential information to make effective decisions.

The final section on marketing strategies covers how the information gathered is used to produce plans that should help the organisation achieve its overall objectives.

The unit is divided into four main sections:

- 11.1 Principles of marketing
- 11.2 Marketing research
- 11.3 Marketing information
- 11.4 Marketing strategies.

Principles of marketing

The development of the marketing concept

Marketing definitions

Marketing plays an important part in ensuring the products consumers want are readily available. The Chartered Institute of Marketing's definition provides a clear picture of the activities involved. Marketing is:

> The management process responsible for identifying, anticipating and satisfying customer requirements profitably

It is a management activity because it requires continuous information gathering, analysis and evaluation in order to make decisions. The information collected should help an organisation identify customer requirements.

But it is not sufficient to find out what consumers are thinking and doing now; there is a need to consider what might happen in the future. Future consumer tastes and preferences need to be anticipated; sometimes businesses can even create them – they use marketing to create needs where none may have existed.

Once consumer needs have been identified, the organisation still has to satisfy them successfully. Designing the right product to satisfy those needs may not prove easy.

It is essential to do all this and make a profit to invest in new products and advertising campaigns, and provide a reward for investors; or in the case of public or voluntary sector organisations, to fund continued and improved services.

Marketing puts consumers at the centre of everything an organisation undertakes, and is the link between producer and customer.

The variety of organisations in the business world means marketing managers find themselves facing very different marketing situations. Some of these different marketing environments are shown in the following table.

289

BTEC National Study Guide: Business. See page 185 for order details of individual texts

111

Organisation	Advertising	Price	Place	Product
National retailer, e.g. Next	National – many methods used – same message nationally	Strong brand name allows it to charge above-average prices	High Street and retail parks	Same product in all stores nationally
National bank, e.g. NatWest	National – many methods used – same message nationally	Same prices (i.e. loan interest rates) across the country	High Street and now on the Internet	Same product throughout national network
Local business, e.g. plumber	Uses local media, vans and Yellow Pages	Flexible, depends on customer's budget	Contactable by mobile phone	Adapt product to cater for local needs
Charity, e.g. Help the Aged	National – cannot be seen to be spending too much on advertising	Donors can give as much money as they like; recipients of help do not pay anything	Contactable by phone, envelope collections and shops	Donor has nothing to show for the donation except perhaps a letter of thanks

While the main marketing aims might be the same for any organisation, how the aims are accomplished depends on the nature of the organisation.

Marketing principles

These are the underlying goals of marketing.

- **Understanding consumer needs:** Markets change rapidly and it is therefore essential that organisations constantly look for new product and market opportunities. Plenty of organisations have failed to appreciate the importance of this principle and have found themselves operating in declining markets (such as videos) and/or competing against organisations with superior products (such as DVDs).

- **Keeping ahead of competition:** Increased competition can have a dramatic impact on an organisation. For example, a competitor might start offering delivery within three days, whereas previously the best performance in the market might have been seven days. Customers might immediately switch to the faster service.

- **Communicating effectively with consumers:** Even the best product, effectively distributed at the right price to the target market, may experience poor sales if the promotional support is ineffective. In many markets where competition is intense, high levels of promotional support are necessary if an organisation is to succeed.

- **Using new technology:** This is an area that has been gaining in importance in recent years. The ability to book flight tickets over the Internet with companies such as EasyJet is changing how the airline industry works.

The use of technology is now considered by many marketing managers as a key marketing principle. Marketing should seek to exploit its potential. The emergence of e-marketing is relevant to marketing for a variety of reasons:

- It provides a new worldwide channel of distribution, especially for products that can be bought and delivered over the Internet. This would include, for example, music, software and films. Some products which have to be physically delivered to the customer, such as books, are also selling well.

It provides new ways for marketing managers to do their job. The potential of Internet-based promotional techniques needs to be investigated. These include personalised e-mail newsletters and software programmes, which can alert consumers to products they might like to buy, based on previous purchasing activity. The ability to send promotional SMS and MMS messages via mobile phones is also of interest to marketing.

Thinking point

1 How can the new technology now available help marketing managers do their job?

2 Should organisations have to obtain the consumer's permission before sending SMS and MMS promotional messages? What might be the advantages of seeking that permission?

Marketing functions

These are the broad areas of marketing activity that contribute towards the achievement of the marketing principles.

- **Establish a distinctive identity for a product or organisation.** There are very few unique products nowadays, so organisations develop brands to give themselves a distinct image in the market. A brand can be a name, a symbol or a design used to identify a product and make it different from its competitors. The Nike 'tick' or 'swoosh' is instantly recognisable across the world. Other organisations seek to create a **corporate image** in the market. Corporate image means the characteristics an organisation wishes to establish for itself in the minds of the public. For example, an organisation might want to be seen as caring and trustworthy, such as Barnardo's, the UK's largest children's charity.

- **Co-ordinate marketing activities effectively.** The decision by the marketing team to launch a new product normally has implications for many other departments in an organisation. Any new product launch is likely to involve the design department in completing the design on time. The distribution department needs to be made aware of the nature of the product to ensure it can be stored and delivered successfully. The sales team needs to be briefed about the product's features and benefits and any special launch promotions. While all these groups need to be kept informed about developments, their activities also need to be co-ordinated. For example, the production unit needs to ensure stock has been produced to coincide with the sales team obtaining orders.

Thinking point

Think of some external agencies whose marketing activities need to be co-ordinated by the internal marketing team. An example is a printer.

Explain the role of these agencies and when they would need to be told about the work they would be expected to complete.

- **Plan, co-ordinate and monitor the marketing mix.** An organisation has to allocate resources between the five parts of the marketing mix – product, place, price, promotion and packaging. Products need to be replaced by new improved versions, which can require high spending on development. It may be necessary to offer discounts to customers to encourage them to buy, and the resulting loss of income has to be considered. To encourage retailers to stock a product, producers may have to provide display units – and these are always expensive. Finally, an organisation has to invest in promotion. The effectiveness of the marketing mix chosen needs to be monitored and changed if the expected results are not forthcoming.

- **Manage changes in technology, competition and consumer tastes.** Marketers have a variety of techniques for

291

BTEC National Study Guide: Business. See page 185 for order details of individual texts

113

The marketing mix

managing change. All the techniques taken together are generally called 'situational analysis' or 'marketing audit'. These are discussed later in this unit.

Marketing objectives and activities

The most effective marketing objectives should be SMART – specific, measurable, achievable, realistic and time-related. For example, an aim might be 'to achieve a 5% market share in the French and German markets within 18 months'.

This objective is *specific* in that it details exactly what has to be done. It is *measurable* because a market share requirement is included. The objective would be *achievable* if everybody in the organisation accepted the aim. It would be *realistic* if it was calculated that it was possible to attain. It is *timetabled*, as the length of time given to achieve the objective is stated.

Marketing activities are the detailed actions that have to be undertaken to achieve the objectives. These are the day-to-day jobs personnel in the marketing team are likely to be doing:

● conducting marketing research into new product concepts or promotional ideas

● implementing promotional campaigns by producing TV commercials and booking airtime with satellite television broadcasters

● calculating new prices when implementing a price increase.

For every marketing objective, a marketing plan is written. These plans determine exactly which marketing activities should be undertaken. The plans are also important for controlling and evaluating the work of the marketing team.

Planning level	Content
Corporate mission statement	Overall vision – e.g. to be a world-class health care organisation
Corporate objectives (overall business objectives)	What has to be achieved to deliver the vision, e.g. to have drugs in all key health care areas
Marketing objectives	Marketing contribution to the corporate objectives, e.g. launch a new drug to help heart attack victims next year
Marketing plan	Marketing tactics to be used, e.g. advertise new drug in medical journals read by doctors

Organisational and marketing objectives – planning, control and evaluation

It is important that the marketing objectives and plans support the overall business objectives. Otherwise there is the possibility that the organisation will not have a common purpose. The overall objectives of the business should have a strong influence on marketing objectives and plans. The transformation of corporate objectives into marketing activity is shown in the table above.

Once a marketing plan is written it not only influences the day-to-day activity within a marketing team, but it is also used to monitor, **control** and evaluate activity.

A variety of resources can be used to monitor performance. For example organisations can:

● compare actual sales performance against targets

● gather feedback from customers about performance – letters of complaint can be a useful source of information

● analyse what the media is saying about the organisation.

The advantage of having a plan is that the organisation should be able to identify quickly when performance is below expected levels – before the end of the planning period. It can then take early action to put matters right. For example, if sales are low in January and February for a particular product, it is quite likely the year's target will not be reached. Current activity can be evaluated and corrective action can be taken as early as March to ensure the year's target is reached.

Practice point

1 It is February and the sales performance is already below the targets agreed. In small groups, consider what corrective action you would take.

2 Compare your plan with those of other groups in the class. Which plan might inflict the most damage on the organisation's profitability?

Marketing mix

Once the marketing objectives have been agreed it is necessary to develop marketing plans to achieve the goals. The marketing mix provides an excellent framework for developing marketing plans. The marketing mix is made up of a number of parts – product, price, promotion, place and packaging.

Product

Product means the combination of goods and services that is offered to the target consumer. For example, Vauxhall offers a range of models based on the Astra, each with many optional extras that the customer can choose. The car arrives serviced and with a comprehensive guarantee, which is very much part of the product.

BTEC National Study Guide: Business. See page 185 for order details of individual texts

115

Price

Price is the amount of money consumers have to pay to acquire the product. This can vary considerably from the advertised price. For example, the local Vauxhall dealer can offer discounts, part-exchange allowances and credit terms, which all combine to alter the price individual consumers pay.

Place

Place describes where and how the consumer can obtain the product. Car producers have a national network of dealers, but place does not have to be a physical location. Nowadays consumers can buy such products as insurance, holidays and books over the telephone, via the Internet or through their TV remote control. Producers have to carefully choose the best method to ensure consumers can find their product in an appropriate place when they decide to purchase.

Promotion

Promotion describes the activities undertaken to ensure the consumer knows about the product and its capabilities. It is usually made up of a combination of advertising, sales promotion, public relations and personal selling. These terms are explained in Unit 3, Creative Product Promotion.

Packaging

Packaging in the marketing mix is concerned with protection, promotion and containment. Effective packaging needs to be distinctive and recognisable, reinforcing the brand image. This has become very important in recent years because of the enormous range of product choice now available to the consumer. In some instances it is the packaging that provides a distinguishing feature for the product, such as in Muller's Yogurt Surprise.

Blending the elements of the marketing mix

The secret of success lies in blending the elements of the marketing mix effectively, as each individual product requires a different blend.

Soft drink producers need to ensure their product tastes pleasant but the most important marketing mix elements are probably place and promotion. People who are thirsty want to find a drink in plenty of convenient locations such as local shops, bus stations and colleges. They are unlikely to search extensively to find their preferred drink, but will choose an alternative. Promotion is used to make a drink stand out from the crowd. The resurgence of Dr Pepper recently was mainly due to widespread distribution and high-profile advertising.

Practice point

1 In small groups, consider the marketing mix used by either your local hair salon or a national salon such as Vidal Sassoon or Toni & Guy.

2 Compare your answer with those for the organisations tackled by other groups in your class. As a class, try to identify the key marketing mix elements for each organisation.

Social, ethical and environmental constraints on marketing

Legal constraints and consumer law

Common law and **statutory law** protect the consumer and ensure marketing is carried out in a responsible manner.

The makers and suppliers of products owe a 'duty of care' to consumers. If a customer feels that a product is in some way harmful, he or she can bring a claim against the producer. A variety of Acts of Parliament have strengthened consumer protection; these are summarised later in this section (pages 297–298).

Data protection

The Data Protection Act came into force in 1984 to protect consumers. Organisations that hold consumer information have to register with the Data Protection Registrar, and agree to guidelines about accuracy and security. The principles of the

BTEC National Study Guide: Business. See page 185 for order details of individual texts

116

Act are discussed in the next section (page 297). The Act gives people the right to see their personal file, for example as held by a bank on their creditworthiness.

Voluntary constraints

Voluntary codes of practice are statements by a committee or organisation about methods of working which are recommended as good practice within an industry. Organisations that volunteer to abide by the codes display symbols showing customers that they participate in such schemes. The codes normally have no legal backing but use other ways of encouraging compliance. An example of an organisation that publishes and administers a code of practice is the Advertising Standards Authority (ASA).

The ASA is responsible for all advertisements and promotions in the following areas:

- press – national, regional and local magazines and newspapers

- outdoor advertising – posters, transport and aerial announcements

- direct marketing – including direct mail letters, leaflets, brochures, catalogues, circulars and inserts

- screen promotions – including cinema commercials and advertisements in electronic media such as computer games, video, CD-Roms and the Internet

- sales promotions – such as on-pack promotions, front-page promotions, reader offers, competitions and prize draws.

The rules governing this type of activity are contained in the British Code of Advertising and Sales Promotion. The ASA protects the consumer by helping advertisers, agencies and the media to produce advertisements that will not mislead or offend. The basic principles are that advertisements should be:

- legal, decent, honest and truthful

- prepared with a sense of responsibility to the consumer and society

- in line with the principles of fair competition generally accepted in business.

The ASA can ask for an advertisement to be withdrawn immediately should the advertiser refuse to adjust it. The ASA has no legal powers but is able to use a number of methods to enforce its decision, including generating negative publicity for the advertiser. This can seriously tarnish an organisation's corporate image.

Pressure groups and consumerism

Pressure groups are organisations formed by people with a common interest, who join together in order to further that interest. Pressure groups watch organisations and influence how they act. They can be extremely effective in changing organisational behaviour. Examples are shown in the table below.

Pressure group	Area of concern	Example of concerns
British Union for the Abolition of Vivisection	Animal rights	Product testing on animals
Friends of the Earth	Environmental issues	Packaging of products
Action on Smoking and Health	Health concerns	Smoking and its impact on health
Citizens Advice Bureaux	Personal ethics	Levels of personal debt
Christian Aid	Business ethics	Promoting responsible corporate behaviour such as 'trade not aid' with developing countries.

BTEC National Study Guide: Business. See page 185 for order details of individual texts

117

Consumerism can be defined as a 'social movement seeking to augment the rights of buyers in relation to sellers'. Advocates of consumerism argue that consumers have four main rights, as shown below.

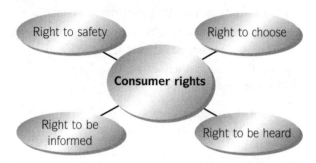

Before the 1960s, consumers had few legal rights and had to rely on their own vigilance and common sense. 'Let the buyer beware' summed up the position; manufacturers and suppliers of goods and services had considerably more power than consumers.

While some businesses may view consumerism as a threat, more enlightened organisations recognise it as an opportunity to identify and respond to changing consumer needs and wants.

Thinking point

1 As a class, think of some pressure groups and decide on the cause they are supporting.

2 In small groups, consider their impact – are they very effective, effective, or ineffective? Justify your ranking.

3 Compile a ranked list of activities which appear to bring results for pressure groups.

Legal and voluntary standards

Advertising standards

Many national organisations base their codes of practice on the International Code of Advertising Practice. The purpose of the code is to ensure that advertising is legal, honest, truthful, socially responsible and does not prevent competition. It also suggests positions on comparative advertising, advertising to children and the avoidance of various types of discrimination. In some countries, such as Sweden, legislation goes well beyond the provisions of the international code.

Ofcom

The Independent Television Commission (ITC) was replaced by Ofcom in January 2004. Ofcom regulates television, telecommunications and radio. It licenses and regulates commercial television and radio, and it undertakes to protect viewers' and listeners' interests. Ofcom monitors broadcasters' performance against the requirements of published codes and guidelines on programme content, advertising, sponsorship and technical performance. It has the power to issue a range of penalties for failure to comply.

The main aim is to ensure that television advertising is not misleading, does not encourage or support harmful behaviour and does not cause widespread offence. Ofcom restricts the frequency and duration of commercial breaks and ensures that advertisements are clearly separated from programmes. In terms of advertisement content, broadcasters are required to check advertising proposals before accepting them for transmission.

Direct Marketing Association (DMA)

The DMA protects consumers from inappropriate, unethical behaviour by unscrupulous or ignorant businesses. It promotes best practice through codes of conduct. In addition to the general code of practice the association has developed others including a code of practice for e-commerce, for electronic communications to children on-line, for SMS marketing and for e-mail marketing.

The majority of the UK population has bought a product or service via direct marketing methods. However, despite its proven use and success, a proportion of consumers still do not welcome direct mail, telephone or fax offers. To assist them, the DMA administers a group of preference services that allow consumers to register their details, free of charge, to stop unsolicited sales and marketing communications by telephone, fax, post and e-mail.

Acceptable language or images and public opinion

When consumers feel that unacceptable language is being used in promotional material they can complain to organisations such as the ASA, Ofcom or the DMA. These organisations use marketing research to gauge what is acceptable and what is unacceptable. Public opinion changes on such matters, so research enables these organisations to remain in touch with current opinion.

Many organisations today believe it is necessary to show the public they operate in an **ethical** manner, in other words act in a responsible way. An organisation that pays low wages to boost shareholder profit may not impress its potential consumers. Consumer opinion can be a significant constraint on organisational and especially marketing behaviour.

Organisations face many potential dangers with regard to ethics and public opinion. By becoming good corporate citizens and being socially responsible, they can generate considerable goodwill.

The idea of organisations working in and for the community is not new. Companies like Boots and Marks & Spencer have long advocated and contributed to community programmes, with involvement in areas as diverse as health care projects, education and training, the arts and sport.

> **Thinking point**
>
> 1 What do you consider to be the characteristics of a socially responsible organisation?
>
> 2 Name a few organisations that you think fulfil your criteria.

Legislation

A considerable number of laws have been passed which directly impact on how marketers can behave.

- **The Sale of Goods Act 1979** states that goods sold should meet three main conditions. First, they should be of satisfactory quality – they must not have any flaws or problems associated with them. For example, a lawn mower must not be scratched or dented. Second, they must be fit for the purpose for which they were purchased. In other words, the lawn mower must cut grass effectively. Third, they should be as described. If the mower is said to cut effectively on slopes of 30%, that should be the case.

- **The Trade Descriptions Act 1968** prohibits false or misleading statements about products. A jacket that is described as waterproof must not let in water when it rains.

- **The Consumer Credit Act 1974** aims to protect consumers when they purchase goods on credit. Consumers must be given a copy of any credit arrangement they enter into. The Act also ensures that only licensed credit brokers can provide credit. Organisations must not send sales staff to people's homes to pressurise them into purchasing on credit, or charge very high interest rates.

- **The Data Protection Act 1998** has become more significant to consumers as marketers have increasingly been using direct mail techniques to communicate with them. The information stored by marketers on electronic databases must be:

  – obtained fairly

  – used only for lawful purposes

  – used only for reasons stated during collection

  – adequate, relevant and not excessive in relation to the intended use

  – accurate and up to date

  – not kept for longer than necessary

  – protected from unauthorised use

BTEC National Study Guide: Business. See page 185 for order details of individual texts

119

– available for inspection and correction by the individual.

A new Act gives consumers greater control on how the data can be used. It is now illegal to telephone or fax a business or person who has registered with the Telephone Preference Service (TPS). Also, consumers supplying personal details through electronic commerce must give permission before their details are passed to other interested parties.

Outcome activity 11.1

The Co-operative movement emphasises 'honesty, openness, social responsibility and caring for others'. The values the organisation sees as important are included in its Responsible Retail Strategy (RRS) campaign. In this campaign it actively promotes fair trade, seeking out suppliers that follow ethical business practices in relation to both human welfare and the environment. It also constantly audits its own operations in order to ensure 'green' approaches.

The honest labelling campaign is a recent venture. First, the Co-operative has addressed its own shortcomings by introducing packaging and labels that are more honest. Photographs on the products have been changed to ensure they are more representative of the products inside. The labelling of products now involves prominent, easy-to-read content, as opposed to tiny panels on the back.

The Co-operative also invites customers to have a say. At the entrance to each store or in a prominent position there are leaflets detailing the honesty campaign. Each leaflet gives space for customers' feedback on packaging and labelling, and invites ideas for improvements.

The campaign calls for changes in the business practice of others in the food industry.

This campaign has enhanced the status of the Co-operative in the minds of many consumers.

Pass

Identify and describe the marketing principles being applied by the Co-operative movement to its products in the light of ethical and legal constraints.

Marketing research

Key themes of marketing research

Helping organisations achieve aims

Marketing research aims to help an organisation make effective marketing decisions by providing information that can inform the decision-making process. It is concerned with the disciplined collection and evaluation of data in order to help producers better understand their consumers.

It can help an organisation to achieve its overall objectives because it can:

- identify market opportunities – for example the move towards screw-top bottles in the soft drinks market for 'little and often' drinkers

- be used to assess and improve marketing activity – for example improve the effectiveness of advertising

- help improve the quality of the marketing being undertaken by revealing important consumer information. Understanding why consumers buy a product can have a significant impact on product design or advertising.

BTEC National Study Guide: Business. See page 185 for order details of individual texts

120

Marketing research theme	Provides information on
Customer or market	Market and market segment sizes Market trends that can be used for forecasting future consumer needs Brand shares including competitors Customer preferences (e.g. colours), lifestyle (e.g. eating out more), aspirations (e.g. wish to have a career)
Competitors	Overall aims and objectives Comparison of products, prices, distribution methods and promotional methods Profit and overall financial situation Likely reaction to competitor plans – how will they respond if another firm increases advertising?
Marketing environment	Political influences (e.g. policies of different political parties) Economic influences (e.g. expected performance of economy) Social influences (e.g. increasing number of over 65s in UK population) Technological influences (e.g. impact of the Internet)

Practice point

1 Think of two organisations that are in close competition, such as Sky and the BBC and, using the checklist in the table above, complete a competitor analysis.

2 How would the behaviour of both change if the fortunes of another competitor were to change – for example if ITV were no longer a force in television?

Qualitative and quantitative research

Research can be grouped into primary and secondary, qualitative and quantitative.

Primary research is usually carried out to find out directly from the market how a new product may be seen.

Secondary research makes use of research already carried out by someone else for some other purpose.

Quantitative research produces numbers and figures – such as the number and percentage of consumers who are aware of a particular product or service.

Quantitative research can be used, for example, to:

- measure sales week by week, including those of competitors
- track prices across a variety of retailers and brands
- estimate market shares of competing brands
- estimate market and segment sizes.

Qualitative research, on the other hand, provides information on why people buy – what motivates them to buy – or their impression of products, services or advertisements.

Qualitative research can be used, for example, to:

- investigate customer attitudes towards a product or organisation

BTEC National Study Guide: Business. See page 185 for order details of individual texts

121

- find out consumer reactions to changes in price

- find out information about consumer lifestyles, habits and buying patterns.

Sources of secondary internal and external research

Large amounts of secondary data are available to the marketing researcher. While a very small proportion of existing data may be useful in any one project, marketing researchers should know where to obtain relevant information. There are two sources of secondary data: internal and external.

Internal secondary data is produced by an organisation in its day-to-day activities. Sales figures, advertising expenditure, stock level records, sales team reports and prices are just some of the examples of the internal data that is produced. In many cases it may be collected in an unorganised way, with managers having little idea about its availability.

External secondary data is information that comes from a wide variety of sources outside an organisation. The numerous sources are discussed in some detail later in this section.

Uses and limitations of secondary research

Secondary data sources are widely used, as they tend to be of low cost and are usually easily obtainable. However, there are some potential problems with this type of information.

- The information is often not detailed enough to help organisations make decisions about their own operations. Reports tend to be about an industry as a whole rather than a particular sector or segment.

- The information may have been collected to promote the status of an industry and the figures may be exaggerated.

- Figures may sometimes be inaccurate because of their source, such as a competitor which, for example, tries to portray itself as the market leader.

- The age of the information may reduce its usefulness, because markets change rapidly.

- The way the information was collected may mean the picture gained is not the whole picture. An Internet survey may not be accessible to all consumer types.

- The organisation publishing the report should be noted, to ensure it is renowned for producing reliable reports.

Nevertheless, secondary research is very useful in a number of ways. It can help to determine the correct **sampling** approach for a primary research project. More commonly it is useful in providing a comprehensive insight into a market in terms of size, segments and trends.

Practice point

Pick one of the following sources of valuable secondary data – ONS Social Trends, ONS Regional Trends, Annual Abstract of Statistics, a company annual report. They should all be available in your library or learning resource centre. Produce a summary of the information contained in the publication you have chosen.

Primary research

Suitability of different methods for different purposes

An organisation has to explore the needs of its customers through marketing research. Organisations need to make sure the research they undertake is not determined by its cost but by the type of information required.

The cost of personal interviews is relatively high because they are time consuming and labour intensive. Interviewers may have to select their target group from passers-by in the street or by knocking on doors. There may be a tendency to 'cheat' if it proves difficult to find enough people in the target group. However, the quality of the information collected can be very high if the interviewer is trained not to lead the interviewees or guide responses. The data is available to be analysed once the interview has been completed.

BTEC National Study Guide: Business. See page 185 for order details of individual texts

122

As an interviewer, how would you select your target group from passers-by in the street?

Focus groups increase the number of people whose views can be researched over a given time scale, compared to interviewing. Groups of between six and ten people are asked to discuss a product or service and the interviewer leads the discussion to bring out thoughts and feelings. The benefit of using a larger sample is that one person's ideas often prompt the thoughts of others.

Personal interviews can be developed in line with respondent replies, whereas a postal interview asks the same questions regardless of responses. The flexibility of personal interviews generally ensures the data collected is very useful. For similar reasons a telephone interview can generate quality data. A postal survey can ask only straightforward questions and cannot investigate an issue in depth.

Personal interviews and telephone interviews always have the potential to be influenced by the interviewer, which is not the case with postal interviews. Telephone interviews, with their ability to contact a lot of people in a short space of time, can ensure the appropriate number of people are interviewed. With a postal survey, response rates are generally very low.

Telephone interviews can collect information quickly. Personal interviews can take time to organise, especially when home interviews are considered appropriate, while postal surveys can take a long time to be returned. They also suffer from the problem that only certain types of people return questionnaires (such as retired householders). Personal interviews are expensive to conduct, whereas a postal survey is a relatively low-cost approach to research.

Research selection should be determined by the type of information required and its importance in any decision being made, and not on the basis of cost. A postal survey might be appropriate to find out how well staff at a leisure centre are treating customers, but not to investigate which new facilities to build.

Marketers organising research must satisfy themselves that the information is reliable, in that if the same question was asked of the same person on a different occasion it would receive the same answer. Marketers must also ensure the data is valid. Respondents can sometimes provide a seemingly sensible answer without understanding the question, and the answer under such circumstances would be considered invalid.

301

BTEC National Study Guide: Business. See page 185 for order details of individual texts

123

Practice point

Knowing the strengths and weaknesses of research methods is important for marketing managers. They can then pick the right one for the issues being investigated. Complete the chart by marking each box as poor, good or excellent for the feature identified.

Research feature	Postal survey	Telephone survey	Personal interview
Obtaining reliable data			
Data free from bias			
Interviewing right people			
Cost			
People agreeing to help			
Speed of collection			
Investigating an issue in depth			

Types of sampling and possible errors

Research involving everyone in the population is called a census. This is seldom possible because of the expense. Consequently, **samples** are used; in marketing terms this means using a small number of individuals to gain an insight into the views of the whole group. There are several ways of selecting a sample.

- **Random sampling** involves picking a random selection of people from the whole population to be researched. For example, every one thousandth person in the telephone book. This means that everybody should have an equal chance of being selected. Using established statistical methods it can be calculated how many need to be interviewed so that the findings reflect the views of the entire population.

- **Stratified sampling** is used to research large consumer markets. It entails dividing the population into groups and drawing samples from each group. For example, the population might be divided into six groups: A, B, C1, C2, D and E, reflecting the social background of the people involved. Random samples are then drawn from each group.

- **Quota sampling** ensures that the proportions in a sample reflect the whole market. Quotas are identified on the basis of known features of the market under investigation. Dividing a quota into age groups is a popular way to ensure that the characteristics of the sample reflect the features of the whole group. This prevents particular groups, such as old or young people, from dominating a sample.

Because quotas can be selected from a relatively small geographical area they are cost-effective in gathering data. Any refusals or non-returns can be replaced by anyone else who fits the quota characteristics.

The problems with quotas are related to interviewer bias, caused by the selection of people in a quota. For example, a quota of 20- to 30-year-old women will have a disproportionate number of 24- to 26-year-olds because it is hard for an interviewer to judge the age of the 20- and 30-year-olds. There is a tendency to approach friendly, happy looking, attractive people, who may have different views and opinions from others. Despite the limitations of quota sampling, it is commonly used for marketing research purposes.

Thinking point

1 You have decided to investigate the market for computer games. Using the quota sampling methods, which age groups would you interview, and how many from each group? Justify your choice of age groupings and the number from each to be interviewed.

2 You wish to discover more about the holiday market. How might you determine the quota groups? Justify how many you would interview from each group.

- **Judgement sampling** is where researchers select the sample based on who they think will most likely reflect the views of the group to be interviewed. It is used in industrial research where a few large companies dominate a market. All the major companies might be included, plus a sample of the rest. The purpose is to weight the results with the views of the important members of the sample. For example, the pharmaceutical giants GlaxoSmithKline and Pfizer, plus a sample of all the smaller companies, would be appropriate in that industrial sector.

- **Convenience sampling** means there is no sample design. It is similar to an interviewer questioning people as met on the street or in the shopping precinct. Choice is left entirely to the interviewer. The sample is chosen on the basis of who can be contacted easily.

Errors can occur in the sampling process that affect the overall results of the research project:

- a low response rate may mean that the final sample is unrepresentative of the whole population

- respondents might give the answer that they feel will please the researcher

- inappropriate answers might be given because the respondent is tired, does not fully understand the question or simply cannot remember accurately

- respondents usually feel they should give a socially acceptable answer to sensitive or potentially embarrassing questions

- in some ways the interviewer might influence the answer, record the answer incorrectly or falsify the response.

Planning the marketing research

Professionally organised research projects will follow a particular planning cycle. To ensure effective research is undertaken, an organisation should do the following.

- Define the objectives and identify the information needs. It is important that the researcher defines the requirements of the research effectively. Defining the problem too narrowly will mean vital data is missed; defining it too broadly will mean time and resources will be wasted gathering unwanted information.

- Design an appropriate research plan. This is a complex area and involves several major considerations, including whether to undertake primary and/or secondary research, the selection of an appropriate research technique (such as a survey), the type of sampling plan required (such as random) and how exactly people should be contacted.

- Consider how to collect the data. The researcher must be quite sure what information needs collecting and what the organisation already possesses.

- Analyse and interpret the data effectively. Information analysis usually involves taking the information from a variety of sources and drawing relevant conclusions before arriving at appropriate recommendations.

- Plan for the effective presentation of the findings. Information has no value unless it assists managers to make better decisions. This may involve a presentation to senior managers or the introduction of a computer-generated report produced by the IT team.

303

BTEC National Study Guide: Business. See page 185 for order details of individual texts

125

Use of e-commerce transaction information

The Internet can gather detailed information through asking surfers to register to browse a site or through collecting information during a purchase. The information can be used to create sophisticated databases for a number of purposes:

- identifying an organisation's best customers

- sending direct mail letters and e-mail newsletters about products that might interest a customer

- recognising customers who have just bought and contacting them to reinforce the purchase

- cross-selling related and complementary products

- providing a personalised customer service.

Use of computers for marketing research analysis

Surveys conducted over the telephone are increasingly popular as they are convenient for both interviewer and respondent. A wide geographical area can be covered while sensitive issues can be investigated. Many companies now use computers to assist telephone surveys, allowing the interviewer to input responses directly into a computer. This technique is known as computer-assisted telephone interviewing, or CATI. This allows the analysis of quantitative data to be completed very rapidly.

Multimedia computer-assisted personal interviewing (multimedia CATI) is a relatively new method of collecting data. It allows research to be done in the home which previously needed a hotel room or other large venue. The interviewer has a multimedia capability, which records respondent answers but can also display pictures, video sequences, TV and cinema commercials. It can even show a product in a variety of packaging designs. Answers can be recorded through a microphone for later analysis; this has the advantage of recording how the question was answered and not simply the words.

Consumers have expressed concern about the privacy and data protection of information gathered in this way. Privacy concerns are about who might use the data, while data protection concerns are about secure storage and the accuracy of the information held.

A potentially cheap method of gathering information is by placing a questionnaire on the Internet. Respondents answer questions directly on an Internet page and the information is logged by computer at the company site. When an organisation requests opinions about a product or an advertising campaign, an e-mail message is sent to people who are potential consumers. Participation is entirely voluntary. The participant enters an e-mail ID and may receive discount vouchers for agreeing to co-operate. The process suffers from the weakness of bias, as only a certain proportion of the population have access to the Internet and only a small number of those will register as willing to participate.

Thinking point

You have an under-used but extensive database of customers who have bought cars from you in the past five years. Write a short report to your manager on how this resource could be used to increase the sales revenue of the organisation.

Strategic, technical and databank marketing research

Primary research can be undertaken for three main reasons – strategic, technical and data collection.

- **Strategic research** is undertaken to assist an organisation in planning its future direction – for example, identifying a new international market to enter.

- **Technical research** is designed to help an organisation undertake its current marketing more effectively – for example, improving the effectiveness of advertising activities.

● **Databank research** involves collecting new or updated information about the markets, segments and consumers of interest to the organisation.

Secondary research

Secondary research can be obtained from a variety of internal and external sources.

News reports

News reports are a source of very useful data.

● Newspapers produce country and industry reports on a regular basis as well as having regular articles about products, markets and consumer trends.

● Magazines such as *The Economist* contain plenty of useful marketing information.

● TV and radio current affairs and news programmes are useful, especially Radio 4.

● The Consumers' Association, publishers of *Which?*, can be a valuable source of information.

Trade journals

These are magazines which are aimed at certain industry sectors, such as *Toy Retailer*, *Building Constructor* and *Accountancy Age*. They can contain useful industry information in terms of buying trends and new technical developments.

Market analysis from specialist agencies

Market research companies produce reports on markets and products and then offer them to organisations with an interest in that particular sector – producers, retailers and suppliers. The reports are expensive to buy. The market-leading companies are Mintel, Dun & Bradstreet and Datastream. They can be accessed on-line.

Mintel (*www.mintel.com*) produces a wide variety of reports covering market size, market segments, main brands, levels of advertising expenditure, factors determining market growth and future forecasts.

Dun & Bradstreet (*dbuk.dnb.com*) publishes, for example, comprehensive financial reports on companies and on the trading prospects in a particular industry.

Thomson Financial (*www.thomson.com*) produces Datastream, a valuable source of current financial data including stock market share prices, historical economic data, economic forecasts, and interest rate and exchange rate information.

Practice point

Choose an organisation listed on the London Stock Exchange – use the share price page from a leading business newspaper. Investigate, using the Dun & Bradstreet and Thomson Financial websites, the types of data which could be obtained about the organisation. How might the information be useful to a marketing team?

Government statistics

These are principally supplied by the Office of National Statistics (ONS), Eurostat (the statistical office of the European Union) and the OECD (Organisation for Economic Co-operation and Development).

● ONS Family Expenditure Survey details how families spend their money.

● ONS Social Trends shows trends in labour markets, incomes and spending.

Thinking point

Read the England & Wales Cricket Board case study in the 8th edition of The Times 100 (*www.tt100.biz*), called 'Using market research to improve consumer focus'.

1 Analyse the American Marketing Association's definition of marketing research.

2 Describe the quantitative and qualitative research undertaken by the ECB, and then explain the difference between the two terms.

3 Explain why the ECB introduced the Twenty20 Cup.

BTEC National Study Guide: Business. See page 185 for order details of individual texts

127

Outcome activity 11.2

A UK private hospital wishes to update its logo while retaining its present image as a professional and caring organisation. Managers want to gauge the public perception of five proposed designs. They could undertake personal interviews with existing patients, so reactions to each design could be observed and recorded accurately. For example, if the majority of patients are between 45 and 70, are both male and female and are from high-income groups, this section of the public should be interviewed. The main competitor is the Nuffield private hospital group.

A soft drinks company is considering a number of different ideas for a new range of 'no added sugar' fruit cordials aimed at the under-12s. Managers want to canvass opinions about competitor ranges that are already available to help develop the product. Focus groups of parents and children under 12 are proposed, with tasting sessions included in the process.

Pass

Describe the marketing research techniques that could be used by the private hospital to help understand its customers, competitors and market environment. Explain how the research could be designed to support its marketing activity.

Merit

Evaluate the relative effectiveness of the research proposed by the soft drinks company in terms of understanding its customers, competitors and the market environment, including legal and ethical constraints. Consider other marketing research methods and whether they might prove more effective.

Marketing information

Using market research information to identify customers

Customer types, behaviour, preferences, lifestyles and aspirations

A segment is a group of customers who share common characteristics which make them different from other groups. Different segments may have different needs; they may require different versions of the product, they may pay different prices, they may buy in different places and they may be reached by different media. Research can play a vital role in investigating market segments and consequently identifying customer types. Some methods of classification are shown in the table below.

There are now some sophisticated segmentation techniques, called 'geodemographic', that combine research from many sources to identify types of neighbourhood. The assumption is that people who live in a particular neighbourhood – generally around 150 households – will react to marketing activity in the same way. Organisations find such analysis useful for a variety of purposes, as shown in the table on the next page.

ACORN (*www.caci.co.uk*) is A Classification Of Residential Neighbourhoods using predominantly census data. It has identified 54 neighbourhood types.

Segmentation classification	Segments within the market
Type of customer	Household, business, charity
Buying behaviour	Frequent user, light user, occasional user
Preferences	Pay-as-you-go, pay monthly
Lifestyles	Single, family with children, retired
Aspirations	Careerists, wanting a quiet life

BTEC National Study Guide: Business. See page 185 for order details of individual texts

Application of geodemographic data	Rank (most frequent first)
Targeting direct mail letters	1
Market segmentation identification	2
Customer database building	3
Media analysis	4
New store location analysis	5
Sales force organisation	6

MOSAIC (*www.experian.com* and *www.business-strategies.co.uk*) combines, among other sources, census information, credit history, share ownership and postcode data to identify household types.

Decision-making units

A decision-making unit (DMU) comprises all the individuals and groups who participate in the purchasing decision process, for example in a business. A typical DMU could include the following groups.

- Users, who will be interested in the benefits the product offers, such as increased production rates or reduced waste.

- Buyers or purchasing officers, who will be concerned about easy purchasing arrangements and delivery dates.

- Influencers, who are individuals whose opinion may be sought about a product or organisation. They will probably be influenced themselves by brand and company reputation.

- Deciders, such as managing directors, who will probably be most concerned with the overall cost of the product and whether the organisation can afford it.

- Gatekeepers, who may deny potential users information for a variety of reasons, including safety concerns or financial considerations. They can prevent sellers reaching the key decision makers.

- Specifiers, who are people who decide on the detailed specification of the product to be purchased. They may well want technical information about such things as component performance and material characteristics.

Marketing research can help identify and then understand these groups.

Thinking point

You are visiting a college to discuss an order for some new photocopying machines. You have two meetings scheduled in the morning, first with a user group and then with the purchasing team. Produce an agenda for each meeting bearing mind the topics each meeting might like to discuss.

Analytical techniques

Situation analysis

How do organisations decide on the way forward? Marketers have a variety of techniques available for considering their options. The techniques focus on identifying the changes an organisation needs to make to achieve its ambitions. All the techniques taken together are generally called a 'situational analysis' or 'marketing audit'. Some of the most frequently used are discussed on the next page.

307

BTEC National Study Guide: Business. See page 185 for order details of individual texts

129

SWOT analysis

A common approach is to use SWOT analysis (strengths, weaknesses, opportunities and threats) to draw together all the evidence from the various techniques used. It is a way of producing a summary which then provides the basis for developing marketing objectives or aims, and ultimately strategies or plans.

Strengths, weaknesses, opportunities and threats analysis provides a framework within which marketers can identify significant developments in markets.

- *Strengths* refer to the internal features of an organisation which provide a competitive advantage. An example could be a well-regarded brand name which is easily recalled by consumers.

- *Weaknesses* are aspects of the organisation which may not stand comparison with competition or are not performing effectively.

  An example might be the inability to have key selling items constantly in stock.

- *Opportunities* focus on events and developments external to an organisation. The growing use and acceptance of the Internet to sell products will present some companies with the chance to increase profits by selling directly to consumers. Pensions are now sold over the Internet, whereas only a few years ago such a purchase would only be contemplated after a personal one-to-one interview with a financial advisor.

- *Threats* are developments external to the organisation which could potentially damage overall performance. These threats can originate from new laws, changes in government policy, or social developments such as the trend towards healthier diets.

A SWOT analysis is a summary of all the information collected during the situational analysis.

Practice point

Undertake a SWOT analysis for your school or college. In small groups, each consider one aspect of the analysis, such as strengths. Discuss your findings with other groups before compiling an overall SWOT analysis.

PESTLE analysis

Marketers use PESTLE analysis (political, economic, social, technological, legal, environmental) to investigate the external environment an organisation is operating in.

- *Political* factors affect the activity of business. Political developments are generally out of the control of an organisation, but it needs to forecast and anticipate change and then react accordingly. The development of the European Union has provided both opportunities and threats to British organisations. Tesco is able to consider expanding into Europe, while German retailer Aldi has already arrived in the UK.

- *Economic* influences look at how the performance of the economy impacts on organisations. All economies go through cycles of prosperity (high levels of demand, employment and income), recession (falling demand, employment and income) and recovery (gradual improvement in production levels, lowering unemployment and increasing incomes). The business cycle is especially important because of its direct effect on consumer and business spending. During times of prosperity, both consumers and business customers buy more goods and services.

- The *social* environment describes the characteristics of society, the people who live in that society and their values and beliefs. The first area of study tends to focus on the population – demographics – revealing information about size, gender, ethnic groups, income levels, educational attainment, occupations and family structure. The

BTEC National Study Guide: Business. See page 185 for order details of individual texts

130

The European Union has provided opportunities for expansion, as for the German retailer Aldi

information is very useful to marketers in predicting the size of markets for many products, from mortgages to brooms.

- Many *technological* developments affect organisations. Growing computer ownership and the Internet allow people to buy virtually anything without leaving their homes. Mobile phones are being used to convey advertisements. Downloading music from the Internet is having a dramatic affect on CD sales.

- The *legal* climate constantly changes as the government introduces new laws through Parliament. For example, the law governing gambling will shortly change. Casinos will be allowed to promote themselves and new members will be able to gamble immediately rather than having to wait 24 hours as at present.

- *Environmental* factors can also affect an organisation. Because aircraft emit a lot of

gases harmful to the environment, airlines are being asked to reduce this pollution before some airports will be allowed to expand in the UK.

Practice point

In the UK a number of social changes are under way. In small groups, think of three, and then consider the impact they have on an organisation like a college.

Competitor and competition analysis

One of the most interesting approaches to examining competition was presented by Michael Porter in *Competitive Strategy: Techniques for Analysing Industries and Competitors*, Free Press, 1980. Porter argued that the most important factors determining the performance of an organisation were the features of the industry in which it was trading. He identified five forces which he felt determined the level of competition,

309

BTEC National Study Guide: Business. See page 185 for order details of individual texts

131

and consequently profitability. He assumed that profits are high when competition is low. The five forces are:

- **Rivalry among existing competitors:** This is the most obvious form of competition, the head-to-head rivalry between firms offering similar products and selling them in the same markets. Rivalry can be intense and cut-throat, or it may be governed by unwritten agreements that help the industry to avoid the damage that excessive price cutting, advertising and promotional expenses can inflict on profits.

- **Threat of entry:** If it is easy to start a business in an industry, as soon as profits look attractive, new firms will arrive. Industries are relatively easy to enter if there are no large start-up costs, patents or copyrights. For example, ICI recently moved to high value-added consumer chemicals, which are heavily dependent on extensive research and development. It is hard for rival companies to copy these products in the short term because of the time and costs involved in researching and producing good ideas. Previously, ICI had focused on industrial chemicals such as fertilisers and gunpowder. As soon as ICI developed a new product, a rival would quickly follow with a similar item and profits would disappear.

- **Threat of substitutes:** A substitute is something that meets the same needs as another product. For example, a glass bottle is a substitute for a plastic one. A substitute may be quite different in some respects, but provide the same benefits to consumers. If the substitute becomes more attractive in terms of price, performance or both, then buyers will be tempted to move their custom. For example, a wide range of synthetic fibres have replaced silk, cotton and wool in furnishing and clothing.

- **Power of buyers:** Powerful buyers can bargain away potential profits. They can cause firms to undercut each other to gain the buyer's business and they can use their power to extract other benefits – such as quality improvements or credit terms. Buyers tend to be powerful when there are relatively few of them buying a large proportion of the total output. A good example is how a few large supermarkets are able to obtain low prices from the many farmers who are growing produce.

- **Power of suppliers:** In a similar way, suppliers of vital resources to an industry can extract high prices from their customer. Such suppliers would include organisations supplying raw materials, power, skilled labour and components.

This analysis helps marketers understand the markets they are operating in, but it also helps them understand the strategy an organisation, such as a competitor, might be following. It then becomes much easier to anticipate their actions and behaviour.

Thinking point

1 You are in the supermarket retailing sector. You feel it is important to form a view about the amount of competition in the sector. Draw up a list of questions which might help you decide on the level of competition in the sector.

2 You would also like to gauge whether a new competitor is likely to enter the sector. Compile a list of factors that might encourage a new entrant and a list of issues that might discourage a new entrant.

Local, national and global marketplace

In some instances it might prove useful to consider developments in local, national and global marketplaces. International developments can have an impact on national and local markets; this has certainly been the case with the further and higher educational markets in Britain, as shown in the table on the next page.

BTEC National Study Guide: Business. See page 185 for order details of individual texts

132

Market	Developments	Consequences
Global	China's one-child-per-family policy and entry into the World Trade Organisation (WTO)	Young Chinese travel abroad to study business, information technology and English, the commercial language of the world. Supported financially by parents willing to invest heavily in their only child
National	British government grants more student visa applications and allows students to work a limited number of hours without a work permit	Young Chinese choose to study in Britain because of the excellent reputation of our universities
Local	British universities are willing to admit international students	Record numbers of international students arrive in areas near to top-class British universities

Product life cycle and product portfolio analysis

Product portfolio analysis is a tool for assessing the potential of a firm's products or business. It helps management decide which of its current products should receive more or less investment to ensure the business achieves its objectives. The two techniques commonly used by organisations are the BCG (Boston Consulting Group) matrix and the Product Life Cycle (PLC) concept.

The BCG matrix identifies the product groups of an organisation and places them on a matrix that considers market growth and relative market share. The assumption is that a larger market share will enable an organisation to benefit from lower unit costs and therefore higher profit margins. There are four areas into which product groups can be allocated.

● 'Stars' have a high market share in a high growth market. They have the ability to generate significant sales in the short and long term, but require promotional investment to maintain their market position.

● 'Question marks' have a low market share in a market that is growing rapidly. The low market share normally indicates that competition is strong. If the market looks to have long-term potential, the organisation needs to decide whether to invest heavily in building market share. If the growth in the

The Boston Consulting Group matrix

market is unlikely to continue or the investment requirement is substantial, the organisation should consider abandoning the product.

● 'Cash cows' have a high market share in a market showing little growth. These products are generally well established with plenty of loyal customers. The product development costs are typically low and the marketing campaign is well established. Cash cows will normally make a substantial contribution to overall profitability. They finance the investment needed to maintain a 'star's' high market share and to develop 'question marks'.

311

BTEC National Study Guide: Business. See page 185 for order details of individual texts

133

● *'Dogs'* are products experiencing little growth with a low market share. Organisations need to consider whether to abandon the area and in the short term 'harvest' the product by raising prices, or delete the item from the product range altogether.

Practice point

Using the product range of a well-known car producer (such as Ford), classify its products (such as the Ford Focus) as stars, question marks, cash cows or dogs. Position them on a BCG matrix. Compare your analysis with groups considering other producers.

The idea that all products have a pattern to their lives lies behind the product life cycle concept. It suggests that a new product enters a life cycle once it is launched on the market.

In the *introductory stage* a product takes time to find acceptance by purchasers and there is slow growth in sales. Only a few organisations are likely to be operating in the market, each experiencing high costs because output is low. They may charge high prices to cover development and the initial promotional costs, but even then profitability may be difficult to achieve. Promotion concentrates on telling consumers what the product does.

If the product achieves market acceptance, sales grow rapidly. In this *growth stage* profits begin to materialise as higher production levels reduce unit costs. However, the growing market attracts competition and soon producers have to invest in building a brand image, product improvements and sales promotions to obtain a dominant market position.

The *maturity stage* follows when a product experiences stable sales. This is generally the longest period of a successful product's life. But eventually sales fall and the market finds itself with too many producers who begin to suffer poor sales and falling profits. Some leave the market, while others use strategies to extend the life of the product. Product life extension techniques are discussed later in the unit.

Most products reach the *saturation stage* when sales begin to fall. During this period, some brands will leave the market.

Products reach a stage of *decline* when sales fall significantly. Organisations progressively abandon the market, sometimes leaving a few producers who are able to trade profitably on low sales totals.

Organisations use the product life cycle to devise new product plans. An organisation will look to introduce new products to coincide with the decline of the established ones.

Thinking point

Read the United Biscuits case study in the 8th edition of The Times 100 (*www.tt100.biz*) called 'An enterprising approach to a marketing re-launch'.

1 Describe the product life cycle of Phileas Fogg and then draw it as a diagram.

2 What four-point plan did United Biscuits draw up for the re-launch of Phileas Fogg?

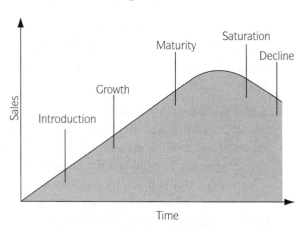

The life cycle of a product

312

BTEC National Study Guide: Business. See page 185 for order details of individual texts

134

Diversification

Organisations face two types of risk associated with **diversification**. The first is concerned with the risks that might be encountered by the business in its current market. The second is the result of a business considering entering a new market with a new product.

The situational analysis should consider the risks arising from serving the current market – things that might go wrong or prove problematical. Such risks might include the economy experiencing low growth, resulting in falling product demand. Most devastating of all, the product the organisation is marketing might lose favour with the consumer. Many video rental stores suffered with the arrival of satellite and cable television. Pubs have closed as bars and clubs have become more attractive venues for an evening out. Different markets will have different levels of risk associated with them.

Some organisations seeking to reduce the risk associated with operating in a particular market have entered new and unconnected markets. For example, P&O has a luxury cruise division and a house-building division. There are few factors that will affect both operations in a similar way. This reduces the organisation's day-to-day operational risk. In contrast, British Airways' fortunes are linked directly to developments in the airline travel market.

Outcome activity 11.3

Britons are deserting their kitchens and dining rooms in favour of eating out in restaurants, pubs and fast food outlets. For some people, cooking has become such a stressful occupation that it is compared unfavourably with doing the cleaning.

Research shows that spending in restaurants has rocketed by more than a third in the past five years, with one in three people now eating out at least once a week. Whereas in 1998 the average weekly expenditure on eating out was £10.90, that has now increased to £18.60.

Outcome activity 11.3 *(continued)*

Single people find it more economical to eat a meal in a restaurant than buy the ingredients and cook it themselves. Cooking at home is no longer any more cost-effective than eating out. Interestingly, the boom in television programmes hosted by celebrity chefs has encouraged Britons to avoid the kitchen because they feel inadequate there. The country's obsession with fine dining has raised expectations beyond the capabilities of most.

A combination of hectic lifestyle, higher disposable incomes and cheaper meals are given as the reasons for the 'going out' trend.

For some, modern technology has made preparing or sitting through a family meal at home almost impossible. Television, computer games and mobile phones have become such a distraction in the home that many people resort to the sanctuary of a fast food outlet or restaurant to offset the stress of everyday life.

There is no longer the pressure to be at home for meal times. Family meals at home have become increasingly hard to sustain with the expanding list of entertainment options at home, which distract individuals from eating together. Research shows that when families do eat together, in a third of cases this is done in front of the television. It seems that home cooking may become a rarity in the future.

BTEC National Study Guide: Business. See page 185 for order details of individual texts

135

Outcome activity 11.3 (continued)

Pass

Using a restaurant or fast food outlet you know, complete a PESTLE analysis. Undertake a competitor and competition analysis and draw a product life cycle for the business before summarising your findings in a SWOT analysis.

Merit

Having used the techniques above, compare the relative effectiveness of those techniques in supporting the marketing development of your chosen restaurant or fast food outlet.

Marketing strategies

Opportunities and threats

Ansoff's matrix

Ansoff's product/market matrix is a useful way to think about different growth strategies. The vertical axis represents opportunities for growth in markets that are currently being served or in new markets. The horizontal axis considers whether the firm would be better off putting its resources into existing products or whether it should consider developing or acquiring new products. The matrix provides four different fundamental marketing strategies: market penetration, market development, product development and diversification.

		Product	
		Present	*New*
Mission (market)	*Present*	Market penetration	Product development
	New	Market development	Diversification

Ansoff's matrix

- *Market penetration* involves selling more of an existing product into existing markets. Possible options are persuading current customers to use more or attracting new customers altogether. This is normally only possible if a market is growing.

- *Market development* entails expanding into new markets with existing products. These may be new markets geographically, new market sectors or perhaps new uses for the product.

- *Product development* requires the organisation to develop modified versions of its existing products so they will have greater appeal in existing markets. By designing products closely to the needs of existing customers the organisation will probably sell more.

- *Diversification* – putting new products into new markets – is a risky strategy because the organisation is moving into areas in which it has little or no experience. Instances of pure diversification are rare and it is used only when no other growth routes are available.

Development of product life cycle analysis

Brand building, extension strategies, product mix and portfolio management

The product life cycle is also helpful to the marketing manager because it suggests that certain types of marketing activity are appropriate at different stages of a product's life.

Brand building is important in the growth stage. The acquisition of a significant market share during this phase will generate profits in the long term. When the product enters the maturity and saturation stages, it will be the strong brands that will dominate the market. Profit will be a consequence, with weaker brands and producers leaving the market. In the decline stage, when sales are falling, it will be the strong brands that survive and produce profit.

BTEC National Study Guide: Business. See page 185 for order details of individual texts

136

It is possible for the marketing manager to take action to prolong the maturity stage or even to stimulate new growth in the market by adopting product life extension strategies.

Practice point

Scotch whisky is a mature product in its biggest markets, the UK and France. This is partly because of the high level of competition in the market – over 2,000 brands – and partly because of the image of whisky as 'something your parents drank'.

The potential to inject new life into the product has come from the trend in countries such as Portugal, Spain and Greece, where whisky is commonly drunk with water, ice or cola by the under-30 age group. If whisky producers can successfully give their product a more youthful and European image, then they might be able to extend the product life cycle.

1 In small groups, pick one of the following product categories: cars, pop stars, films or toys. Suggest ways in which organisations might be able to extend the life of the product.

2 Exchange your ideas with other groups and note the ones you think would work.

The product life cycle encourages the management of the product mix. The product mix is sometimes called the product assortment, and it consists of all the products an organisation offers to its customers. Managing the product mix involves:

- ensuring the existing products continue to satisfy consumers

- modifying and adapting existing products to take advantage of new technology, emerging opportunities or changing market conditions

- deleting old products that are close to the end of their life and no longer serve a purpose

- introducing a flow of new products to maintain or improve sales and profits levels and consequently securing the future of the organisation.

An organisation therefore needs a balanced product portfolio, capable of sustaining it satisfactorily into the future. The ideal portfolio should contain neither too many new nor too many declining products. Too many new products could put the organisation at risk, as product launches require significant resources. At the other extreme, too many declining products could threaten the future of the organisation.

Differentiated marketing and the product life cycle

Limited resources, competition and large markets make it sometimes ineffective and inappropriate for organisations to sell to every segment. For the sake of efficiency, they must select some target markets. Managers may choose one of the marketing options in the table below.

Marketing option	Strategy	Stage of product life cycle
Undifferentiated marketing	Aims to produce a single product and acquire as many customers as possible – segmentation is ignored	Appropriate for introductory and perhaps decline stages
Concentrated marketing	Attempts to produce the ideal product for a segment in the market (e.g. Rolls Royce)	An option when market size is substantial, normally during growth and maturity stages
Differentiated marketing	Tries to introduce several versions of a product, each aimed at a different segment (e.g. several different sorts of savings accounts)	Possible in growth and maturity stage, because the market is large enough to make it profitable

BTEC National Study Guide: Business. See page 185 for order details of individual texts

137

Segmentation, targeting, product positioning and the product life cycle

An important concept that affects the length of a product's life in the market is the product's positioning.

Product positioning means finding out the crucial product features that are important to consumers, and designing the product accordingly. The most successful products are the ones which, compared with competition, match consumer requirements best. These are products that will have a longer product life.

Harrods, for example, is positioned as one of London's most exclusive department stores. In order to reinforce this positioning with its target market, Harrods makes sure that its product ranges, its staff expertise, its displays and the overall atmosphere in the store are all of high quality. It is the best in its class and will as a consequence have a longer product life than other stores which do not reflect so well what the consumer expects. In simple terms, the best products in a particular market will have a longer life cycle.

Thinking point

Think of some products which you would consider to be outstanding in their particular market. Try to identify the reasons they have become outstanding successes. Which points seem to recur regardless of the product you are considering?

A popular technique used by marketing managers to evaluate how well their products match the requirements of the market is the production of perceptual maps. This technique is considered later in the unit (page 319).

Application of the marketing mix

The marketing mix provides an excellent framework for developing marketing plans or strategies that meet the needs of consumers. The marketing mix consists of product, price, place, promotion and packaging plans.

Products

Many marketing managers suggest that product is the key ingredient in the successful development of a successful marketing mix. No amount of promotion, extensive distribution or attractive pricing will sell a poor product.

Organisations can find themselves in a position where the product itself is insufficient to attract consumers. It is what surrounds a product, often called the augmented product, which enables them to compete. The extras are used to increase the product's market appeal. A computer retailer may offer installation, user training, and an on-site repair service to enhance the basic product. None of this affects the actual computer the customer buys, but it will affect the satisfaction and benefits the buyer gains from the product. With so many similar products now available, the augmented product can make the difference between success and failure.

Thinking point

In table format, note down the augmented product offered by DIY warehouses, food supermarkets, airlines and pop stars.

Unit 3, Creative Product Promotion, discusses branding, the importance of packaging, and the role and different meanings of product quality. New products are the lifeblood of most organisations. To appreciate how new products are developed, the role of product trials and the impact of timing on a product launch, read the section on new product development (NPD) in Unit 3 (page 86). To understand the importance of developing new products, read the sections earlier in this unit on the product life cycle and the Boston Consulting Group matrix (pages 311–312).

Consumer markets are used to having products immediately available for customers to buy. In business to business (b2b) markets this may not always be the case. Organisations that make products to the special requirements of their customers, for example business software programmes, will need time to produce the product.

This type of situation is also found in some business to consumer (b2c) markets. For example, MFI no longer stocks products on each site for immediate pick-up. Customers are given a guaranteed delivery date with compensation paid automatically if the delivery is late. MFI generally quotes 10 days for delivery, having made the judgement that this is the time the customer will be prepared to wait for a purchase of this type. This ensures everything the customer needs is delivered together, preventing multiple trips to the local store to collect unavailable parts. It also means that MFI needs to devote less money to holding stock, enabling it to offer lower prices to customers.

Pricing – strategies, methods and price elasticity

The ultimate objective of pricing, as with the other elements of the marketing mix, is to produce the required level of sales so that the organisation can achieve its objectives. It is excellent customer value that attracts customers and generates sales.

There are three main types of influences on price setting in practice – cost, competitors and demand. Managers determine the prices set by an organisation, whereas the costs an organisation faces are facts. Different groups of managers are likely to set different prices for the same product. The various approaches to pricing are discussed in Unit 3, Creative Product Promotion.

Price elasticity describes the sensitivity of demand to changes in price. It measures the change in the amount purchased when there is a change in price. Demand is said to be elastic if the change in the quantity demanded is of greater proportion than the proportional change in price. For example, if the price of a particular insurance policy fell by 10% and there was an increase in sales of 20%, the demand for the product would be said to be elastic, because the change in price led to a more than proportionate response in demand. If a price increase of 10% resulted in a 5% fall in sales, then demand would be said to be inelastic.

Practice point

Consider how information on a product's price elasticity might have an impact on the way managers price their products. What could they do to make their products price inelastic? Would this be beneficial to the organisation?

Place

Place describes how the consumer can obtain the product. The role of retailers and wholesalers is described in Unit 3, Creative Product Promotion.

Logistics, sometimes called distribution, describes the physical process of moving goods to the final consumer. It can provide some important benefits which the consumer values. It can ensure products are always available on the supermarket shelf. It can ensure the right products are delivered on time, in a convenient way and undamaged.

Logistics function	Function activity
Order processing	Ensures orders are quickly and accurately relayed to the producer
Transportation	Ensures delivery on time, in a convenient way and undamaged
Stock management	Ensures products are always in stock and available
Warehousing	Ensures stock is stored safely and undamaged
Customer service	Keeps customers advised of developments – e.g. a delay in delivery

317

BTEC National Study Guide: Business. See page 185 for order details of individual texts

139

Organisations that often have products out of stock, make delivery promises they don't keep, supply damaged goods or take weeks to process an order are doomed to fail. Effective distribution and logistics should be seen as important to the customer.

Traditionally, producers would involve a number of other organisations in the process of delivering the product to the final customer. For example, a producer of software in the Far East would appoint a UK distributor to whom the goods are shipped. The distributor would then sell the products to wholesalers who showed an interest. The wholesaler in turn would supply the retail stores who sold the product to the end user. The organisations between the producer and the customer – distributor, wholesaler and retailer – are called **intermediaries**.

However, the Internet allows producers and customers to trade directly with each other. The intermediaries are redundant. This process is called 'disintermediation'.

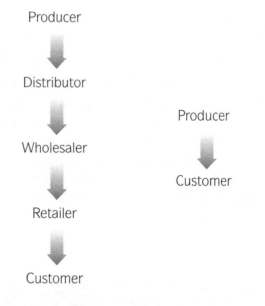

Thinking point

Describe the benefits of disintermediation for consumers, and for producers. Are there any drawbacks of disintermediation?

Promotion

The tools available for promotion include customer service, branding, public relations, sponsorship, personal selling, direct marketing, corporate image development and after-sales service. These options have to be blended together to ensure the maximum number of consumers are exposed to the promotional message at the lowest cost. The choice of method depends on the habits of the target market and their reaction to promotional activity. Most of these promotional tools, except customer service and after-sales service, are discussed in Unit 3, Creative Product Promotion.

Customer care is about how customers are treated during all interactions they have with an organisation. It involves what happens to them before they purchase a product, during the purchase process and after they have bought the product. With so much product choice and so many similar products, this aspect of the marketing mix is now seen as very important for success. Customer care programmes show the importance of the extended marketing mix.

After-sales service deals with a smaller number of activities once the product has been bought. The organisation's customer care programme will influence the way the after-sales programme is designed and conducted.

Customers expect organisations to have a comprehensive array of after-sales services as part of the product purchased. An after-sales service may include extended guarantee options, accidental damage insurance, a full refund or exchange promise, a repair service and a price promise.

Extended marketing mix

The **extended marketing mix** takes the traditional elements of product, price, place, packaging and promotion and adds another three Ps: people, processes and physical evidence.

BTEC National Study Guide: Business. See page 185 for order details of individual texts

140

The importance of the extra elements in the extended marketing mix can be seen if some of the key ingredients of an effective customer care programme are considered.

● Customers should receive clear and accurate information delivered in a courteous manner. *People* have to be trained to provide the level of service expected.

● Quick and easy purchase systems, and straightforward procedures for refunds and the exchange of goods, show how important *processes* are now to the customer and the marketing mix.

● Customer care involves making sure the consumer enjoys the buying experience, and that its *physical evidence* is of high quality. Consequently customer care staff have smart uniforms, and organisations try to signpost their buildings effectively and make the surroundings, such as reception areas, comfortable.

Continuous review and evaluation of marketing mix

A perceptual map can be used on a continuous basis to review and evaluate the effectiveness of the marketing mix. The map should consider the two most important aspects of the marketing mix. For breakfast cereal bars, this might be price and product. The map below shows that perhaps a market opportunity exists for an economy-priced, low-calorie bar. This product development proposal would have to be researched to check whether a genuine market demand existed.

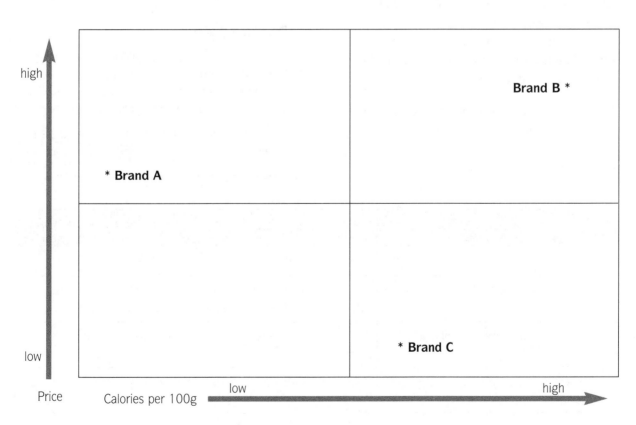

Perceptual map – breakfast cereal bars

319

BTEC National Study Guide: Business. See page 185 for order details of individual texts

141

Evaluation strategies

There are several techniques available to evaluate marketing strategies or plans. Plans can be evaluated against overall company objectives, against the aims of a particular marketing plan or using the principles of marketing.

The results of marketing strategies can be evaluated for their contribution to overall organisational objectives such as growth, profit, providing public services, survival or operating ethically. These objectives are discussed in detail in Unit 1, Introduction to Business. For example, if an organisation had an overall objective to grow by 10% and advertised products increased sales by 12%, it would be possible to conclude that the marketing strategies made a significant contribution.

Alternatively, the effectiveness of a marketing strategy could be evaluated using the particular aim of the marketing plan. For example, a marketing plan may have been developed to obtain a market share of 5% in the French market within 12 months. An achievement of 3% after 12 months would suggest the plan had not achieved its objective.

Finally, an organisation can evaluate its plans against the principles of marketing.

- **Understanding consumer needs.** Is there evidence within the plans that the organisation understands its consumers?

- **Keeping ahead of competition.** Did the plans take into account competitor strengths?

- **Communicating effectively with consumers.** Did the promotional plans deliver accurate and relevant information to consumers?

- **Using new technology.** Did the plans effectively use new technology in terms of exploiting new product opportunities, and/or improve the way the marketing was conducted by the organisation?

For the evaluation process to be effective, the steps in the table below need to be followed.

This type of information should be collected as a matter of course for use in the situational analysis or marketing audit. So the circle is complete and the process begins all over again.

Practice point

1 Read the case study on 3G phones in Unit 3, Creative Product Promotion, page 84. Using the principles of marketing, evaluate the success of Hutchison's marketing activity.

2 Compare your analysis with those of others in the class.

Evaluation steps	Example
Relevant information collected	Increase in sales of advertised products obtained
Results analysed and feedback provided	Products advertised on TV achieved significant sales increases; products advertised in magazines recorded smaller increases
Weaknesses and problems identified	Magazines used for advertising not always read by target audience
Improvements and recommendations proposed	Magazines which are more likely to be read by target audience to be used next time

320

BTEC National Study Guide: Business. See page 185 for order details of individual texts

142

Outcome activity 11.4

Lucozade used to be positioned as an invalid's drink, with the slogan 'Lucozade aids recovery'. Its advertising in the 1960s used to show sick children being tended by a caring mother who gave them Lucozade. As general health and living conditions improved, its overall market appeal declined. If people bought Lucozade only when there was sickness in the household, the purchase frequency and volume would be very low, especially when compared with other more mainstream fizzy drinks.

Lucozade was repositioned to capitalise on the growing health boom. Instead of being a semi-medicinal 'illness' drink, it became a specially formulated, glucose-rich source of energy for active and busy people. It still retained its premium price and quality image, but created much more of a positive image for itself and a reason for customers to drink it frequently.

The repositioning was achieved through packaging with a 'one-shot' bottle. The large-size bottle was discontinued. The new positioning was endorsed through powerful celebrity advertising, featuring current sports heroes.

Pass
Identify and describe the marketing strategy used by Lucozade to increase the demand for its product.

Merit
Analyse the marketing strategy used by Lucozade to increase the demand for its products.

Distinction
Make supported recommendations for the development of the Lucozade marketing strategy, as informed by the use of market analysis techniques.

Key terms

Common law
the law developed through the courts and based on previous decisions; precedent, as it is called, requires the courts to follow past decisions in cases with similar facts and covering the same points of law

Control
to take corrective action, if necessary, to bring performance into line with a plan

Corporate image
the characteristics an organisation seeks to establish for itself in the minds of the public

Diversification
the spread of business risk by reducing dependence on one product or market

Ethics
moral principles or rules of conduct generally accepted by most members of a society

Extended marketing mix
the normal elements of product, price, place, packaging and promotion but also another three Ps associated with marketing services: people, processes and physical evidence

Intermediary
company that buys from one member of the supply chain and sells to another in the process of transferring goods from the producer to the consumer

Marketing
providing the right product at the right price in the right place profitably

Sample
a group of people selected as representative of the views of an entire target market

Statutory law
the law created when Parliament passes new legislation through an Act of Parliament

BTEC National Study Guide: Business. See page 185 for order details of individual texts

143

End-of-unit test

1 What is the Chartered Institute of Marketing's definition of marketing?

2 Name the four elements of consumer rights.

3 What are the four tests the Advertising Standards Authority (ASA) uses to decide whether an advertisement is acceptable?

4 What is a code of practice?

5 What sort of information does qualitative research reveal?

6 Describe judgement sampling.

7 What is the purpose of strategic research?

8 Name a source of government statistics.

9 In what sort of market would you expect to find a DMU?

10 How do organisations use geodemographic data?

11 What does PESTLE analysis prompt researchers to examine?

12 Explain what a 'star' product is in the Boston Consulting Group matrix.

13 Define the term 'market development' as used in Ansoff's matrix.

14 Describe three ways the life of a product could be extended.

15 Explain price elasticity of demand.

16 What consumer benefits can effectively organised logistics deliver?

17 Explain the term 'disintermediation'.

18 Name the elements of the extended marketing mix.

19 What technique can be used to evaluate the effectiveness of the marketing mix?

20 Name the four principles that can form the basis for evaluating marketing strategies.

BTEC National Study Guide: Business. See page 185 for order details of individual texts

144

Resources

Texts

Hill and O'Sullivan: *Foundations of Marketing*, CIM Publishing, 2001

Needham, D and Dransfield, R: *Marketing: Everybody's Business*, Heinemann, 1995

Needham, D, Dransfield, R et al: *Marketing for Higher Awards*, Heinemann, 1999

Websites

www.asa.org.uk Advertising Standards Authority

www.mintel.com Mintel

www.thomson.com Datastream

http://dbuk.dnb.com Dun & Bradstreet

www.dma.org.uk Direct Mail Association

www.which.net Consumers' Association, publishers of *Which?*

www.ons.gov.uk UK Office of National Statistics

www.oecd.org Organisation for Economic Co-operation and Development.

www.europa.eu.int/comm/eurostat/ European Union Statistical Office

www.lucozade.com Lucozade products

www.tt100.biz The Times 100 – business case studies

CD Roms

Mastertext CD-Rom, *Advanced Vocational Business*, Cyber Communications Ltd, 2000

BTEC National Study Guide: Business. See page 185 for order details of individual texts

145

Recruitment and selection describes the process that organisations follow to attract applications from people who want to work for them, and then to choose the best person for the job. This process covers four different areas.

The first area is planning for the recruitment itself. This means thinking about why the person is needed in the first place and what he or she should do. You will learn the meaning of key terms such as **job description** and **person specification**, which will help you to apply for jobs successfully in the future.

Next the selection process itself is examined, including different types of interviews and tests that many large organisations now use to recruit employees. Communication and decision-making skills are vital at this stage.

Policies and procedures that organisations use are important and this section will analyse different documents used in business before, during and after the interview.

The final area to be examined is the legal aspect of recruitment – the laws that govern employers and employees.

This unit is therefore divided into four main sections:

- 15.1 Recruitment planning
- 15.2 Selection practice
- 15.3 Recruitment practices and procedures
- 15.4 Recruitment and selection legislation.

Thinking point

Before you start working through this unit, think about any full- or part-time jobs or work experience placements you have applied for.

Did you follow a particular process? Draw the process that you followed as a flow chart or diagram, and in small groups compare your results. Are there things that are the same in all of the processes? Are there any differences?

Keep your flow chart or diagram until you have finished the unit.

Recruitment planning

Initial stages of planning

After an organisation has placed an advertisement, anyone who applies for the position becomes an **applicant**. However, a lot of work happens within the organisation before this stage.

Part of recruitment planning involves the organisation working out whether it needs to recruit anyone at all. There may be many reasons why an organisation considers recruiting.

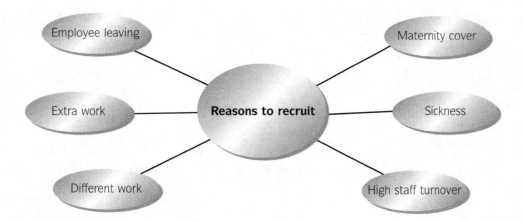

Some organisations have problems keeping staff in their jobs. This is measured by their **labour turnover rate**:

$$\frac{\text{Number of staff leaving in a length of time}}{\text{Average number of staff employed in that length of time}} \times 100$$

This shows how many staff leave in a certain amount of time compared to the overall number of staff in the organisation. If this figure is very high, it shows that staff tend not to stay long.

If employees regularly leave an organisation and need to be replaced by new ones, this will cost the employer a lot of money. Not only do new employees need extra training, it costs both time and money to recruit them.

Some industries have high turnover rates because they do not pay well or they involve working unsocial hours, for example in retailing or hospitality. Some organisations in these industries may try to reduce their turnover rates by changing working conditions to encourage people to stay longer. Others accept the situation and try to recruit more often.

Sometimes new employees are not needed because there are other ways of getting more work done in the business, and this is called improving the **productivity** rate.

There may be a high absence or sickness rate. There are two calculations to work out these rates:

Absence measurement (%)
$\dfrac{\text{Hours of absence}}{\text{Hours of total time}} \times 100$
Sickness measurement (%)
$\dfrac{\text{Hours of sickness}}{\text{Hours of total time}} \times 100$

Finding out why people are off sick or absent, and trying to reduce these absences, will help to increase productivity. This could be done by improving working conditions or changing working hours. This may mean that the organisation does not need to employ new staff.

325

BTEC National Study Guide: Business. See page 185 for order details of individual texts

147

Case study   Castle Green

Castle Green is a hotel in the North East of England with 105 employees. Using flexible working, so that work patterns better fit the needs of staff, staff turnover was reduced from 64% to 40% in two years. This is a great achievement because some organisations in this industry have been known to have staff turnover figures as high as 100%.

The area also has less than 1% unemployment, which makes it difficult to recruit and keep staff in a 24-hour customer service business.

Castle Green's reputation as a good place to work has also meant that new employees have joined from industries unconnected with hospitality.

As a result of these changes, Castle Green has saved money by needing to spend less on recruitment, selection and training, as well as seeing an increase in customer satisfaction. Customers like to come back and see people they have met before.

Absenteeism (the rate of absence) is low (0.5% of payroll compared to the national average of 4%).

1 Why do you think that staff turnover can be as high as 100% in the hospitality industry?

2 What are the advantages to Castle Green of reducing its staff turnover rate from 64% to 40%?

3 What are the implications of a 1% unemployment rate for a business in a sector with a high staff turnover?

4 The staff turnover rate was 40% last year; use the staff turnover rate calculation to work out how many employees left the organisation that year.

Skills auditing

Another way of working out whether or not to recruit is by doing a **skills audit**. Existing employees are considered to see whether they already have the skills needed to cover new organisational objectives. Some employees may have those skills but may not be using them. The organisation could use these employees instead of employing new staff.

Organisations may also do skills audits routinely to work out the skill level within the organisation. A firm of solicitors, for example, may analyse

how many junior solicitors it has in training and how many are qualified, so it can plan for the future needs of the business. Sometimes organisations will use specialised software packages called human resource information systems (HRIS) to keep records of all employees and work out the skill level in the organisation automatically. This can be useful if they do project work and need to find people with specialist skills or qualifications very quickly. Employees may be able to work in more than one job area for the organisation.

BTEC National Study Guide: Business. See page 185 for order details of individual texts

148

Evaluating sources

Even if an organisation decides that someone new is needed to do a particular job or task, this does not always lead to an external vacancy. The organisation may decide to recruit internally. Some organisations have a policy of promoting vacancies internally before they advertise externally, to encourage career progression. The table at the foot of this page shows the advantages and disadvantages of internal and external recruitment.

Job analysis

Whether the job is to be advertised internally or externally, **job analysis** must be completed.

To work out what the job involves, the first step is to look at the job description. This is because it outlines the duties involved in the job as well as the pay and hours. The person doing the job at the moment may be observed so the employer can work out exactly what he or she does – this is called work study. An interview may also be used, especially if an employee carries out additional tasks that were not in the original job description.

Part of this analysis will also involve looking at the types of qualifications, materials and tools needed to perform the job. The relevant supervisor or manager will also be consulted as he or she may have knowledge of up-to-date requirements for the job, such as any changes in the law that affect the job.

Materials also need to be looked at, such as training manuals or accident reports. These may give the employer some idea of ways to improve the working conditions for the person in the job. If the accident report shows employees suffering the same types of medical problem, such as a bad back, there may be a recommendation that employees take part in a safe lifting course. The employee currently in the job may also be asked a set of questions about aspects of the job.

Job description

Once the job has been analysed and the key factors that are important to the organisation have been decided, a job description needs to be written or updated to describe what the job involves. Different organisations have their own style for job descriptions, but each contains a set of standard information as shown in the table on the next page.

Internal recruitment	External recruitment
Advantages	*Advantages*
Cheap to advertise	Higher number of candidates
All candidates known	Candidates may have new ideas
Candidates already know the organisation	Potential for new skills to be brought into the organisation
More likely to have a manageable number of applicants	
Can encourage career progression	
Disadvantages	*Disadvantages*
Limited choice of candidates	Takes longer
May cause problems among employees	People appointed may not be as good as they appear
Employees may be stuck in their ways	More expensive to advertise

327

BTEC National Study Guide: Business. See page 185 for order details of individual texts

149

Title of the job	This is important as it is used to give a person an idea of what the job involves and the level of responsibility, e.g. finance manager.
Department and location	A job description will be written for a particular department in an organisation, especially if the organisation is very large.
Broad terms	This gives a rough idea of what is involved in the post. Many job vacancies have **open-ended terms**, which means that they can change slightly to take into account the needs of the business or employee.
Responsible to whom	This tells the employee whom he or she must report to on progress in meeting tasks and responsibilities.
Responsibilities	This tells employees about any people or resources for which they have responsibility.
Scope of post	This gives guidance on how far-reaching the post is, for example whether there is the chance to supervise others or make management-level changes.
Name of compiler and approver	This is the person who designed and agreed the job description.
Date of issue	In a fast-changing business world, it is important to know when the last changes were made to the job description.

Practice point

In pairs, write a job description for the position of business studies teacher. Using the table above and the example on the next page, write something for each of the areas. You may need to interview a member of staff to complete this activity.

Feed back your results to the rest of the group and create a standard job description for a business studies teacher.

BTEC National Study Guide: Business. See page 185 for order details of individual texts

150

Money Management Ltd

Job description

Job title	Finance assistant
Department	Accounts
Responsible to	Sarah Pearson
Scope of the post	The finance assistant's main role is to assist the finance manager
Responsibilities	The post holder is expected to help with company accounts using Sage accounting software. This requires preparation of accounts for budgets within the organisation and assistance in the production of annual accounts for external agencies. Duties performed by the post holder include:

- reconciliation of accounts and problem-solving of any variances

- preparation of invoices

- raising orders

- general office duties such as travel-claim processing

- ad hoc reports as and when required

- any other duties as commensurate with the post

Compiled by	C Taylor
Date	8 March 2004

BTEC National Study Guide: Business. See page 185 for order details of individual texts

151

Person specification

Like the job description, the **person specification** gives a list of requirements, but these relate to the person doing the job.

The person specification will have an introduction giving details about the job, such as job title, post reference number and management responsibilities (including whom the employee needs to report to and be responsible for). It will then detail **attributes** or qualities that the organisation expects that person to have, for example the type of personality or experience.

Some organisations will also use ratings in their specification. This means that they will rate how important a part of the person specification is to a job. On this scale, 1 might mean that this attribute is very important, and 4 that it is relatively unimportant.

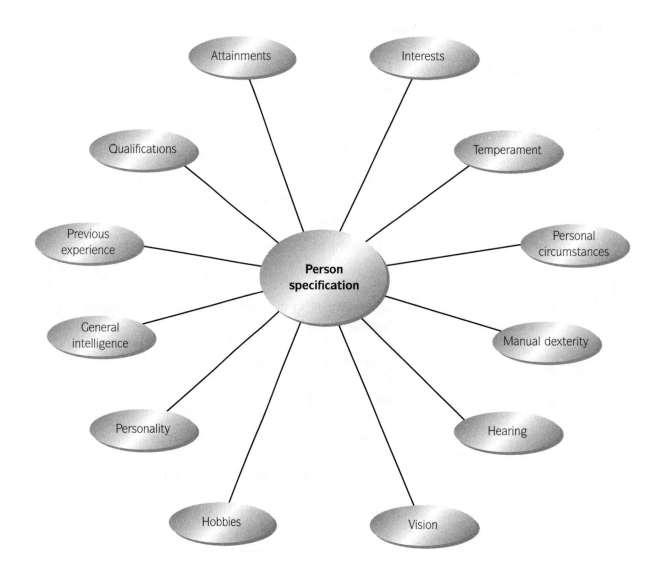

BTEC National Study Guide: Business. See page 185 for order details of individual texts

152

Person specification

Post title: Finance and administrative officer

Grade: Clerical 3/4

Criteria	Essential	Desirable
Qualifications/knowledge:	BTEC National Diploma in Business GCSEs in Maths and English plus 3 others at Grade C or above, or equivalent IT skills, particularly spreadsheets and database	
Work-related experience:	1–2 years' general office and/or financial experience Good level of numeracy	Experience in higher education
Skills/abilities and special attributes:	Good organisational skills Able to prioritise workloads Good communication skills Team-working ability	Previous experience of or willingness to work in an open-plan environment

Practice point

Write a person specification for the job of BTEC Business student! Using each of the categories contained in the person specification above, describe what is needed and then rate how important each attribute is. An example is started below to help you.

Previous experience	3
Able to work to deadlines	1

Previous experience was rated a 3 because it is not essential, but useful, to have studied business before starting the BTEC course. Working to deadlines is given a 1, because it is essential to get work in on time.

When you have finished your person specification, compare it with those of others in your class.

BTEC National Study Guide: Business. See page 185 for order details of individual texts

153

Methods of application

The method of application is the way people can apply for the job. There are several different methods and they will vary according to the type of job. These are shown in the table below, with their advantages and disadvantages. The methods are often combined; a letter, for example, may be sent in or faxed to an organisation with a curriculum vitae (CV).

Method	Purpose	Advantages	Disadvantages
In person	Applicants go to the organisation and apply in person Mostly used by smaller organisations or those that recruit frequently	Applicant and organisation can meet Easy to do Often used for jobs advertised in the place of work Only interested people who know the organisation already will apply	May be difficult to plan for May not attract the right sort of people Difficult for the applicant to prepare May not be easy to compare candidates
By letter	Applicants write a letter about their suitability for a job and send it to the organisation by post or fax	Gives the organisation the ability to compare Allows applicants to demonstrate their suitability for the job	Applicants are likely to show only their strengths and not weaknesses Applications are not in a standard format The letter may take a long time to arrive or get lost A fax may be difficult to keep confidential
Curriculum vitae (CV)	Applicants write all their details including education and employment history on two pages, including **referees**	The organisation can see all information about an applicant in one place	CVs focus only on positive aspects May have been used to apply for other jobs, so may not be specific to a particular role
Telephone	Applicants call and notes are made about them Sometimes tests are done on applicants to try to work out their personality type	Can be used for large numbers of applicants as the information can be put into a database and can be sorted Allows the applicant to speak to someone from the organisation and ask questions	The telephone may be busy or engaged and good applicants never get through An automated service may put off applicants or may not operate outside office hours
Application form	All applications have standard questions and boxes to be completed	Easy for the organisation to compare candidates Will only collect information that the organisation asks for	Paper-based forms may take time and money to distribute Forms will need to be processed and put into a system to compare them

BTEC National Study Guide: Business. See page 185 for order details of individual texts

Curriculum vitae

Personal details

Name   John Smith

Address   18 Hill Lane
Besthampton
BE15 7PJ

Telephone   023 80511822

Date of birth   2.2.85

Education

2001–2003   Topton College

1996–2001   Besthampton School

Academic qualifications

BTEC National Diploma in Business, Merit awarded

Eight GCSEs, including Maths and English

Work experience

2001-2003   Part-time employment at HMV using the till, pricing stock and stock management as well as dealing with customers

Personal statement

I am an outgoing person who likes to play sport. I am a member of the rugby team at college and also play at the weekend for my local team. I enjoy computing and am able to use a number of different software packages including Microsoft Office XP. I am hard working and always on time.

Referee

Kate Sharp
76 Laxford Avenue
Southampton
SO26 8PU
02380 876233

BTEC National Study Guide: Business. See page 185 for order details of individual texts

155

The other main method of application is on-line, and use of this method is increasing all the time. E-mail allows applicants to send letters and CVs directly to organisations, and on-line application forms are growing more common.

The advantages of on-line recruitment are:

- organisations can advertise job vacancies on their website free

- it can increase the number of candidates, which is useful for specialist employers

- data can be sent to the organisation very quickly

- data is sent directly and needs little processing

- it can happen 24 hours a day, 7 days a week

- people looking for company information may see the job and apply for it

- it can be accessed by people with disabilities on an equal basis

- it allows employees to access relevant jobs more easily by doing searches.

The disadvantages of on-line recruitment are:

- technical problems can occur, such as the website or e-mail not working

- jobs advertised on the World Wide Web may receive too many applicants, so employers may take a long time to choose candidates

- not everyone has access to the Web so it may reduce the number of possible applicants, and it may not be accessible to certain groups of people

- it may be difficult to prove where the information has come from; electronic signatures can be used, but are not common at present.

On-line recruitment is becoming more popular so organisations must make sure that it is used successfully and encourages as many people to apply for a job as possible. This includes making sure that **discrimination** does not take place against any group of people, for example disabled people.

Compliance

As you have already discovered when thinking about on-line recruitment, there are many things that organisations must do to ensure that everyone has a fair chance of applying for a job. Making sure that the organisation acts fairly is called ensuring **compliance**. When a vacancy is advertised and applications are made, UK employment laws apply, and equal opportunity rules mean that companies must not exclude categories of people.

The legislation you will need to be aware of is discussed in the legislation section in this unit, on pages 346–348.

Case study | **The Civil Service Recruitment Gateway**

The British Civil Service recruits graduates using on-line recruitment at *www.faststream.gov.uk*. Vacancies are advertised on-line and applicants must complete an on-line questionnaire and application form before they complete the second (a computerised test) and third (assessment centre) stages.

Only applicants who are successful at each of the stages follow on to the next.

1 How important do you think the on-line questionnaire is to the Civil Service?
2 What are the advantages to the Civil Service of using on-line questionnaires as part of its recruitment process?
3 What are the disadvantages to the Civil Service of using on-line questionnaires as part of its recruitment process?

As well as complying with legislation, organisations also have their own way of dealing with the application process. Some organisations have specific procedures for how and where they advertise vacancies. Procedures are agreed by senior managers within the organisation, and before a vacancy may be advertised it needs to be signed off by those managers. Other recruitment procedures might include ensuring applicants are not interviewed by relatives, colleagues or friends to make sure the process is fair.

Outcome activity 15.1/3

Tesco has part of its website (*www.tesco.com*) dedicated to school-leaver and graduate recruitment. The site shows video clips of young people working at Tesco and features competitions with prizes such as £500 in shopping vouchers.

Young people can search for vacancies and apply on-line. On-line application forms are provided and frequently asked questions are answered.

Pass

1 Using the Tesco website, classroom resources and newspaper articles, write a report that describes the recruitment and selection process at Tesco.
2 Identify and describe the different stages in the process and planning of recruitment and selection at Tesco. You may wish to use illustrated diagrams to do this.
3 Describe the recruitment practices and procedures used at Tesco. Using your guideline stages describe in full detail the practices and procedures that Tesco uses.

Merit

Explain ways of ensuring that recruitment and selection are effectively and efficiently carried out at Tesco. Research how Tesco currently works and make recommendations for any improvements it could make.

Selection practice

Selection practice deals with three main areas: the preparation for selection, communication skills, and selection and decision-making.

Preparation

The selection of the right person for the job needs careful planning. Organisations will have different ways of managing interviews. Once the organisation has decided which individuals it wants to interview, it will produce a list of **candidates**. An interview is the opportunity to ask questions of the applicant and to work out the suitability of the person for the job. It is also the first opportunity that applicants and the organisation have to speak with each other formally.

Interviews

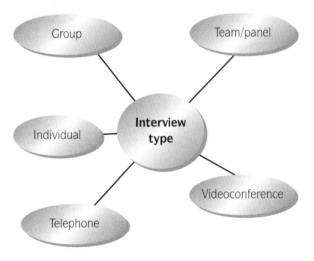

- **Group interviews** are where a number of people are interviewed together. This allows an organisation to present information about the job to a number of people at the same time and also allows them to see how people relate to each other.

- **Individual interviews** may be done face-to-face or over the telephone. While **telephone interviewing** is quicker it may not, unless videophones are available, be as useful because the interviewer is unable to see the body language of the person being interviewed.

335

BTEC National Study Guide: Business. See page 185 for order details of individual texts

157

What are the advantages of an interview using videoconference facilities?

● **Team/panel interviews** can also be used to allow the organisation to gain different opinions about an applicant. A panel of experts may be used to ask the candidate different questions related to specialist fields.

The number of interviews that are needed must also be planned for, and this will depend on the type of vacancy that is being offered.

There can be different types of interview at different stages. An organisation might want to have a screening interview first to select the most appropriate candidates, then hold interviews with the line manager, and finally conduct a panel interview with the senior management team.

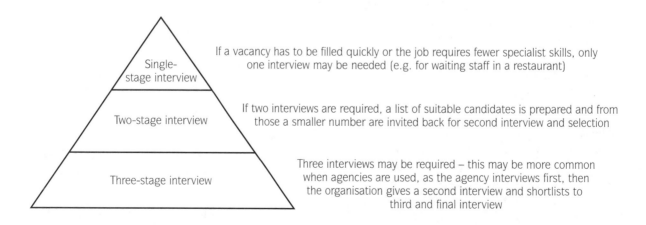

Single-stage interview — If a vacancy has to be filled quickly or the job requires fewer specialist skills, only one interview may be needed (e.g. for waiting staff in a restaurant)

Two-stage interview — If two interviews are required, a list of suitable candidates is prepared and from those a smaller number are invited back for second interview and selection

Three-stage interview — Three interviews may be required – this may be more common when agencies are used, as the agency interviews first, then the organisation gives a second interview and shortlists to third and final interview

Selection centres

Screening interview

Selection centre

Interview with senior management

Selection centres use a number of tests or tasks to assess the skill level of candidates in order to choose the best one for the job.

During various stages of the process candidates may be asked to perform tasks and tests. These include the following.

- **Psychometric tests:** Tests that attempt to measure intelligence or personality type, to assess how well a person will suit a job. These may be multiple-choice, paper-based tests.

- **Aptitude tests:** These assessments attempt to measure suitability for a job and may be more practical, such as putting tasks into priority order or demonstrating management of a small group.

- **Attainment tests:** These may measure by observing candidates performing in a group. They show the level at which candidates work within a group – as a high or low achiever, for example.

- **Occupational preference tests:** These measure skills that are important for the job. For example, if a job requires the person to be very customer focused, the test will measure this. A role-play may be used, for example asking a candidate to deal with a dissatisfied customer.

Time management

Time management is essential to preparation. Planning three-stage interviews takes a lot of management as time is needed between each stage. The right selection process will need to be chosen based on:

- the type of job
- the amount of time available until the vacancy must be filled
- the amount of working time available for the process to be carried out.

> **Practice point**
>
> 1 Careers Centres can usually provide a set of practice psychometric tests. By using these resources or those available on the Internet, complete a psychometric test yourself.
>
> 2 In small groups compare your results. How did you feel when you took the test, and what are the advantages or disadvantages to an organisation of doing such tests?

Communication skills

Body language

In Unit 2, Business and Management, you learned on pages 74–75 about the importance of body language and how actions such as folding your arms or leaning forward affect the way you communicate. Maintaining eye contact and smiling are extremely important and help to communicate that you are open and trustworthy. A firm handshake is also a way of showing that you are a confident and suitable person for the job, but being over-confident is as bad as being shy and nervous, because that may make the interviewer see you as being dishonest or big-headed.

The way you sit in the interview chair can also give signals to the interviewer. If you slouch down during the interview or tap your foot, you may appear to be uninterested in the job.

There are other non-verbal barriers that may affect how you communicate. Dress is an extremely important issue in recruitment and selection. How you dress will communicate to your interviewer whether or not you will fit into the organisation. It is usual in the business world to wear smart clothes in an interview, such as a

337

BTEC National Study Guide: Business. See page 185 for order details of individual texts

159

List the communication skills this candidate needs to improve

suit and for men a tie. Your choice of dress may be a barrier to communication if you dress in a way that the interviewer does not expect. Wearing perfectly clean clothing and being neat and tidy also influences the interviewer subconsciously.

Effective questioning

The use of effective questioning techniques is important for the interviewer, as asking the right questions will help the candidate to give the right answers.

Open questions	Questions that give the candidate the opportunity to give an extended answer. Examples: <ul><li>What is your biggest strength?</li><li>How would you deal with this problem?</li></ul> They may also be used to check information given in the application form.
Closed questions	Questions that allow a candidate only to give a factual or yes-or-no answer. Examples are: <ul><li>Did you take a job last summer?</li><li>How many GCSEs do you have?</li></ul>

Using a variety of types of question will allow the interviewer to gain a useful impression of the candidate, so it is essential that the questions are prepared before the interview, especially if it is to be done by a team or panel. To control the interview process, a member of the team will need to co-ordinate the questions to make the interview flow well.

Candidates also need to think about preparation and control. Candidates often feel under pressure in interview situations and will therefore need to stay focused and give well-thought-out answers, as well as maintaining eye contact and good body posture.

Candidates are usually given an outline of the format of the interview, for example how long it will last and the type of questions they will be asked. This allows them to try to do their best. It is important that appropriate and equivalent questions are asked of all candidates so that each person has a fair chance of getting the job. The section on legislation on pages 346–347 gives more information about this, but the main point is that candidates must not be unfairly disadvantaged. For example:

- a woman must not be asked about her marital status or whether or not she has children

- no one should be asked about sexual orientation

- no one should be asked about religious or political beliefs

- no one should be asked about his or her socio-economic grouping.

Listening skills

Whether interviews are by phone, face-to-face or by videoconference, listening and analytical skills are required. Listening is very important for the interviewer so that he or she really hears what the candidate can offer the organisation and makes a decision to employ the right person. Sometimes interviewers will use summarising skills to help them listen. Summarising is a form of recapping, or going over, what has been said.

Practice point

1 Look at the questions below and decide which are closed questions and which are open. Check your answers with others in your class.

   1 Which skills do you think are needed for this job?

   2 Do you have a BTEC National Business qualification?

   3 Can you type?

   4 How long did you work for your last company?

   5 What do you think is your greatest weakness?

   6 What do you know about our organisation?

   7 Is your name Sam Brown?

2 Imagine you are one of the people asked to interview candidates for the post of sales assistant in a shop. The sales assistant is responsible for customer service, taking money, dealing with the till and filling shelves. Produce a list of closed and open questions that you could ask, and practise using them by carrying out a role-play in pairs.

If the interviewee makes a statement, the interviewer may check it by asking 'I think you are saying … Is that correct?' Summarising allows the interviewer to confirm understanding and shows the candidate that he or she is listening.

Analysing the answers and making sense of them may lead to further questions, and it is important that the interviewer has good listening and analytical skills in order to be able to probe the candidate in a fair and controlled manner. This may be the only chance the interviewer has to ask questions and compare candidates before deciding who will be chosen for the job. It is crucial that the interviewer can analyse and judge answers in order to make a decision.

339

BTEC National Study Guide: Business. See page 185 for order details of individual texts

161

Feedback

At the interview, candidates are also informed about the next stage of the process. They will be given a date and time by which they will be told whether they have been successful. This is a form of feedback. Candidates will also be told what will happen to their personal information if they are not successful. It may be destroyed, but some organisations ask candidates for permission to keep the information for, say, another six months so that if another job should become available, they can be considered. Keeping this information secure is part of the organisation's responsibility to maintain **confidentiality**.

Specialist staff

Making sure information is correctly stored and processed is usually the responsibility of the **human resources department**.

People working within the human resources department are often involved in the interview process to check that everything is carried out appropriately and fairly, as they are responsible for keeping up-to-date on employment law.

Selection and decision-making

When all the candidates have been interviewed, the job of choosing the best candidate must be carried out. This can be done in many different

---

Practice point

Rate the two candidates below based on their histories. The job is for a hairdressing junior in a salon, with the offer of training. The pay is the minimum wage and the hours are 35 per week. Using the information below, rate the candidates on each of the criteria and give them overall totals.

Discuss in small groups which of the two should get the job, and why.

Louise Meacher	Zinat Rashid
Has three years' full-time work experience in a hairdressing salon but gave up her job to go and work in an office after a disagreement with the salon owner. NVQ2 Hairdressing completed.	Has been working on Saturdays for six months in a hairdressing salon while at college full time studying for Beauty Therapy exams. Has no formal qualifications in hairdressing but has a Customer Service qualification. Willing to learn new skills.

Qualifications required

None essential, but NVQ1 desirable

Attributes required

Good customer service skills

Ability to respond well to supervision and follow instructions

Good organisational skills

Ability to adapt to change

Ability to work under pressure

ways, but a popular method is rating the candidates against several criteria, with a score for each. The individual scores are then added up and the totals compared. The candidate with the highest score is the one who is offered the job.

By doing this, an organisation is trying to make the process fair and objective. But it is important to recognise that the candidate with the highest score will not necessarily be the one with the most qualifications or experience; it will be the person who is the best fit for the job. Someone with too many qualifications may be as inappropriate as someone with not enough.

Once the candidates have been rated and the person has been chosen, the next stage is to record relevant information about the other applicants and why they have not been chosen for the job. The main reasons for this are:

- to be able to feed back information to candidates so they can improve in their next job application

- to keep notes on why the person was not suitable for the job for the organisation's own records

- to monitor equal opportunities, and demonstrate that the organisation carried out the process fairly and legally

- to keep candidates' notes on record, with their permission, for consideration in connection with other possible vacancies.

When the candidate has accepted the position, probably by telephone and then in writing, the last stage is to communicate with all the relevant people in the organisation to inform them about the person recruited, including line managers, other employees, senior management and the human resources department. A training plan may need to be prepared for when the person starts.

Outcome activity 15.2

Pass

By using a business that you know well or your school or college, describe key ways in which a selection interview may be planned and carried out in order to result in an appropriate appointment to the staff of your selected business. Include preparation, communication skills and selection and decision-making.

Recruitment practices and procedures

Outsourcing

You have examined some of the more general practices and procedures for recruitment and seen how complex the process is. Some organisations don't have the time or specialised staff to carry out this work, so they employ other people to carry out some stages for them. This is called **outsourcing**, and may involve any of the following:

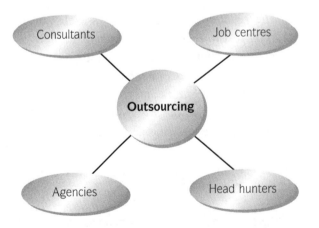

Each of the methods shown in the diagram above involve an agent doing recruitment work. The organisation specifies the type of employees required and the agent finds them.

BTEC National Study Guide: Business. See page 185 for order details of individual texts

163

Advantages of using an agency	Disadvantages of using an agency
The organisation can concentrate on running the business, not looking for new employees	Cost – the organisation must pay the agent a fee
The organisation does not have to employ a recruitment team	May not find the right person for the job as the agent does not work in the organisation and may not have as much incentive to employ the right person
The agency has access to many different applicants and can screen out those unsuitable	
The agency will not let competitor organisations know that the company is recruiting, but advertisements will	
The agency can offer advice about what is happening in employment generally, and in the organisation's own sector	

- *Job centres* are a type of agency run by the government's Employment Service. They are designed to help people who are unemployed to find a job, but can be accessed by anyone. They also give information on work-related issues such as entitlement to benefits, and training advice for people wanting to work in the UK or other European countries.

- *Head hunters* are used by businesses that need specialist workers or those that are in high demand. Their job is to go out and find people who are very successful in a certain type of work and tell them of job opportunities in other organisations, to try to persuade them to change employer. Unlike other agencies, head hunters look for people who are demonstrating that they are successful within a job, for example the top-selling salesperson.

Advertising a post

Advertising a post can be done in a number of ways. Some organisations use newspapers, others use posters, some keep an up-to-date list of interested people to e-mail and others rely on fax machines. On-line advertising through websites is also becoming more popular, but the most suitable place to advertise a post is where the most potential applicants will read it! Advertising may also be done by using an agency or job centre.

Case study   Jefferson Maguire

Jefferson Maguire (*www.jeffersonmaguire.co.uk*) is a head-hunting agency based in Hampshire. It recruits employees for leading companies including Douwe Egberts, Storm and Virgin. Its activities include targeting high achievers, presenting candidates to clients, interviewing candidates and helping candidates to resign from their current employer.

1 What are the advantages to businesses of using head hunters to recruit new members of staff?
2 Are there any disadvantages?
3 Which areas of business would make most use of head hunters when looking for new staff, and why?

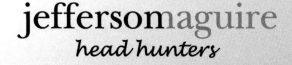

342

BTEC National Study Guide: Business. See page 185 for order details of individual texts

164

Some vacancies are advertised only within a business, because the organisation already has suitable employees working for it. Equal opportunity legislation requires organisations to advertise vacancies as widely as possible, so using internal recruitment only may not be appropriate. There may also be an ethical problem when considering an internal applicant – will the best person get the job?

Advertising externally can be very expensive, however, and take a lot of time. If an advertisement is placed within the organisation there may be fewer and better applicants compared to a job advertised externally.

One of the most successful ways to advertise externally for new employees is to place an advertisement in a national newspaper. Advertising rates are calculated as a cost per single-column centimetre.

Broadsheet newspapers such as the *Guardian*, *Telegraph* and *Times* charge from about £40 to £100 per one-column centimetre for classified recruitment advertisements, so the advertiser would pay at least this amount for the smallest possible advertisement. In practice, several centimetres of space would be needed to give enough information to potential applicants, so the cost would be multiplied accordingly. A large advertisement, such as half a page, would cost perhaps £7,000 to £8,000.

For some newspapers this fee would include on-line advertising for a set period of time, but for others an extra charge would be payable for the advertisement to appear on the newspaper's website as well as in the printed paper.

Organisations will have a house style for their advertisements. This means that they will use the same layout for each vacancy they advertise

Practice point

Compare the two advertisements below for the job of accountant. What do they have in common? What is different? Which one would you apply for, and why?

Job title:	Accountant	**Job title:**	Accountant
Location:	Liverpool, Merseyside	**Location:**	Belvedere, Greater London
		Salary:	Negotiable
Salary:	£18,000	**Job type:**	Permanent
Job sector:	Accountancy	**Description**	

Description

Assistant accountant

Wirral-based company seeking an experienced person to assist in preparation of monthly accounts, bank reconciliations, cash flow forecasting, VAT returns, etc. Salary is £18K to £19K. Call the Blue Agency.

Description

Financial accountant

Established damp-proof and timber-preservation company requires suitably experienced person to maintain financial data and records. Reporting directly to the directors, the successful candidate will be responsible for the financial records including the sales ledger, purchase ledger and nominal ledger. The role includes raising invoices and the weekly maintenance of payroll records for both employees and subcontractors. You will be responsible for all month-end routines including the preparation of accurate monthly accounts for management use and for all accounting administration. Requires hands-on experience of Sage Line 50 and Sage Payroll and knowledge of the Construction Industry Scheme, cards, certificates and vouchers. Hours 9 am–5.30 pm, Monday–Friday. Vacancy to commence January. Apply with CV to …

BTEC National Study Guide: Business. See page 185 for order details of individual texts

within or outside the organisation. This is very important for external advertising as it makes it easy for potential applicants to recognise a job opportunity with the organisation. Sometimes the advertisement might show the company logo or be printed in a particular text or in a particular colour.

The type of advertisement will depend on the job. The advertisement will be based on the job description and person specification. Vacancies for some jobs may include large amounts of information including pay and conditions, whereas for senior managerial jobs pay and conditions may be negotiable.

Documentation and procedures for selection and interview

Documents must be completed or sent out to possible applicants so they can decide whether the job is for them.

Before the interview

Application packs and further information, with closing dates, need to be given out so that candidates can decide whether they want to apply for the job.

The type of attributes listed as needed by the successful candidate should comply with legislation. This list may also be used to decide who should be offered a second interview.

References may be taken up. This is especially important if the job involves working with young or vulnerable people.

A set of questions should be drafted so that the interviewers know exactly what they are going to ask, and ask the same set of questions for each candidate.

The procedure for telling candidates whether or not they have been successful needs to be in place.

For the interview

During the interview the interviewer will need to have a set of prepared questions.

Details about the candidates, such as their CVs or application forms, will be used to prompt questions.

The interviewer should lead the interview to make sure that it lasts the right amount of time and the right amount of information is collected. In a panel interview, one person usually leads the interview and controls the time.

After the interview

Notes will be written about each of the candidates so that a decision can be made about which candidate is to be offered the job.

Candidates can claim expenses for travel or meals – this is very important if they have travelled a long way.

If references have not already been taken up, they will be taken up now.

Police and medical checks can be made to see whether the person is suitable for the job.

A verbal offer of the job is made.

The candidate accepts or declines the job. If it is accepted, a written offer letter is sent confirming details including salary, start date, hours of work, holiday entitlement and any other requirements such a proof of qualifications.

An induction programme is prepared to train the new employee to work for the organisation. The programme should include everything from health and safety requirements to where to get a cup of coffee.

Candidates who are unsuccessful are usually told by phone or in writing.

Possible barriers to communication

Throughout the process of interviewing there must be compliance with company procedures. This will ensure that all relevant laws are taken into account to make sure that the process is as fair as possible.

The recruitment process must attract the widest possible range of candidates. Examples of this include advertising jobs in Welsh and English for vacancies in Welsh-speaking parts of Wales, to make them accessible for English speakers; and advertising vacancies where women or members of ethnic minority groups who are under-represented in the organisation will see them, for example in newspapers or magazines popular with those groups, such as *The Voice*. *Cosmopolitan* has job advertisements encouraging women to join the police, for example. New methods of encouraging variety in types of candidates include on-line applications and text messaging information services.

Most organisations have an equal opportunities policy that states how they work to maintain equality of opportunity within the organisation. Equal opportunity policies are designed to encourage candidates to apply for jobs that they may not have considered. They also give the organisation good publicity as they are seen to be fair.

Case study | BT's equal opportunity policy

Here is an extract from the statement BT has on its website (*http://www.btplc.com/societyandenvironment/betterworldreport*):

BT is an equal opportunity employer and it is the aim of this policy that all persons, wherever they are in the world, should have equal opportunity for employment and advancement on the basis of their ability, qualifications and suitability for the work.

BT and the Connected World Device are registered trade marks of British Telecommunications public limited company

It is BT's policy that no job applicant or employee receive less favourable treatment in any aspect of employment on racial grounds, or on grounds of gender, religion, disability, marital status, age or sexual orientation, gender status or caring responsibilities, or be disadvantaged by conditions or requirements which cannot be shown to be justifiable. To this end our policies will become the global benchmark, reflecting sensitively the particular circumstances and local cultures of each country and community in which we operate.

There must be no unlawful discrimination; direct, indirect or institutional, against any person whether in recruitment, selection, training, promotion or in any aspect of employment. Harassment of any form at work is also a form of discrimination and will be treated as such under the terms of this policy. No form of harassment or bullying, including derogatory remarks at work, will be tolerated. Cases will be dealt with under the BT Harassment and Bullying Policy.

Text used by permission of BT

1 What benefits do you think BT gains by having an equal opportunity policy?
2 How could BT try to measure whether its policy is working?
3 What is the purpose of the BT Harassment and Bullying Policy?
4 What is the difference between indirect and direct discrimination?

BTEC National Study Guide: Business. See page 185 for order details of individual texts

Recruitment and selection legislation

As you have already seen, recruitment and selection are governed by equal opportunity legislation. This section aims to give you an outline of each of the main Acts that are relevant to this process. You will need to look up each Act yourself to find the full details. Legislation is changing all the time, so keep up to date with what is happening in this area by reading newspapers or journals, and watching quality news programmes on television.

- Sex Discrimination Act 1975 and 1986
- Race Relations Act 1976
- Equal Pay Act 1970
- Rehabilitation of Offenders Act 1974
- Disability Discrimination Act 1995
- European Working Time Regulations 1998
- Employment Act 2002

Sex Discrimination Acts 1975 and 1986

These Acts ensure that men and women are treated equally. People must not be discriminated against because of their marital status, sex or if they have had their gender reassigned. Indirect and direct discrimination are both unlawful.

- **Direct discrimination:** This would occur where a less qualified man was given a job in preference to a more qualified woman.

- **Indirect discrimination:** This occurs when a job has requirements that one sex is likely to be unable to comply with, such as requiring applicants to be 6 foot tall. Very few women are so tall.

Sometimes jobs are exempt from the Sex Discrimination Acts if they must be performed by a particular sex; for example, a youth worker specialising in helping young women may have to be female.

If a group is under-represented, positive steps can be made to encourage that particular group, such as offering free management courses to women because there are not enough women in a particular organisation.

Race Relations Act 1976

This Act makes it unlawful for anyone to be discriminated against on the grounds of race, colour, nationality, ethnic origin or national origin. Employees must be protected from discrimination, victimisation and harassment and can use an industrial tribunal to force employers to change the way they operate or to seek compensation. Indirect and direct discrimination are both unlawful under the Race Relations Act.

- **Direct discrimination:** This would occur if a job was advertised as suitable only for someone with a black skin, as it would discriminate against anyone with white skin.

- **Indirect discrimination:** This would occur if an advertisement required applicants to be fair haired, as it would discriminate against certain ethnic groups.

Case study   Lorell Garages Ltd

Job advertisement

Person with excellent English wanted as car technician in local garage. Must be physically fit and at least 6 foot 2 tall. No previous experience necessary but should be willing to learn and be prepared to get dirty. Pay subject to negotiation.

Apply in person

Closing date 26 June

1 How does this advertisement discriminate directly and indirectly?
2 Rewrite the job advertisement in a more acceptable format.

BTEC National Study Guide: Business. See page 185 for order details of individual texts

168

Equal Pay Act 1970

This Act requires employers to pay men and women equally. This includes all aspects of pay including benefits, childcare allowances, sickness benefits and car allowances.

Rehabilitation of Offenders Act 1974

This Act is designed to allow some criminal convictions to be considered 'spent' after a certain amount of time. This means that after that time, the convictions are ignored and the ex-offender does not have to mention them when applying for a job. The amount of time needed depends on the crime, but the purpose of this is to allow ex-offenders to be rehabilitated into society and to get jobs.

There are some exceptions to the Act, and for work in some job types a conviction can never be considered spent. Examples of such jobs include:

- working with young people

- working in social services

- any employment involving the administration of justice, such as police or probation service, or professions with legal protection such as accountants, nurses or doctors

- national security jobs, such as those in the Civil Service.

Disability Discrimination Act 1995

This Act makes it unlawful for a disabled person to be treated less favourably because he or she is disabled, unless there are very good reasons. Reasonable adjustments must be made to premises so that disabled applicants or workers are not put at a substantial disadvantage.

From October 2004 all employers have to comply with this Act. Making reasonable adjustments might mean adding handrails for wheelchair access or a hearing loop for a person who is hard of hearing.

Working Time Regulations 1998

This directive introduced the idea of a maximum average working week of 48 hours, to be measured over a period of either 17 weeks, 26 weeks or 52 weeks according to workforce agreement. It also imposes restrictions on the maximum length of nightshifts, provides for rest periods and ensures a minimum annual leave allowance of four weeks. Employers have to keep records of how many hours an employee has worked to avoid any disputes.

Employment Act 2002

The Employment Act 2002 covers a number of areas within employment law including:

- the right to 26 weeks' paid maternity leave and 26 weeks' unpaid leave

- the right to 2 weeks' paternity leave for working fathers and 26 weeks' leave for adoptive parents

- the right for fathers and mothers to ask for flexible working arrangements if they have children under six or disabled children under 18

- grievance and disciplinary procedures in the workplace to settle disputes more quickly

- rights for people who are on fixed-term contracts

- monitoring of equal opportunities through questionnaires

- the right for members of trade unions to take paid time off to attend meetings and training.

All of these Acts together give UK and EU legislative protection to individuals throughout the recruitment and selection process. They are regularly updated and aim to ensure fairness in the world of work.

Outcome activity 15.4

Job title: Office junior and office administrator

Salary: £13,500

Job sector: Secretarial and administration

Description

Office junior and office administrator

Experience in an office environment essential for administrator role. Duties will include corresponding with insurers and property owners and arranging surveys of thatched properties. Salary £13,500.

Junior's role will include welcoming visitors, filing and call handling. The role may also include some general accounts work. Salary £13,500.

Pass

Using the job advertisement above as a starting point if you wish, research current employment legislation and describe which main pieces of legislation the employer must comply with when recruiting and selecting. Explain how this legislation affects the way employers recruit.

Merit

Explain the importance of recruitment practices and procedures in ensuring compliance with business, ethical and legal requirements. To do this you will need to look back at the sections above on outsourcing, advertising, documentation and procedures, barriers and legislation. How do these things ensure compliance? Can they guarantee compliance? What are the issues involved?

Distinction

Evaluate the relative effectiveness of selection interviews as an indicator of likely candidate suitability in the case of a selected business, making recommendations for improvements in procedure.

Thinking point

Looking back at the flow chart or diagram that you made at the start of the unit. Compare the process of recruitment and selection as you knew it then and as you know it now. Have your ideas changed about what the process involves?

BTEC National Study Guide: Business. See page 185 for order details of individual texts

170

Key terms

Applicant

a person applying for a job

Attributes

the characteristics that someone has, for example the type of personality (outgoing, conscientious); the type of attributes needed will change depending on the type and level of the job

Candidate

the individual who has applied for the job and will continue with the recruitment process

Compliance

organisations making sure they fulfil the requirements of the law

Confidentiality

keeping information secure and accessible only to authorised staff

Discrimination

bias against a particular group, causing them to be disadvantaged or excluded in the recruitment process; this can be for a number of reasons including race, gender or disability

Human resources department

department that deals with the management of policies and procedures relating to the people who work for an organisation; it covers areas including payroll, sickness monitoring, grievances and disciplinary procedures

Job analysis

analysis by an employer of the amount and type of work to be done by a person in a particular post

Job description

the list of working conditions for a job, e.g. pay, hours and duties

Labour turnover rate

the measurement of staff leaving as a percentage of the total staff; a low percentage is better for an organisation in general, because this means that staff don't tend to leave

Open-ended terms

terms that are defined flexibly; sometimes an employer might write into the job description a statement that the job covers 'any other reasonable duties as required by the post'

Outsourcing

where someone else carries out work for an organisation, for example a recruitment agency screening job applicants

Person specification

list of attributes needed by a person to do a job, such as personality type or experience

Productivity

the measurement of how much work an employee is doing in the time he or she is employed

Referees

people who are willing to supply a reference for an applicant; the names and contact details are written on the CV or application form, and usually one of them is the person's last employer

Skills auditing

the process where employers look at the types and levels of skills of people working for them

349

BTEC National Study Guide: Business. See page 185 for order details of individual texts

171

End-of-unit test

1 Describe three reasons why an organisation may wish to recruit.

2 What is the purpose of skills auditing?

3 Which ratio is used to measure how long people stay in their jobs?

4 What does 'productivity' mean?

5 Name two advantages of recruiting externally.

6 Name two advantages of recruiting internally.

7 What does job analysis involve?

8 What is the difference between a job description and a person specification?

9 Name two types of information usually given in a job description.

10 Describe one advantage of using CVs as part of the application process.

11 Describe one disadvantage of using the telephone as part of the application process.

12 Give two advantages of on-line recruitment.

13 Give two disadvantages of on-line recruitment.

14 What does 'compliance' mean?

15 What is the purpose of a selection centre?

16 What are psychometric tests?

17 Describe the difference between open and closed questions.

18 What does candidate rating involve?

19 What does outsourcing involve?

20 Name and describe four different pieces of legislation that must be followed in the recruitment and selection process.

BTEC National Study Guide: Business. See page 185 for order details of individual texts

172

Resources

Texts

Bartol and Martin: *Management*, Irwin McGraw Hill, 2001

Bratton, J & Gold, J: *Human Resource Management: Theory and Practice*, Palgrave Macmillan, 2003

Cuming, MW: *The Theory and Practice of Personnel Management*, Butterworth-Heinemann, 1993

Lockton, DJ: *Employment Law*, 4th edn, Palgrave Macmillan, 2003

Martin, M & Jackson, T: *Personnel Practice (People and Organizations)*, Chartered Institute of Personnel and Development (CIPD), 2002

Journals

Personnel Today

Personnel Review

Personnel Management

Websites

http://www.hrintranet.co.uk/ HR Portal – on-line recruitment advertising agency

http://www.strategies.co.uk Strategies – website design and web development

http://www.homeoffice.gov.uk The Home Office

http://www.equalitydirect.org.uk/ Equality Direct – advice for business managers on equality issues

http://www.lawontheweb.co.uk Legal information site

http://www.dti.gov.uk The Department of Trade and Industry

http://www.jobcentreplus.gov.uk Job Centre service from the Department for Work and Pensions

351

BTEC National Study Guide: Business. See page 185 for order details of individual texts

173

BTEC National Study Guide: Business. See page 185 for order details of individual texts

174

TEN STEPS TO A GREAT IVA

What is the IVA?

IVA stands for **Integrated Vocational Assignment**. This is a specific piece of work you will do for your BTEC National qualification.

The IVA is set by Edexcel, marked by your tutors and the assessment is checked by Edexcel. The IVA is **compulsory**. You cannot gain the complete award unless you attempt it. Obviously, though, you should do a lot more than just attempt it! Indeed, it is sensible to aim as high as you can. You might even surprise yourself.

This guide gives you hints and tips on researching and completing your IVA so that you will target all your efforts productively. In other words, you won't waste time doing things that aren't needed or you weren't intended to do! This doesn't mean that you can get by without doing any work at all. It does mean that you will get the maximum benefit for the work that you do.

Step 1: Understanding the basics

The IVA is a set of tasks you have to do. The tasks only relate to one or two specific units. These are identified on the front cover of the IVA. You will only be expected to complete tasks after you have learned about the unit(s) in class.

The IVA *must* be all your own work. If you have to do part of the work as a member of a group then the conclusions you write must be your own. If any part of the work has been done with someone else this must be clearly stated. This also means that you should not share your ideas or your researched information with anyone or copy anyone else's work

The IVA is not an examination. It is a series of tasks that you have to do to check that you understand the information you have learned. If you can demonstrate that you can apply and use this information in more than one situation and make informed judgements then you will gain a higher grade. You will be expected to research your own information to add to the work you have done in class. However, you must always list and identify your sources and never try to pass them off as you own work. How to do this is shown under Step 4.

You can produce your IVA over a period of time. Your tutor will tell you how long you have to complete it when it is issued. Make sure you know your deadlines for each stage and for any reviews that you have with your tutor. These will be included on a **Centre IVA Issue Sheet** that your tutor will give you. It also includes information about the resources you can use and support that is available to you. Keep this sheet safely and enter all the dates into your diary or onto your wall planner immediately. It is also sensible to enter a 'warning' a week before each important date, to remind yourself that it is looming!

Always remember that if you have any worries or concerns about your IVA then you should talk to your tutor. Don't wait for the next review date to do this – especially if the problem is serious.

1

BTEC National Study Guide: Business. See page 185 for order details of individual texts

175

Help yourself . . .

. . . by making sure you possess a diary or wall planner on which you can write deadline dates when you receive your Centre IVA issue sheet.

Step 2: Obtaining your IVA

You are unlikely to be expected to start your IVA until you have completed most, if not all, of the unit(s) to which it relates. However, you might be given it sooner so that you know what to expect and you can see the actual tasks you will have to answer.

You can see the IVA at any time, yourself, by logging onto the Edexcel website at www.edexcel.org.uk . Click on to 'qualifications', then select 'BTEC National' then click on the subject you are studying. The document you want is entitled *IVA – Learner Instructions*. It is normally quite short, between 8 and 10 pages, and contains the following information.

- The title page, which gives you

  - the level and title of your BTEC National qualification
  - the subject
  - the unit(s) to which the IVA relates
  - the date of issue and specification to which it relates. Ask your tutor if you are not sure whether this matches your course.

- Full instructions for completing and presenting the IVA. This is on page 2. It is very important that you read this carefully.

- Your assignment tasks and a copy of the assessment criteria grid(s). You will find out more about these under Step 3.

Help yourself . . .

. . . by starting a special IVA file that includes the IVA, the Centre IVA issue sheet and any specific notes your tutor gives you relating to the IVA.

Step 3: Understanding the tasks

This is the most important step of all. If you don't understand what you have to do to answer a question then you are very unlikely to get a good grade. You may do a lot of work but much of it may be irrelevant or – more likely – you will miss out important information.

It is quite normal for students to panic when they first read a set of assignment tasks! For this reason you are likely to be introduced to your IVA in a special session held by your tutor. Although your tutor cannot do the work for you (obviously!) you are allowed to receive guidance and can discuss general ideas, just like you would for an internal assessment. Your tutor can also answer any queries you have and give you ongoing advice and support in your review sessions to help you to do your best.

All IVAs are written in a certain format, or design.

- They start with a scenario or context to 'set the scene'. This may be quite short – just a few lines – or take up most of a page.

BTEC National Study Guide: Business. See page 185 for order details of individual texts

176

- Below this are several tasks. Each task usually starts with some introductory or background information and is then divided into lettered sub-sections.

- You are often expected to provide your answer in a specific document, such as a report, a letter, a leaflet, a table or a summary.

- At the end of each task you will see the unit number and assessment criteria covered by that task, eg Unit 2, P1, M1, D1. In this case it would mean that particular task related to Unit 2 and your answer must focus on providing evidence against the first assessment criterion under each of the pass, merit and distinction columns. You can match up this information in the assessment criteria grid(s). Your tutor will show you how to do this if you are not sure.

You will not be expected to do all the tasks at once. Let's assume you have been told to start with Task 1. There are two things you can do to make sure you understand *exactly* what you have to do.

1 Break the task down into chunks and analyse it.

2 Complete a task checklist before you start work.

You will read how to do this in Steps 4 and 5.

Help yourself . . .

. . . by first reading all the tasks you will have to do to get the overall picture and then reading – far more carefully – the first task you have to do. Then note down anything that puzzles you or that you do not understand.

Step 4: Analyse the task

Although IVAs aren't meant to be daunting or difficult to understand, it can be useful to know what to do if you do experience any problems. If a scenario or a task is short it is normally easier to understand. If it is long it may be more difficult. This is because there is more 'additional' information and if you miss any of this, it may affect your grade.

If there is a lot of information don't expect to understand it fully the first time you read it. Just read it to get a general impression. Then read it again, more slowly, to get the meaning. It is often helpful to go through it again, much more thoroughly, to identify the important words. This is called **task analysis**. The aim is to identify:

- the **background information** – which sets the scene or the context. You need to understand this for the task to make sense

- the **command words**, such as 'describe' or 'explain' – which tell you what you have to do. You *must* obey these when you answer the questions. If you are unsure what any of these words mean, check back to the explanation in *The Smart Way to Achieve Your BTEC National* at the start of this book

- other **specific instructions** which tell you what you have to do – such as 'provide three examples' or 'write a report'

- any important **topic words** which give you the subject of the task.

Finally, make sure you now understand the purpose of the task you have to do and the audience you are preparing it for. Both these factors affect the way you will structure and present your answer.

BTEC National Study Guide: Business. See page 185 for order details of individual texts

177

Task 1: Prove your understanding of the IVA

Edexcel issues an assessment called an IVA that covers the whole of either one or two units of a BTEC National programme. This tests all learners nationally on the same set of tasks. Produce a short report *which identifies* your own tasks in relation to your IVA. Your report should include:

a A brief **description** of the IVA.

b An **explanation** of the main instructions given to learners. This must include the **identification** of three requirements which ensure that each IVA is the student's own original work.

c Your own plan for producing your IVA which shows how you have **analysed** your options and provides **justifications** for the decisions you have made.

Background information which sets the scene.

To produce a short report, and what the report should include are both instructions. Your own tasks in relation to the IVA are topic words

'Brief' is an instruction, 'of the IVA' is the topic. 'Description' and 'explanation' are both **command words**. 'Must include' is an instruction but 'identification' is a command word. The remaining words are topic words except for 'three' which is an instruction.

'Your own plan' is an instruction. The remaining words give you the topic. This must involve 'analysis' and 'justification', so these are both **command words**.

Help yourself . . .

. . . by practising task analysis yourself.

In agreement with your tutor, select **one** task in the IVA you have been issued and carry out the following tasks.

a Identify the background information, command words, instructions and topic words that it contains. You can use any combination of colour or highlighting (such as bold or underscore) that you find easiest to understand.

b Explain the purpose of that task and identify your audience. Then say how these two factors will influence your answer.

c Compare your ideas with those of other members of your group.

Step 5: Completing a task checklist

This will confirm if you really do understand what you have to do. Simply read the following list. If you can complete the column on the right with ticks then you understand the task. If you can't then you must resolve the problem before you start work.

BTEC National Study Guide: Business. See page 185 for order details of individual texts

178

Checklist for understanding your IVA task		✓ or x
Read the scenario or context that 'sets the scene'	Does it make sense? Do you understand all the words used? Can you identify the key words? Would it help you to highlight these? Could you accurately explain the scenario or context to someone else, using your own words?	
Read the task you have to do and then analyse it	Have you carried out task analysis? Can you identify the background information? Can you identify *all* the command words? Can you identify *all* the instructions? Do you understand the topics? Can you clearly state what you have to do, using your own words? Do you know how to set out the document(s) you have to produce?	
Do you know the purpose of the task and have you identified your audience?	Can you explain the reason for doing this task? Who is your audience? How will these two factors affect your answer?	
Check the evidence statement at the bottom of the task and check this against the assessment criteria grid	Do you know the grades you can get for this task? Can you see how the command words differ within the task to cover merit and distinction questions? Are you *certain* that you know what is meant by each command word?	

- If you don't understand a word that is used then look in a dictionary or check the list of command words and their meanings given in *The Smart Way to Achieve your BTEC National*.

- If there is any instruction that you do not understand, such as how to set out a document that is required, talk to your tutor.

- If there is any aspect of the topic that you missed when it was covered in class then talk to your tutor about obtaining the information you need.

Help yourself . . .

. . . copy the checklist and complete it for the first task on your list. Remember that you *must* obtain help if you still cannot understand anything about the task you have to do.

Step 6: Planning your work

Completing any task(s) will take some time. You have to allow enough time for obtaining the information, deciding what to use, getting it into the right order and writing it up. You also need to bear in mind the review date(s) agreed with your tutor – as well as all the other college and personal commitments you have! It is therefore sensible to make a plan.

- The IVA is designed to cover the unit content and each task covers different parts of the unit. You can check which parts of a unit are covered by a particular task by looking at the key words. These will relate to the assessment criteria for the unit and the unit specification, which gives detailed information on the content.

BTEC National Study Guide: Business. See page 185 for order details of individual texts

179

- Next estimate how long it will take you to find the information you need. You will do this more accurately if you identify your information sources. Although this will obviously depend on the format of your IVA and the task you are doing you will probably want to refer to

    – notes you have been given in class
    – your course textbook
    – two or three library books or journals
    – some online resources.

    If you are researching for a project or need to use evidence from a particular event then you may need to arrange to talk to people to get their views. You must therefore allow enough time to obtain your information.

- Decide how long it is likely to take to sort through your information before you can start to write your first draft answer.

- Allow time for rereading and revising your answer and then for checking the way you have presented the information.

- Decide how many hours a week you will need to spend on your IVA to stay on schedule.

- Split these up into sensible sessions. Longer than two or three hours is too much – you won't work well when you're tired. Shorter than half an hour isn't much good unless you've a specific small job to do.

- Identify times during the week when you will do the work and mark these in your diary or on your wall planner, eg Tuesday 5 pm – 7 pm. Then stick to them! If an emergency means you can't work at that time remember that you then need to reschedule these hours at another time to keep on target!

Help yourself . . .

. . . by always allowing more time than you think you will need, never less. You should also find a quiet place to work, where you can concentrate. Now make out your plan for the first task you have to do. Aim to finish a week early to allow time for slippage.

Step 7: Researching, storing and selecting your information

Problems with researching are always linked to the quality and quantity of information. For information to be good quality it needs to relate directly to the topic. You also need to understand it! Quantity is also important. If you only rely on your course notes then you are unlikely to produce original work and this will affect your grade, but too much information is very confusing and you are likely to get bogged down trying to decide what to use.

Start by listing all the potential sources of information you can use. These will depend largely upon the type of task you are doing and the information you need.

- If you are looking for books you are best to aim for two or three that specifically cover the topic. Check this by looking in the index when you are in the library, then skim the text to make sure it is written at the right level and that you find the style 'user-friendly'. You are wise to schedule in a prompt visit to your college library – particularly if there are many students doing the same IVA as you!

- If you are searching online you will have far more success if you learn how to do advanced searches on websites such as Google. It is also important to keep focused and not get distracted by interesting but irrelevant information you come across as you search! If you need help searching on line, talk to the IT resource staff at college.

- If you need to visit organisations or interview someone then prepare well in advance. Make the arrangement and then draft a list of questions. If you want to take a tape recorder, first check this is acceptable.

BTEC National Study Guide: Business. See page 185 for order details of individual texts

180

- If you are preparing a presentation that involves other people in your group arrange a first meeting to decide your roles and responsibilities. Check in your library for useful guidelines on preparing and giving a presentation.

- Buy a box file and label it. If you are broke use an empty cardboard box! Put in every scrap of information that might be helpful for your IVA. If your IVA covers two units then you might find it helpful to keep the information that relates to each one in separate folders.

- Make sure that all the information you put into your box file is dated and labelled with its source (see below). This includes any photocopies you have taken or print-outs you have made.

- Have a cut-off date when you stop collecting information and start to write. If you don't, you can easily find yourself running out of time to complete the task.

- Only select the most relevant information after re-reading the task *and* your task analysis. It's often easiest to start by spreading out all your information on a large table (or the floor!). Then select everything you think you might need and put the rest away.

- Read through your information and make draft notes to answer the question. *Don't* copy out reams of information – note down the source of the information instead. Remember that most of your IVA must be in your own words.

- Make sure you only include relevant information and that you re-word or adapt information to match the task you are doing. It is very tempting to 'cut and paste' lots of information, particularly from the Internet, just because you found it! A good trick is to keep looking back to the question at regular intervals to keep yourself focused and *never* include everything 'just 'cos it's there'! Remember that marks are always awarded for quality of work, not quantity!

Help yourself . . .

. . . by being self-disciplined when you are looking for information. This means not getting distracted, *always* noting down the source of information you print out or photocopy and *always* storing it safely so you can find it again!

Step 8: Identifying your sources

You must do this if you quote from any source. If you forget then you could be guilty of plagiarism. This is a serious academic crime as it is assumed that you were trying to pass off someone else's work as your own. It is so serious that some colleges and universities have installed special software to catch plagiarists!

Your tutor or your college library will be able to give you detailed information on citing references. If not, use the following as your guide.

In the text:

- Always put quoted information in quotation marks. Mark Twain said 'There are lies, damned lies and statistics.'

- If you refer to an author put their name and then the date and/or page number in brackets. Chaffey (2002) argues that . . . .

At the end of the task, in your bibliography, list your references in alphabetical order of author. Put the title in bold or in italics so that it stands out.

- If your source is a newspaper or magazine, state the name of the author(s), year of publication in brackets, title of the article, the title of the publication, volume or date, pages of the article eg Gascoigne, C (2005) **Leading from the front**, Sunday Times Smarter Business, 6 February 2005, page 7.

- If your source is a book, give the author(s), date of publication in brackets, title and the publisher eg Chaffey, D (2002) **E-Business and E-Commerce Management**, Prentice Hall, page 25.

BTEC National Study Guide: Business. See page 185 for order details of individual texts

181

- If your source is from the Internet then you should give enough information for your tutor to be able to find the article online. However, you are also wise to keep your print-out as Internet sites are regularly updated and you may need proof of your information. It is recommended that you give the name of the person or organisation responsible for the article or site, the title of the document, the word Internet in square brackets, the URL and the date you accessed the information. This is the address line that shows on screen and is normally printed at the bottom of the page eg Sport England, **What the 2012 Olympics would do for the UK**, [Internet], http://www.sportengland.org/index/news_and_media/olympics_2012/2012_uk.htm [Accessed 7 February 2005]

Help yourself . . .

. . . by checking if there is a course or college guide to citing references. Ask your tutor or librarian if you are not sure. Alternatively you can test your research skills by finding information online. Type 'Harvard referencing' into any search engine. This is the most usual method used by students at university.

Step 9: Writing and presenting your IVA

The first thing to do is to plan your answer. Re-read your task analysis to refresh your memory. Check carefully the command words, the instructions and the topic words. Make sure you know what type of document you have to produce and how to set it out.

There are two ways in which you can plan your answer. Use the one that is most natural for you:

1 Write a list of all the information you want to include. Then put it into the correct order. Decide what will go in the introduction, what in the middle of the answer and what your conclusion will be.

2 Write the question in the middle of the page and write your information around it. Link the information with arrows so you end up with different themes. Decide the best order to introduce each theme and how these will be reflected in your paragraphs.

If you find that you are missing any information write this on a 'to do' list. You can still plan and draft your answer. Your 'to do' list is to make certain you don't forget to find out the remaining details.

Decide the approach you want to use. For example, if you have to contrast and compare two things then you could write all about one and then the other; alternatively you could describe each one and then analyse the similarities and differences afterwards. *Neither is right or wrong* – do the one you find easier. If you find that it then doesn't work very well when you start to draft your answer, be prepared to change it.

Don't think that you need to write in a more flowery or grandiose style than you normally do. In fact, there are lots of pitfalls if you do this – such as using the wrong word or writing a complex sentence that no-one can understand! Instead, keep your writing style simple and only use words you understand. If you also keep your sentences relatively short but vary the length a little then your answer will also be more interesting and easier to read.

Don't expect to write the answers to merit and distinction level questions quickly. These are deliberately written to make you think! Look back at the command words information and examples in *The Smart Way to Achieve your BTEC National* if you are struggling. Then draft your answer as best you can and discuss your ideas with your tutor at your next review meeting. This might help to put you on the right track again.

The type of task and your audience will determine your writing style. If you are asked to prepare a formal business document such as a report it is better to use a quite formal writing style. In this case try to write using the third person. This means you don't say 'I think that ' but 'it is considered that' or 'it would appear that'. Equally you wouldn't say 'You can do this by . . .' but 'This could be done by . . . '. The situation is different, though, if you are preparing an informal account, such as an article for a staff newsletter. In every document, though, you should avoid using slang or contracted words (eg can't or hasn't) and *never* use the abbreviated words or jargon that you would use in a text message or if you were talking to your friends.

BTEC National Study Guide: Business. See page 185 for order details of individual texts

182

Leave your work alone for a day or two before you make a final check. This way you are more likely to spot errors. You may also find this easier to do if you take a print-out rather than read it on screen. Check it against the question. Have you obeyed all the command words? Have you included everything that was asked for? Is the information given in a logical order?

Now check the presentation and your writing style. Have you set out the document correctly? Is it in the right style? For example a letter or report must be set out in the right format and not written as an essay style answer. Is the grammar correct? Is every word spelt properly? Don't rely on your spellchecker here. It cannot tell the difference between 'hear' and 'here' or 'there' and 'their'! Word processing packages are also very limited in their ability to correct grammatical errors, so never assume that you don't need to check your work carefully yourself. If you are preparing a draft print-out to discuss with your tutor it is useful to use wide margins and double spacing then you have plenty of room to note down comments.

Make sure you have included a sheet with all your references on it. It is usually easier to compile this as you go – rather than create these at the end when some notes will be buried under a mountain of paper.

Finally check that the presentation of your IVA matches *all* the requirements set out on page 2 of your *Instructions for Learners completing IVAs*. For example, you must not put your work into plastic pockets or into a box file or a lever arch file. You also need to put a cover sheet on the front and sign a declaration that all the work you are submitting is your own.

Help yourself . . .

. . . by asking someone you trust to read through your work and make comments. This can be a close friend or a family member but shouldn't be a fellow student who is doing the same IVA as you. If your friend or relative can't understand what you are trying to say then it is probably true that your tutor will have the same problem!

Step 10: Is this the best you can do?

It always seems a tragedy when students just miss a better grade because of carelessness or silly mistakes. As a final check, before you give in your work, run through the following list. Only hand in your work when, hand on heart, you know you honestly couldn't do any more.

- You have incorporated all the suggestions and ideas that you discussed with your tutor at your review meetings.
- You have answered every part of every task and there are no gaps or omissions.
- You have addressed all the command words correctly and taken account of all the instructions.
- You have checked the spelling, punctuation and layout.
- You have checked and double-checked that all the references are included.
- All your pages are numbered and your name is on every sheet.
- You have followed every other instruction for completing and presenting your work. Do a final check of page 2 of your *Instructions for Learners completing IVAs* before you hand in your work. For example, are all your pages in the right order and are they securely fastened together?

Help yourself . . .

. . . by handing in your work before the deadline and then relaxing! Once you have done your best and submitted your work you cannot then alter the grade for that particular piece of work. Remember, though, that the grade you achieve is very important feedback for future work you will do. Learn from your mistakes and build on your successes – and your work will always continue to improve.

BTEC National Study Guide: Business. See page 185 for order details of individual texts

183

BTEC National Study Guide: Business. See page 185 for order details of individual texts

184

BTEC National Study Guide

BUSINESS

The chapters in this Study Guide are all taken from

BTEC NATIONAL BUSINESS

written by Rob Dransfield, Catherine Richards, Philip Guy and David Dooley and published by Heinemann Educational Publishers.

If you liked this book and would like to order a full copy either go to your local bookshop and quote the ISBN number: 0 435 45535 4 or order online at <u>www.heinemann.co.uk</u>